80 From the 80s

By Lane Myer

Cover Photo by Nicole O'Brien

Proofread by Thushan Kumaraswamy

Contents

For my Mom, who probably thinks every film in this book is tat.

Introduction

Perhaps it's nostalgia or maybe the films were just better, but for me, the 1980s presented the best that cinema had to offer. I was born in the early 1970s and got into film at the turn of the decade, seeing *Flash Gordon* on my first ever cinema visit. I was hooked from the opening moments and soon became obsessed by the medium, especially with the birth of the home video market. Film was pure escapism, where anything was possible and the hero generally prevailed. The darker paranoia of the 1970s gave way to the outlandish, garish and magnificent 1980s. When you lived through it, the fashions didn't seem as ridiculous, the plots didn't seem so flimsy and the effects were never less than cutting edge. For ten short years, Hollywood turned out some of the most amazing and entertaining pictures – and there was little before or since that has come close.

Looking back now, a lot of them *don't* stand up to the test of time, but for people of a certain age, who caught the likes of *Back to the Future* and *The Goonies* at the time, they will hold a near-untouchable place in our hearts. And that's not to say movies of the 80s should be passed over for the like of *Apocalypse Now, A Clockwork Orange* or *Taxi Driver*. Indeed, for pure entertainment, I'd take *Raiders of the Lost Ark, Ghostbusters* and *Beverly Hills Cop* over all manner of 'classics'. These *are* my classics. A whole generation may not have understood 2015's *Back to the Future* day celebrations, but for those who were there at the start, there was something heart-warming about seeing Doc Brown and Marty all over social media and television. Even well-respected, award-winning films from the 1970s and 1990s don't get that kind of love. Then again, we'll probably never see a Criterion version of *Spacehunter: Adventures in the Forbidden Zone.*

For me, the 1980s were a transition from fresh-faced school kid to shy teenager and beyond. Everything felt more fun, more exciting, and yet at the same time, hard-hitting and influential. We wanted a day-off like Ferris; we somehow hoped our ZX Spectrum could conjure up our own version of *Weird Science*'s Lisa. At the same time, we identified with the struggles of *The Breakfast Club* and even if we didn't quite understand Molly Ringwald's predicament in *Pretty in Pink*, some of us knew the shame of never being quite cool enough, never quite having the right clothes or money. These might seem trivial, even laughable nowadays, but the right movie at the right time could make you soar or break your heart. Maybe you wept over *The Champ* or *Love Story*, but neither could hold a candle to Meg Ryan breaking down over Goose's death or Connor Macleod's farewell to Heather.

As you get older and begin to face the harsher realities of life, the feel-good factor of the 1980s becomes even more important. The films transport you back to a simpler time, when you can recall £1 cinema tickets and £1.50 video rentals (well, £1.50 for the new releases). Nostalgia goes a long, long way and helps paper over a lot of cracks and bad special effects. Films back then didn't feel made by committee or focus tested to within an inch of their lives – though I'm sure that did happen. No idea felt too outlandish and it rarely seemed as though box office potential was a factor in a lot of movies getting the greenlight. Then again, we didn't have the internet back in 1985, so it was much harder to obsess about the opening weekend box office of *Rocky IV* when compared to previous entries in the series. Simpler, dare I say better, times.

I've been interested in film for a long time, but I've only really written about them in terms of how much money they've made. I was a box office reporter for ten years, and witnessed all manner of successes, failures and trends. As time wore on, my writing focused more on charting a film's journey to the screen than what it did once it got there. The obsession over how a film performed lost its shine – more so when one realised that a film's window of success was shortening from its entire theatrical run, down to its first week, weekend and now opening night. Indeed, a picture can now be condemned to failure based only on the amount of money it makes during its midnight screening. For me at least, the story behind the movie became a more interesting one. Even a minor release could hold a fascinating backstory. Perhaps its development had gone on for years, maybe the director had quit during filming or the studio had fought over its rating. There was always more to the story than the 100 minutes you saw up on the screen.

When I stopped writing a weekly box office report, it was a big change to my life. In one shape or another I'd been producing a report every Sunday for ten years, rarely missing a weekend. With that obsession gone (and it did become such), I had a big hole in my life that nothing seemed to fill. Books, videogames and even family life couldn't plug the void left by not writing anymore. I toyed too many times with returning to box office reporting, but doing it well is a full-time career, and I didn't want that back in my life – not that I had time for it anyway. I wasn't sure how to proceed but I knew, despite my mind telling me the contrary on more than one occasion, I was actually a pretty good writer. I couldn't write fiction, I was painfully aware of that and one book on one subject would also be a struggle – that's why I loved writing the box office report, it was something different every week. And then, while attempting to relive my youth, it came to me.

The idea behind *80 From the 80s* originated in Melbourne, Australia, though obviously has its roots in the cinemas and video shops of the 1980s. In the St. Kilda area of the city lies the Astor Theatre, a building with its own extensive history that stretches right back to 1913. Originally built as the Diamond Theatre, it was renamed a year later to the Rex Theatre, and was part cinema-part vaudeville. It closed in 1917 and by 1924 was being used as a garage. The building was sold in 1935 and demolished in the December of that same year. Frank O'Collins, who then owned the site, commissioned architect Ron Morton Taylor to design the new art-deco building. Work progressed incredibly fast and by April 1936, the Astor Theatre was opened. Over the years, it has changed hands several times and avoided redevelopment on more than one occasion. It is now listed on the Victorian Heritage Register.

In 1983, the building and its single screen theatre was licensed by George Florence, who set about devising a screening programme for which the Astor would become renowned. Florence brought back the double-bill feature, screened 70mm classics, hosted Q&A sessions with various directors and even held the occasional premiere. The catalogue was, and still is, extensive. As I write this, *Lawrence of Arabia* has just screened in all its glory. *The Jungle Book* and *The Aristocats* are on a double bill tomorrow and at the end of the month is the fantastic Predator/Commando night. December is no less brilliant – The first two *Lethal Weapon* movies rub shoulders with *Coffy*, *Rio Bravo* and *It's a Wonderful Life*. John Hughes' *Pretty in Pink* plays on the same night as *Ferris Bueller's Day Off* and they've even found time for some post-Christmas Monty Python with *Life of Brian* and *The Holy Grail*. No movie is too good, too bad, too old or too new for the Astor. The theatre exists purely for the love of film.

I moved to Melbourne from England in 2013 and didn't hear about the Astor for over a year. When I did finally discover it, thanks to an advert for a *Raiders of the Lost Ark* screening, I couldn't believe my luck. The place was only thirty minutes away and their upcoming catalogue was the stuff of legend (at least for me). The funny thing was, whenever I mentioned the Astor to everyone, they were surprised I'd never heard of it – I was just as surprised that no one had ever told me about it! The first trip I made was on a Sunday afternoon to see *Indiana Jones and the Last Crusade*. I hadn't seen the film in a number of years but walking into the theatre that day I was transported back to the ABC cinema I visited back in the 1980s. The style, the atmosphere, was exactly how it should have been – as far from the sterile multiplex as possible. They also had a strict no talking/no mobile phone policy, something all but gone from the modern cinema experience. Everyone was friendly, the tickets were exceptionally good value and their choc-top ice creams went far beyond the reputation they had earned over the years.

The screening was little short of revelatory. *Raiders of the Lost Ark* is still the best of the series, but seeing *Last Crusade* up on the big screen, some 25 years after its original release (when I caught it on its opening day) was an incredible experience. I didn't get to the Astor half as often as I should have and was both shocked and saddened when it was revealed that the theatre was to close in March 2015. I checked their upcoming calendar and made a note to see at least three more pictures before its closure. Despite the place only being a thirty-minute drive from where I live, it's a treacherous one that takes you through some of Melbourne's busiest areas – and often at the tail end of rush hour. I managed to catch *Guardians of the Galaxy*, a great film to see with a crowd, but it was nothing compared to seeing *Ghostbusters*. The place was packed, and if there was an empty seat, I couldn't see it. Another fantastic screening enhanced further by the crowd's enjoyment. The only downside was that the planned double bill with its sequel was replaced by a showing of *Labyrinth*.

I also managed to complete a lifelong ambition; to see *Raiders of the Lost Ark* on the big screen. I never got the chance during its initial release and I ended up renting the film three times before I got to see it on video. If anything, it was even better than I remembered it to be. It's one of the best pictures ever made and stands the test of time beautifully. I'd make a further trip to the Astor to see another classic, one that I'd again missed out on during its original release – though this was due to not being old enough at the time.

Beverly Hills Cop was on a double bill with *Planes, Trains and Automobiles*. I wasn't as concerned about seeing the John Candy/Steve Martin picture. It's a great movie, but for a long time in the 1980s, *Beverly Hills Cop* was my favourite. In fact, it was the first ever VHS movie I purchased, being one of the first sell-through releases – a movie made available to buy at a much cheaper rate than normal movies. Back at the time, it wasn't unusual for a VHS release to cost upwards of £80, the primary buyers being video rental shops who often charged a high membership fee as well as a rental cost, as a way to cover the initial cost of purchasing such movies.

I arrived at around 9pm on the Saturday evening and waited until *Planes, Trains and Automobiles* had finished before taking my seat. The lights dimmed and we were greeted by Glenn Frey singing The Heat is On, before the camera travels to an alleyway containing a truck full of cigarettes and Axel Foley. The deal goes awry when Foley is interrupted by a passing squad car, resulting in a manic chase through Detroit, accompanied by the Pointer Sisters' Neutron Dance. I'd seen this sequence a hundred times and as the truck smashed through car after car, I began to wonder how the movie had been released back in the day. Murphy was starring in what would be his third smash hit in a row after *48 Hrs* and *Trading Places*. I knew Martin Brest had directed the picture and it was a Simpson/Bruckheimer production. Beyond that, I knew a little about the soundtrack but that was about it.

The information had to be out there though. The advent of DVD commentaries and extras had opened up a whole world of information. Combined with the internet, there wasn't much one couldn't find out with a bit of investigation. Nowadays we know almost everything about a film before it's even made it inside theatres. Script announcements, casting, on-set reporting and the like leave very little to the imagination. If the movie is based on a book, you'll probably have read it or know someone who has. Back in

1983, you'd be lucky see much beyond a cast interview once the film came around for release. In those opening moments, I'd found a new writing project. By the time Axel makes it to Beverly Hills, I'd already gotten a rough idea sketched out in my head.

Beverly Hills Cop, like *Raiders*, was even better than I'd remember. Murphy really was at the top of his game and has not been better since.

I decided to call the project *80 From the 80s*. I'd take 80 movies produced in the 1980s and chart their complete production history, release and box office performance. The work I'd been doing on the box office reports would hopefully stand me in good stead when I began researching these older movies. I was pleased too that Box Office Mojo had charts running right back to the start of the 1980s and had separate entries for most films I could come up with. I set up a spreadsheet and began to compile a list of movies I wanted to cover – beginning with the ones I enjoyed the most. I began adding in more and more detail – box office figures, budgets (where available), stars and studios. It didn't take long to compile a list of more than eighty titles. Mentioning the idea to others helped add in further suggestions.

I estimated it would take two years to complete the project but realistically, I had no idea. An average box office report could take anything up to sixteen hours to write, spread across the entirety of a week. Those longer reports were done when I didn't have a job and had the luxury of being able to write and research for extended periods of time. With a full-time job and family, writing time would be severely limited. In order to complete the project in the estimated time, I'd need to be turning out a completed essay once every ten or so days. As I continued to work on the list, I realised there were films released in the 1980s about which there wasn't a single unknown detail. *The Empire Strikes Back* and *Return of the Jedi* have complete volumes about their creation. There'd be nothing I could add. Similarly, the likes of *Raiders of the Lost Ark* and even *The Goonies* had thousands upon thousands of words written about their production history. *Back to the Future* even had a feature length documentary about its making.

I began to edit the list down, removing such films. But I was also cautious to not end up with a list made up entirely of cult and obscure movies. Some of those have more extensive works written about them than the major mainstream hits. In the end, I did start with something of a cult movie, perhaps just to test the water. I knew *Krull* had been popular on the UK home video market so its history would be of interest to some people. They'd have at least heard of it, if nothing else. When I began researching I unearthed some great information. This wasn't top secret stuff, it was all out there, but by writing about the entire production, I was able (I hoped) to bring all the multiple sources together in one place – and hopefully make it an interesting enough read at the same time. Despite having not written in over six months, the first essay came together quite quickly. In all, it took around ten days to research and write, and at least another day of messing around to get the format correct.

I opted to make a small table to display the initial information – name, tagline, studio, stars, production budget and box office takings – along with the 2014/5 equivalent, in order to give people a more relatable set of figures. Initially, I left out the synopsis, instead opting to cover the entire plot over the space of a couple of paragraphs slotted after the film's production but prior to its release. At that point, I figured if you were reading about the movie, you'd have already seen it and this would serve as a refresher. The structure was more-or-less in place from the get-go. I started with a short introduction which led to how the project had started. This allowed me to cover the history of the writer or director, before moving on to casting. This, again, let me look into the cast's background – what had they done previously? Was there any history behind their being cast?

Any pre-production material was covered next, followed by information on the actual shoot. For *Krull*, I managed to find a small number of articles that generally tallied up with one another. As I'd soon discover, this wasn't always to be the case. By the time I'd gotten to writing about the film's box office, I was in familiar territory. Thanks to Box Office Mojo, I knew how the picture performed, its existing and upcoming competition and even how many theatres it had opened in. I also had to recognise that a $10M opening was a really big deal and that a movie out at 1500 locations was a major, wide release. This was the early 80s, not 2014, and the cinematic landscape was quite different. I decided that once the box office was covered, there was mileage in discovering what the cast and crew did next. This, too, opened up a number of great stories and more than a few sad ones. A short conclusion rounded things off and was one of the few times I allowed my own personal thoughts on the movie to come into play. This was to be a project that celebrated movie-making and I wanted people to realise that just because effects or fashions looked ropey, that wasn't a reason to pass something by.

The response to the first article was great – I was pleased that people had heard of the movie and were interested in how it came together. What made me happier were the memories it conjured up for many; their nan taking them to see *Krull*, renting it from some grotty video shop or paying a pound to catch it at their local cinema on a Saturday morning. The film was obviously not a huge success as you'll see, but it was remembered fondly enough. For me, helping people revisit those days was better than comments on the actual writing (which thankfully many seemed to also enjoy). The project had interest to others and that spurned me on to the next essay.

And so it went for a few months. Sometimes the articles would be painful to research and write, and others practically wrote themselves. Oddly, the easier movies to cover were those that were the hardest to find information on (though I didn't realise that at the time). If you had a movie with twenty different sources, they often had opposing versions of the same story, or the timeline of events was laid out in numerous ways. The director brought the story to the star, the star brought the movie to the studio who found a director. It was a task to sift through what was possible and what wasn't. Sometimes I'd have to discount version X of events and go with version Y because more people corroborated that one.

At times, I'd find what I suspected was a fairly low-key picture only to discover a huge backstory and following. I'd end up with such a glut of information that I didn't know where to start. You had real experts on a movie, who'd dissected it to the nth degree – I didn't like taking those sorts of things on because I was only visiting for that short period, where some had been following the film for years. I generally got lucky with the choices, which were picked more often than not at random from the master list I'd created. Some films linked to the next in minor ways, but apart from all being released in the 1980s, there was no great plan as to what would come next.

I'd generally start by reading the Wikipedia entry to see if there was more to the film than met the eye. The Internet Movie Database (IMDb) was next, cross-checking films that the director and stars (and often, writer and special effects teams) had worked on previously. Then it would be a case of searching for old articles, both online and off. Magazine scans would be invaluable for things like *Young Sherlock Holmes*, while a YouTube video covering the making of *The Last Starfighter* proved incredibly useful for correcting the timeline of events.

Biographies could be another great source of information, and I'd sometimes have to check out ones that didn't actually cover the star or director but rather someone who didn't make it into the picture at all. These were useful if I'd discovered an actor, writer or director had turned a movie down (or been involved behind the scenes) – there could still be some kind of reference or timeline information, perhaps the actor had auditioned but not got the part? Any titbit that could place a film's shoot dates or when an actor joined the cast, could be useful. Oddly, DVD commentaries ended up being less useful, as they'd often be more about friends reminiscing than the production of the movie. This was great to listen to but not so good for research.

Of all the movies I wrote about, only *The Karate Kid* didn't make it past the starting block. I'd begun to research the picture only to discover a really great article about its entire production history. I realised early on that to write my piece I'd need to use this one, and reading through it, there'd have been little I could have added. I did almost give up on *The Secret of My Success* as well, especially when I discovered it warranted only three minor references in Michael J. Fox's own autobiography. That one required some real investigative work, more so when there was conflicting information on how the actor had joined a previous project that would have some impact on the one I was writing about. Occasionally it became a guessing game – which two or three words could I put into Google to find information? A bit of that kind of experimenting helped me discover a great interview Nicholas Rowe, of *Young Sherlock Holmes*, had given about how he got involved in the film.

The articles continued to prove popular and it was great to see people re-discovering (or discovering) the movies I was covering. However, the full magnitude of the task began to weigh on me. When the work was coming together, I was turning a new essay out every couple of weeks, but it was getting harder to get started. If I could turn out a new one as regularly as that, it would still take nigh on four years to complete the project. That suddenly made it seem like a lot less fun. I began to take longer and longer between columns, finding it increasingly difficult to get started – though things seemed to go OK when I did get some words down. The gaps got longer and the project looked in jeopardy.

I took some time away and eventually decided to force myself to write every night, for an hour. Even if what I produced was no good, I'd just get back into the habit of writing daily. I also took the decision to not put any finished work online until I had one essay complete and was well into writing the next one. Getting back into the routine really helped and before long, I'd completed three brand new columns that were easily longer than anything I'd done previously. When they finally debuted online, I was relieved that people enjoyed them.

I came to the conclusion that I'd never get the remaining sixty films covered in the same depth and so chose to release the first twenty into a book. Not to make money – this project has never been about that – but so I could put a full stop to it. It meant I'd have a completed piece of work that I could be proud of, but at the same time, freeing myself to move on to other projects without feeling like I'd abandoned this one. I'm not sure if this book signifies the end, but it does represent a line drawn in the sand.

Along the way, I've been overwhelmed by the support I've received. From people on the forum I frequent and on Facebook and Twitter. The likes, shares and retweets have made it all worthwhile. It was great too, when Steven E. de Souza, co-writer of *48 Hrs*, told me he'd enjoyed the column I'd written on the movie (he'd seen it via a retweet). Better was to come. When I casually asked *Clue* director Jonathan Lynn (via Twitter) if he could confirm the film's budget, he replied. Feeling lucky, I sent him the completed column, which he not only read but offered to fact-check for me. True to his word, he came back with a number of corrections and clarified some production facts for me. A true highlight and a real privilege.

As for the Astor Theatre, it was saved at the very last minute by Palace Cinemas. The company closed the place down while essential maintenance work was completed but true to their word, since re-opening have kept to the same incredible programme of films.

And so I present to you, *80 From the 80s*. An in-depth look at the entire production of twenty great movies. Maybe you know them all, perhaps you rented a few. If not, I hope this book convinces you to catch some of them. Thanks to the wonders of modern technology, you won't even need to find a video shop (and even if you did, you can bet *Krull* hasn't been returned and *Romancing the Stone* won't have been rewound).

Lane Myer

December 2015

Krull

A world light-years beyond your imagination

Studio: Columbia Pictures

Release Date: 29th July 1983

Director: Peter Yates

Starring: Kenneth Marshall, Lysette Anthony

Budget: $26M – 2015 Equivalent: $62M

U.S Box Office: $16.5M – 2015 Equivalent: $39.3M

On the eve of a wedding meant to unite two rival kingdoms, The Beast's army attacks, slaughtering many and kidnapping the bride-to-be. Prince Conwyn must join forces with a wise man, a magician, a Cyclops and a band of thieves in order to locate the only weapon capable of destroying the Beast. With time and many forces against him, can Conwyn save his bride and the kingdom?

Despite being one of the most expensive movies of the time, Krull is seemingly forgotten amongst the releases of the early 1980s. Taking its primary influence from *Star Wars* and *Lord of the Rings*, it sought to score box office gold in the late summer of 1983. With *Return of the Jedi* starting to look a little long in the tooth, Krull staked its claim to be the next fantasy epic.

At the helm was Peter Yates, a director of some pedigree. Yates had originally started out as a race driver (something that would influence his later work) before setting his sights on acting. Upon graduating from the Royal Academy of Dramatic Arts, he worked in repertory theatre as both an actor and director. During the 1950s, he took on a number of different jobs, which would eventually lead to an assistant director credit on *The Inn of the Sixth Happiness*. This, in turn, led to him working on *The Entertainer* and *The Guns of Navarone*, while making his mark on the small screen with directing credits on both *The Saint* and *Danger Man*.

This early work paved the way to his first feature directing credit for Cliff Richard's *Summer Holiday*, a lightweight musical comedy designed to highlight the singer's talents and help sell records. Yates would follow this up with the surreal *One Way Pendulum*. It was his third feature, *Robbery*, which would garner him the attention of Steve McQueen. The picture was a very loose interpretation of The Great Train Robbery, yet what caught the actor's eye was a sequence featuring a high speed car chase through London. So impressed was he that he sought out Yates to direct the action drama, *Bullitt*. The film would go on to be McQueen's most successful picture and the climactic car chase around San Francisco set the benchmark for movie chase sequences for years to come.

Bullitt essentially made Yates, allowing him to work consistently for the next thirty-five years. Not afraid to mix things up, he moved from romantic drama (*John and Mary*) to crime caper (*The Hot Rock*) and then black comedy (*Mother, Jugs and Speed*). From *Bullitt* in 1968, he would go on to make ten movies in the next thirteen years and work with some of the biggest actors of the time including Dustin Hoffman, Robert Redford, Barbra Streisand and Robert Mitchum. He even found time to ride the Jaws bandwagon in the late 70s when he directed *The Deep*, an underwater thriller starring Jacqueline Bisset and Nick Nolte. Admittedly, the film had more of a link to Spielberg's classic than most, having been based on a book by *Jaws* author Peter Benchley.

He would round out the 1970s with an Oscar nomination for his work on the coming-of-age picture, *Breaking Away*. Suffice to say, when Krull came around, Peter Yates was something of a seasoned veteran.

With *Star Wars* having taken the world by storm in 1977, science fiction was thrust back into the mainstream. The release of *The Empire Strikes Back* in 1980 merely proved how popular the genre had become and studios were quick to cash in with cheap knock-offs, though few were of any substance (or much in the way of box office). Hoping to ride on the bandwagon was Columbia Pictures, who set to work on what would become known as Krull. To craft the screenplay, they hired writer Stanford Sherman, who cut his teeth on *Batman* and *The Man from U.N.C.L.E* and had seen recent success with the Clint Eastwood sequel, *Every Which Way You Can*. Sherman was tasked with combining the hi-tech adventure of *Star Wars* and the fantastical elements of *Lord of the Rings*, into a movie that the studio hoped would attract fans of both (along with everyone else). At one point, it was rumoured that the producers had been seeking a tie-in with the Dungeons & Dragons brand. Whilst the story persisted for many years after Krull's release, there was never actually an official approach – though a Dungeons & Dragons script was said to be in the works at around the same time (elements of which would make it into the 1983 cartoon series of the same name).

With the script nearing completion, Columbia set about gathering a production team and cast. Hoping to live up to the epic moniker, a huge $27M budget was put in place. To put that into some perspective – *Raiders of the Lost Ark* had cost $18M to bring to screens, while *Return of the Jedi* would weigh in at $32.5M. Curiously, Krull's estimated budget may actually have been higher still, with some stating it was closer to the $40M mark. Whatever its final cost ended up being, the studio wanted to ensure it was up on the screen for all to see.

Forgoing major stars, Krull's cast was made up of relatively unknown actors. Indeed, even the most famous of the crew, Carry On stalwart Bernard Bresslaw, was hidden behind layers of prosthetics that would turn him into the Cyclops, Rell. Colwyn would be played by Ken Marshall, who had recently gained some attention as Marco Polo in a TV mini-series of the same name. He would be joined by Lysette Anthony as Lyssa, a model-turned-actress who was dubbed 'the Face of the Eighties' by photographer David Bailey and who had made her screen debut in soap opera *Crossroads* when she was only a year old. Ynyr, essentially the Obi-Wan role, would be portrayed by Freddie Jones, a character actor whose work stretched back to the early 1960s. He had found fame playing Claudius in the TV series, *The Caesars*, amongst many other pieces of work on both stage and screen. Perhaps more interesting for a contemporary audience is the supporting cast. Aside from *Grange Hill's* Todd Carty and David Battley as Ergo The Magnificent, was Alun Armstrong, Robbie Coltrane and Liam Neeson.

Armstrong had been acting on TV and in films for over ten years by the time he took the role in Krull. He had scored his first on-screen role by writing to director Mike Hodges when he was looking to cast local actors in *Get Carter*. From there, he would appear in a number of roles throughout the decade, taking in both situation comedy and one-off dramas. In contrast, Robbie Coltrane was still a relative newcomer in 1982, and while Krull was his fifth film role to date, it was arguably his biggest at that point. Like Alun Armstrong, Liam Neeson had been bitten by the acting bug fairly early on in his life, but it would be a number of years before he would make his screen debut. Instead, he took on a number of casual jobs and trained as a teacher before joining a Belfast-based theatre troupe. While performing on stage as Lennie Small in *Of Mice and Men*, he was spotted by John Boorman, who offered Neeson a part in *Excalibur*, which helped prepare him somewhat for his role of Kegan in Krull.

Columbia spared no expense when it came to the physical production of the film, taking over ten sound stages at Pinewood, including the biggest of them all – the 007 stage. In all, more than 23 sets were created, and further location shooting took place in Italy and the Canary Islands. With construction underway on the enormous swamp set, work began on the Slayer costumes and a self-contained animatronics suit for The Beast, the first of its kind according to special effects supervisor Nick Maley. For Krull's score, the studio hired James Horner, who had won acclaim for his work on *Star Trek: The Wrath of Khan* the previous year. Horner had begun his career scoring movies for Roger Corman, steadily working on bigger productions. After the success the *Star Trek* sequel bought him, he became one of the most sought after composers of the 1980s, and would go on to provide the score for *Aliens, Willow* and *Field of Dreams*, to name but a few.

The shoot itself appears to have been uneventful. Despite this being Peter Yates' first foray into science fiction, he had little problem handling the effects and make-up work that many of the scenes required. With shooting coming to a close in late 1982/early 1983, post-production work got underway. It was around this time that the decision was made to dub Robbie Coltrane's voice with that of TV star Michael Elphick. Similarly, Lysette Anthony also found her voice was replaced with that of American Lindsay Crouse. The theory put forward for this by Columbia Pictures president Frank Price was that people in the United States were more likely to see a film with an unknown American actress' voice than an unknown English one. It is not clear when Coltrane discovered his dialogue had been replaced, but Anthony was told after the dubbing had already taken place and had been completely unaware beforehand.

Meanwhile, the studio looked ahead to the film's marketing and its late summer release. With a huge budget to recoup, and no major stars with which to promote the picture, Columbia knew the story, scale and effects would have to do most of the grunt work to get people into theatres. To help promote the picture and add further revenue streams, they set up marketing deals with Parker Brothers for a Krull board game and sold the videogame rights to Atari. A pinball game was also designed but never went into production. Alan Dean Foster wrote the novelisation and Marvel produced a comic book tie-in.

The cinematic landscape back then was quite different to the one we know today. While cinema-going was still popular, the boom of the home video market was starting to cut deep into its revenue. Some even predicted the death of movie-going within five years. A wide release back in the early 1980s would grace between 1000 and 1600 locations and while multiplex theatres did exist, it wasn't in any great number. Re-issues were still incredibly popular and it was not unusual to see last summer's hits being rolled out again twelve months later (Disney movies aside, home video would soon eviscerate that revenue stream). The summer of 1983 promised to be one of the biggest in history thanks to the May 25th release of *Return of the Jedi*. Even though no studio would go up directly against Episode VI, there were more than enough major releases willing to take a chance both before and after it made its debut.

Hoping to distance itself from Jedi, but still capture the summer market, Columbia opted for a July 29th release date for Krull, where it would be up against the Chevy Chase comedy, *National Lampoon's Vacation* and *Private School*, an *Animal House/Porky's* knock-off. Competition from the week before consisted of the Rob Lowe comedy *Class* and *Jaws 3D*. While on paper Krull had a lot going for it, its lack of a major star hurt the picture, especially going up against a Chevy Chase vehicle. Furthermore, reviews weren't positive, with a number citing the picture's downbeat tone as something of a stumbling block. It certainly looked the epic that had been promised but few felt it added up to much of anything.

Out at 1,281 locations, Krull stalled and never really got chance to recover. It made $5.4M during its opening weekend and had to settle for a fifth place finish. The studio was right to be fearful of *Return of the Jedi* – even in its tenth weekend on general release, it was still very real competition and actually finished higher. As expected, *National Lampoon's Vacation* took the top spot, making $8.3M, while *Jaws 3D* dropped 45% from its opening weekend, earning $7.2M. Krull held quite well in its second frame up against *Risky Business*, but surprisingly, had already begun to shed its location count. It managed one more weekend in the top ten before vanishing completely.

All up the picture made $16.5M, some way short of its $26M budget, and became one of the costliest failures of the year (and an even bigger flop if the rumoured higher budget figure was true). The lack of star power, strong competition and poor reviews were all contributing factors to its downfall. However, while the home video market was seen by some as the death knell for cinema, for studios it became a second chance at making money. Krull enjoyed success on VHS, and over the intervening years gained a cult following. It rarely makes it into the top films of the 1980s, but is often cited as an unappreciated gem, with a new generation discovering the movie on DVD and again on Blu-Ray. As for Columbia Pictures, one imagines their disappointment was short-lived when *Ghostbusters* opened the following summer and became one of the biggest releases of all time.

Post-Krull, Peter Yates never made another science fiction-based picture, but continued to enjoy success for many years. Indeed, he won great critical acclaim (and another Oscar nomination) for his adaptation of *The Dresser*, which was also released in 1983. In an interesting twist, Ynyr actor Freddie Jones had made the role of 'Sir' famous in the original stage production. Like Yates, Jones would continue to work for many years, teaming up a number of times with David Lynch (with whom he had worked on *The Elephant Man*), along with a memorable turn in *Young Sherlock Holmes*. Robbie Coltrane made waves with the role of Danny McGlone in *Tutti Frutti* and again as Eddie Fitzgerald in *Cracker*. To a whole new generation of fans, he will always be Hagrid from the *Harry Potter* series. On the other hand, Liam Neeson stuck it out in Hollywood, making a name for himself in a number of pictures. It was his role as Oskar Schindler in Steven Spielberg's 1993 drama, *Schindler's List* that bought him international recognition. The actor would later reinvent himself as a modern action hero in the movie *Taken* and continues to be a popular draw today.

Lysette Anthony would go on to become a household name by the mid-1980s and combined a successful TV career with movie and theatre roles. She appeared in the Michael Elphick sitcom, *Three Up, Two Down*, and alongside Michael Caine in *Jack the Ripper* and

Without a Clue. She would also attract acclaim for her role in Woody Allen's 1992 movie, *Husbands and Wives.* Sadly, Krull's failure all but ended Ken Marshall's career before it had got going. He wasn't seen on screen again until 1987 and is remembered more nowadays for the role of Michael Eddington in *Deep Space Nine.*

Had Krull been a success, one imagines a sequel would have been forthcoming – a prophecy central to the film tells of Colwyn and Lyssa ruling the planet, and their son ruling the galaxy. Instead, it became a minor footnote in cinema history. Like many movies of the era, time has not been kind to Krull, but there is still much to enjoy. The sets still impress, and the script introduces enough adventure to keep the pace brisk yet entertaining. It's also not afraid to utilise a number of darker elements, including a somewhat downbeat final third. Krull may not be remembered in the same way as *Return of the Jedi*, but it is still worth seeking out or rediscovering.

If you enjoyed Krull, you might like these…

Highlander

Russell Mulcahy directs Christopher Lambert and Sean Connery in a tale about immortals destined to fight until only one remains. A time-hopping, globe-spanning adventure featuring a fantastic turn by Clancy Brown as The Kurgan, backed up by a suitably epic Queen soundtrack.

The film wasn't a hit upon release but went on to spawn numerous (terrible) sequels, a TV show, animated film and more. The original remains a great piece of entertainment that still plays incredibly well today. Its non-linear storytelling keeps the film fresh and Mulcahy handles the transition from 80s New York to 14th Century Scotland, by way of war-torn Germany, brilliantly.

Trivia: The script was actually written for a class assignment project given to Gregory Widen while attending a screenwriting course at UCLA. It began life as Shadow Clan.

The Beastmaster

One of the many Conan clones that were big at the start of the 1980s. Marc Singer plays Dar, a warrior with the ability to communicate with animals. He's thrown into a battle against Rip Torn's Maax. Aided by an eagle, a black tiger, two ferrets and 80s siren Tanya Roberts, Dar travels to the city of Aruk to avenge his people.

Another minor release that gained a following over the years, The Beastmaster still has a lot to enjoy, and is a lot less brutal than Conan or the ultra-violent (but excellent) The Sword and The Sorcerer. The film went on to spawn three sequels and a short-lived TV show.

Trivia: Two sequels followed, one in 1991 entitled Through the Portal of Time and another in 1996 known as The Eye of Braxus.

Legend

Ridley Scott's art house, dark fairy tale starred a young Tom Cruise, Mia Sara and a near unrecognisable Tim Curry. Buried beneath a mountain of prosthetics (thanks to make-up genius Rob Bottin), Curry's performance as Darkness drew much of the praise the film garnered.

The film went through numerous issues during filming, with one huge set completely burning down. The final version of the movie was hacked to pieces to make it more palatable to audiences and Scott's full vision wasn't seen until 2002 with the release of the director's cut. Legend remains an interesting curio that's worthy of re-discovery.

Trivia: According to special effects make-up artist Rob Bottin, at the time the film had the biggest make-up crew ever assembled for a single project

-----

Flash Gordon

He'll Save Every One of Us!

Studio: Universal Release

Date: 5th December 1980

Director: Mike Hodges

Starring: Sam Jones, Melody Anderson

Budget: $27M – 2015 Equivalent: $82M

U.S Box Office: $27.1M – 2015 Equivalent: $82.3M

When the plane carrying football star Flash Gordon and journalist Dale Arden crash lands into the house of Dr Hans Zarkov, the duo find themselves coerced into travelling to the planet Mongo, the apparent source of a series of bizarre weather phenomena that Earth is experiencing. Once there, they discover Mongo is ruled with an iron fist by Ming the Merciless, and it is up to Flash to put a stop to his plans before Earth is destroyed.

The origins of Flash Gordon stretch back to the early 1930s. Created by Alex Raymond, the character first appeared in comic strip form on January 7th 1934 and was both inspired by, and in direct competition with, Buck Rogers. In the original strips, Gordon was a polo player and Yale graduate – and was portrayed as the archetypal American hero. When a plane carrying Flash and his companion, Dale Arden, crashes near the home of Dr. Hans Zarkov, the pair finds themselves kidnapped. Zarkov is convinced Earth is being attacked from the planet Mongo and coerces Flash and Dale to travel there with him in a craft he has created. Once there the trio faces off against Ming the Merciless who is revealed to be behind the attacks. The strip would take in a number of locations across Mongo, and the adventurers would find themselves both helped and hindered by the planet's inhabitants. Ming would ultimately be overthrown, and this enabled Flash's adventures to take in other planets and galaxies, alongside regular visits to Mongo.

The strip was incredibly popular, appearing in daily and Sunday papers across America. Raymond's Sunday run would last eleven years, while Austin Briggs would produce daily strips from 1940-44. Going forward from there, Briggs worked on both strips, before passing on the weekend edition to Mac Raboy in 1948. In the years that followed, Dan Barry took over the daily run, while Raboy continued to work on the weekend strip, until his death in 1967. Flash Gordon continued to be a staple of American papers for many years; with Barry himself working on both daily and weekend strips until 1990. The latest story, Flash Gordon: Zeitgeist appeared in 2011, with a Ming spin-off following in 2012. Over the years there were also novels, along with reprints of the earlier strips, radio serials and at least one magazine adventure.

Such was the popularity of the characters that a serial movie was put into production in 1936, with athlete Buster Crabbe as the titular hero. Shown in thirteen instalments, Flash Gordon followed a similar storyline to the comic strips, with the characters initially landing on Mongo and facing off against Ming the Merciless. Each week's segment would follow on from the previous one – which always ended on a cliffhanger to ensure a returning audience the following week. It was the first primarily science fiction based serial ever made, and would eventually be released as a standalone picture entitled *Rocket Ship*. Two further serials would be created, with Crabbe and the majority of the principal cast reprising their roles. These too would be released as standalone pictures sometime after their initial serial run. Flash Gordon's *Trip to Mars* debuted in 1938, with *Flash Gordon Conquers the Universe* arriving in 1940. Like *Rocket Ship*, the movie versions would carry different names to their serial counterparts, becoming *Flash Gordon: The Deadly Ray* and *The Purple Death from Outer Space*.

The characters weren't only confined to the silver screen either. In 1954, Telefusion and Intercontinental Television Films teamed up to produce a 39-part TV show. Curiously, while it would feature Flash,

Dale and Zarkov, arch-nemesis Ming and the planet Mongo were nowhere to be seen. Despite remaining a popular strip, Flash Gordon would be absent from screens for a number of years, until George Lucas and Gary Kurtz attempted to secure the movie rights from King Features in the 1970s. King demanded too much money and creative control, leaving the duo to start from scratch. Lucas went on to borrow pieces from Flash Gordon (along with elements of Kurosawa's *The Hidden Fortress*) when he moved forward with his own original science fiction film, *Star Wars*. The subsequent huge success of Lucas' picture did not go unnoticed by uber producer Dino De Laurentiis.

Laurentiis had been a producer working in Italy for a number of years – starting in 1940 with *L'ultimo Combattimento*. He went on to work on a variety of projects, including the production of Federico Fellini's *La Strada*, which won the first ever Foreign Film Academy Award in 1956. In the 1970s, he turned his attention to America, working on such pictures as *Serpico* and *Three Days of the Condor*. After producing a remake of *King Kong* (to weak critical response but decent box office) it is said he witnessed the incredible success of Star Wars, and sought to secure the rights to Flash Gordon. It must be noted, there is conflicting information regarding Lucas, Laurentiis and Flash Gordon. Some sources claim Lucas approached Laurentiis to buy the rights, and when turned down, went on to create *Star Wars*. Others state that Laurentiis only obtained the rights when he saw how successful Lucas' picture had become.

According to the Internet Movie Database, producer Lou Scheimer sought out Laurentiis when he needed to raise additional funds to complete his animated Flash Gordon movie-of-the-week for NBC. Laurentiis agreed to help on the proviso that Scheimer could secure him the theatrical movie rights – which he promptly did. With the rights in hand, the project could move forward, and the Italian producer had one person in mind to direct. In 1930s Italy, most American comics were banned by Mussolini. However, prior to embarking upon his career in film, famed director Federico Fellini worked on a number of bootleg Flash Gordon strips. Upon securing the rights to the character and his universe, Laurentiis sought out Fellini to direct the big screen adaptation, but the director was not interested and turned down the offer.

With Fellini out of the running, the producer looked to Nicholas Roeg to take on the job. Roeg had begun his career as a photographer and camera operator, graduating to a second unit photography credit on *Lawrence of Arabia*. In the 1970s, he'd had a stunning run of films, making his directorial debut on *Performance*. He followed this up with the acclaimed Walkabout and horror film *Don't Look Now*. He gained further notice for the David Bowie science fiction drama, *The Man Who Fell to Earth*. Roeg sank himself into the entire Flash Gordon universe, and spent a year crafting a script. While impressed, Laurentiis passed, and informed

Roeg: "I don't want to make that picture. Please stay and I'll tell you the picture I want to make."

Roeg walked and the producer signed Mike Hodges on to helm the picture instead. Initially he was said to have been the choice to direct the already-in-the-works sequel. However, with Roeg out of the running, the *Get Carter* director was placed front-and-centre. There's conjecture over this situation, as some sources claim Hodges was actually the eighth director the picture was offered to. Third choice or eighth, Flash Gordon now had a director. The production also scored an ace when they managed to secure the talents of *Star Wars* director of photography, Gil Taylor. With Roeg's script deemed unusable, Laurentiis hired Lorenzo Semple Jnr. with whom he had worked on the *King Kong* remake. Semple got his start on the Adam West Batman TV show, scripting the pilot and the first four episodes, while also acting as executive story producer on the remainder of the first season. He would go on to provide the screenplay for *Batman the Movie* in 1966. He changed tack for 1968's *Pretty Poison*, and won acclaim for his work on *The Parallax View* and *Three Days of the Condor*, which marked *his first collaboration with Dino De Laurentiis. Knowing Semple's work on Batman*, it is easy to see how Flash Gordon ended up with a similar tone despite the source material being a more serious affair.

Casting could now get underway. The first choice to play Flash was Kurt Russell, who at that point in his career was something of a screen veteran. Russell had started acting in 1957 and became a popular child actor who had comfortably managed the transition to adult star. When the offer came through, he was busy working with John Carpenter on the TV movie Elvis. Russell quickly passed, deeming the character and script one-dimensional. A young Arnold Schwarzenegger, who had gained notoriety for his work on the documentary *Pumping Iron*, auditioned for the part, but was dismissed due to his strong Austrian accent. In the end, Flash Gordon was found in the most unusual of places – as a contestant on *The Dating Game*. Sam J. Jones had little acting experience, having had a bit part in the Dudley Moore comedy *Ten*, and a spread in *Playgirl*, but he looked the part of the all-American hero. According to Jones, one of Laurentiis' relatives had seen his appearance on *The Dating Game* and suggested him for the part; he was signed up the next day. Melody Anderson, who played Dale Arden (and also had a role in Carpenter's Elvis movie) found herself pursued by the producer, despite having the same opinion on the script as Kurt Russell. She'd already passed on the role but Laurentiis refused to take no for an answer. Anderson relented and found herself on-board a plane for England that night. According to an interview she gave to Starlog in 1980, she arrived Saturday morning for a screen test and make-up trial (including dying her blonde locks brown) and by Monday was on the way to Scotland to commence filming on Tuesday.

Actor and singer Topol (famed for his role in *Fiddler on the Roof*) was chosen as Dr Hans Zarkov, and along with Max von Sydow, added an international flavour to the cast – along with giving the production a certain amount of credibility. Sydow had been a fan of the comic strip as a boy and thought the role offered him something a little different from the norm. In contrast, Royal Shakespeare Company stalwart Timothy Dalton viewed the role of Prince Barin as little more than a paycheck. Elsewhere, somewhat disgraced actor Peter Wyngarde would provide a memorable turn as Ming's second in command, Klytus, while Brian Blessed offered a bombastic performance as Vultan – a role for which the actor is still best known despite a huge body of other work. Rounding out the cast would be Italian actress Ornella Muti, who would make her English language debut on the picture in a role that was almost as memorable as Blessed's.

Flash Gordon may have looked a little cheap on-screen, but this couldn't be further from the truth. The studio put forth a budget of between $20-30M (sources vary on this, though $27M is the figure regularly bandied about). The lavish sets and outrageous costumes would certainly attest to that. Indeed, some said the film itself was shot more around the costumes than it was the script. Filming took place in Scotland and England, at both Elstree and Shepperton studios. Things went off the rails almost as soon as shooting had commenced. With Semple's script more than a little on the camp side, Jones and Anderson were told to play the roles absolutely straight – which resulted in the picture becoming unintentionally funny. Upon seeing the first rushes, Laurentiis was upset by the laughter of the crew, and pushed the actors to play the roles with even more seriousness. This only made the performances funnier still. Scenes and sequence were created and scrapped with alarming regularity. The Italian crew didn't get on with the English one, and rarely discussed what the other should be doing – but both agreed they were right. Language barriers also meant the Italian crew weren't able to report back that things weren't quite how Laurentiis and the studio had envisioned.

Director and cast would turn up on set with little idea of what they would find – either in terms of set design or costumes. Hodges shot whatever he could. Years later, he would describe the film as "the only improvised $27-million movie ever made." The fabled duel between Barin and Flash left the actors covered in silver paint, which had to be removed between set ups. Impractical costumes made the shoot arduous for many, especially Vultan's hawk men who were unable to sit down once their wings were attached. The climactic attack on the War Rocket Ajax took three days to set up, and left many of the cast suspended in mid-air for hours at a time. Blessed's hijinks resulted in the entire sequence being reset (something that took a further day to achieve) when it was revealed during the rushes that he'd accompanied his bazooka shots with 'pew, pew, pew'. Even Melody Anderson was caught up in the chaos. A proposed sequence would see Ming cause Flash to hallucinate that Dale had turned into a giant spider. A huge costume was created and the actress spent four hours in make-up and a further six shooting the sequence only to be told that while it looked great, they couldn't use it as it had nothing to do with the script.

Off-set, Sam Jones was running into problems himself. Forever getting into fights, at one point he ended up in hospital requiring stitches to his face. According to legend, Laurentiis himself burst into the theatre and insisted the doctor leave the actor with no visible scarring. Such incidents led to one of the most infamous stories surrounding the shoot and one that would have a long-term effect on Jones' career. There are a number of theories behind the fact that Jones' voice was dubbed in the finished film. Hodges claimed the majority of filming was complete with only some second unit work remaining, for which he used Jones' stunt double. The director managed to find someone to impersonate Jones' voice for any lines required, which ended up being used in the finished product. However, Jones claims the vast majority of his lines were dubbed. According to the book *Dino: The Life and Film of Dino De Laurentiis*, Jones and the producer had a falling out about money (and Jones' off-set behaviour) and when shooting broke for Christmas, the actor went back to Los Angeles, never to return. The book goes on to claim Flash Gordon must have been the only film completed without its principal star. Chances are, there is truth to both these theories – with Jones' stand-in having to complete the film in his absence and the impersonator doing the rest.

In spite of all these issues, shooting was completed at a lightning pace due to the requirement of an extended post-production period to add in the film's many visual effects. As the pieces started to pull together, thoughts turned towards the soundtrack. Mike Hodges wanted Pink Floyd, but ended up settling for Queen. The band's management approached the production upon seeing 20 minutes of the finished picture. Laurentiis had never heard of the legendary band but commissioned them to create the soundtrack upon hearing some of their work. Queen were given reign to produce whatever they wanted, provided it complimented the picture. Flash Gordon became the band's ninth album and the first of only two soundtracks they would provide (the other being *Highlander*). All but two tracks were instrumentals, though snippets of dialogue are heard throughout. The idea to use dialogue wasn't actually part of the original plan. Brian May and Roger Taylor were composing the score and inserted dialogue to get a feel for how the music would work within the film. Impressed with the experiment, they left it in the final product, leading to the memorable single, Flash.

Dino De Laurentiis anticipated (and hoped) that Flash Gordon would be an even bigger hit than *Star Wars*. Hype was building as its December release approached, helped in part by trailers and Queen's Flash receiving plenty of airplay. Reviews were generally positive (the film holds an 81% approval rating on Rotten Tomatoes) with attention paid to the sets, costumes and soundtrack. While not the costliest film of the time (as mentioned, the budget was somewhere between $20-30M), Flash Gordon still needed to be a sizable hit to recoup its budget and secure any sequels. In comparison, the number one movie of 1980, *The Empire Strikes Back*, cost $18M and made back $209M (admittedly this was the sequel to one of the biggest films of all time).

Flash would have little in the way of competition, with only *Popeye* waiting in the wings. There were some comedy heavy-hitters in December, but as they didn't skew the same demographic, they weren't seen as competition as such. The picture opened on the 5th December 1980 at 823 locations, earning an OK $3.4M during its first weekend. While there's little to compare it to, *Stir Crazy*, which opened a week later, made $8.6M and the aforementioned *Popeye* earned $6.3M. Thanks in part to the Christmas break, the picture would go on to earn $27.1M in North America and although it pretty much covered its costs, it was still seen as a flop. It performed very well in the UK, making $14M and becoming one of the biggest releases of the year. It did solid business in Italy too. But the film lacked the breakout success of *Star Wars*, and that put any proposed sequel (or trilogy) to bed. Like *Krull*, Flash Gordon became a hit on the burgeoning home video market and gained a very strong cult following in the intervening years.

Post-Flash, Sam Jones found himself in a number of TV movies and one-off episodes. He had a short-lived TV show in 1987, *The*

Highwayman, which ran for 10 episodes before being cancelled. Since then, he has continued to work but has never come close to the high profile of that first major role. Melody Anderson led a similar path, appearing in one-off episodes of popular shows of the time such as *The A-Team* and *Murder She Wrote*. She had recurring roles in *St. Elsewhere* and *Manimal*, but appeared to have retired from show business in 1995. Topol appeared in the mini-series *War and Remembrance* in 1983, and played the same part in the follow up *The Winds of War*. He would go on to reprise his *Fiddler on the Roof* role to great acclaim, touring the production throughout the world.

Max Von Sydow went from the strength to strength. Already a well-respected actor, he would continue to mix mainstream Hollywood fare with smaller European movies. His role in 1987's *Pelle the Conqueror* helped earn the film a Best Foreign Film Academy Award. As is well-documented, Timothy Dalton would take over from Roger Moore as James Bond, making his debut as the character in *The Living Daylights*. He gained further notice for his role in the *Gone with the Wind* sequel, *Scarlett*. At the time of writing, he has a recurring role in the TV show, Penny Dreadful. Director Mike Hodges switched to TV movies before returning to theatrical releases with 1985's *Morons from Outer Space*. The 1998 movie *Croupier* won him (and star Clive Owen) much attention.

Flash Gordon's influence still resonates, with director Edgar Wright citing it as a favourite of his, and using some of its visual cues in

Scott Pilgrim Vs The World. Writer and director Seth MacFarlane went a step further and featured the film prominently in his 2012 comedy, *Ted*. He even had Sam Jones play himself, recreating the rocket cycle scene with star Mark Wahlberg. Attempts to bring Flash Gordon back to screens have been made over the years, most notably in a 2007 TV series which ran for a single season. As recently as April 2014, there has been talk of another film, with Fox securing the rights to the character and setting *Star Trek 3* (reboot) writers J.D. Payne and Patrick McKay to work on the script.

Looking back today, the film still holds up well. The costumes and sets still impress, as does Queen's soundtrack. While some of the acting will elicit laughter, a number of sequences still work effectively, particularly the trial of the wood beast. And despite its campy tone, the picture is quite graphic in places and doesn't shy away from what are exceptionally traumatic experiences for the main characters – Flash's 'death' and Zarkov's memory wiping being the stand outs. With 2014 being the character's 80th birthday, there's no better time to rediscover the movie.

Flash – He'll save every one of us.

If you enjoyed Flash Gordon, try one of these…

Spacehunter: Adventures in the Forbidden Zone

Peter Strauss stars as Wolff, a salvager-cum-bounty hunter who attempts to rescue three 'Earth girls' captured for Michael Ironside's pleasure. Aided by young scavenger Molly Ringwald (and hindered by fellow salvager Ernie Hudson), Spacehunter has a lot going for it, not the least of which is a bizarre and deadly assault course sequence. Michael Ironside turns in a suitably manic performance as Overdog, a part man/part machine creation with huge mechanical pincer hands.

The post-apocalyptic genre was popular in the early 80s but thanks to opening a week before *Return of the Jedi*, Spacehunter vanished as quickly as it appeared. The picture was notable for being part of the resurgence in 3D, along with the likes of the *Jaws 3D*, *Parasite* and the third entry in the Amityville horror series. While its effects haven't aged well, it remains an entertaining slice of science fiction.

Trivia: Mid-way through production, director Jean LeFleur was replaced by Lamont Johnson.

Masters of the Universe

Based on the Mattel He-Man toy range, Masters of the Universe featured Dolph Lundgren as He-Man and Frank Langella as Skeletor. The story sees the hero and his comrades displaced from Castle Greyskull and finding themselves on Earth when an attempt to retake the castle fails. Now in a different realm, He-Man must team up with teenagers Kevin and Julie to battle Skeletor's forces both on Earth and back in Eternia.

Masters of the Universe was created to cash in on the huge success of the cartoon series, which itself was spawned from the toy range (and not the other way round, as is the norm) but did little to revive flagging sales. Much maligned upon release, the film has a cheesy, camp quality about it and makes a decent double bill with Flash Gordon.

Trivia: A proposed sequel was scrapped and ended up becoming the Jean Claude Van Damme science fiction movie, *Cyborg*.

The Adventures of Buckaroo Banzai Across the 8th Dimension

With a cast featuring the likes of Peter Weller, John Lithgow, Clancy Brown and Jeff Goldblum, Buckaroo Banzai may well be the one of the most cult sci-fi features in history. Weller stars as the titular hero, a physicist, neurosurgeon, race car driver and rock star all in one, who battles the Red Lectroids, an inter-dimensional alien race from Planet 10.

The picture was in development for so long that, by the time shooting commenced, director W D Richter had a 300-page Complete Buckaroo Banzai dossier, which consisted of countless notes and every scrapped script that had been written. Attempting to splice action, comedy, science fiction and romance, the film failed to find an audience at the box office but became a minor hit on video. In the intervening years its popularity has risen and for those that get it, it remains a much-loved classic.

Trivia: Despite its end titles promising a sequel, Buckaroo Banzai against the World Crime League, the failure of the original movie saw plans shelved indefinitely.

WarGames

Is it a game, or is it real?

Studio: United Artists/MGM

Release Date: 6th June 1983

Director: John Badham

Starring: Matthew Broderick, Ally Sheedy

Budget: $12M – 2015 Equivalent: $28.6M

U.S Box Office: $79.5M – 2015 Equivalent: $189.8M

David Lightman is curious to play a series of new computer games, and sets about hacking into a game company's system to find them. However, unbeknownst to him, he's actually found his way into a US military war simulator and he's about to discover that this is one game that could turn very deadly – for everyone.

For the modern audience, it's perhaps a little baffling to see how prevalent the threat of nuclear war was back in the early 1980s. With

Ronald Reagan in power, the Russians and Americans pursued a game of nuclear one-upmanship, whose effects quickly spread to all facets of life. People became survivalists, built fallout shelters and campaigned to 'Ban the Bomb'. Never one to miss a trick, Hollywood was quick to use the nuclear threat as the central device in a number of projects. Initially the focus was on the dangers of nuclear power, with 1979's *The China Syndrome* being among the first. The Jack Lemmon/Jane Fonda picture opened just twelve days before the nuclear disaster at Three Mile Island proved the dangers were all too real.

As fear grew, TV events *The Day After* and *Threads* showed the devastating aftermath of a nuclear holocaust on small groups of the general populace. *Red Dawn* went one step further, featuring a Russian-led invasion of America; with nuclear weapons decimating the bigger cities, high school students of one small town made a stand against the invading armies. World War Three seemed only a button press away.

Despite the central threat of global thermonuclear war, the 1983 release WarGames began life as quite a different picture. Conceived in the late seventies by screenwriters Lawrence Lasker and Walter F. Parkes, the story was known as The Genius, a drama featuring a dying scientist named Falken and a troubled, yet brilliant teenager onto whom he hopes to pass all his knowledge. Computers didn't yet feature in the story, but that changed when the duo met Peter

Schwartz and David Scott Lewis. Schwartz worked at the Stanford Research Institute and introduced Lasker and Parkes to the growing culture of hackers and hacking. He also highlighted the link between computers, gaming and the military.

This was further cemented during a meeting with hacker David Scott Lewis in early 1979, who would go on to be the primary inspiration for David Lightman, the lead character in the story. Lewis claims that even at that early stage, much of the scientist/protégée aspect was absent from the story and that part of the plot featured a space-based laser defence system not unlike the Star Wars programme Ronald Reagan would unveil a few years later. The script went through several incarnations and along the way moved from being known as The Genius to WarGames. The central premise, that of a hacker who almost triggers a nuclear war, began to take shape.

The military aspect of the story became clearer too. While researching ideas for their 'war room' Lasker and Parkes met another person who would have an influence on the script. Having coerced their way onto a tour of a military defence nerve centre (located under Cheyenne Mountain) the pair met James Hartinger, then commander of NORAD (North American Aerospace Defence Command). Interested in their script, Hartinger arranged to meet them off-base. He was very much in favour of one of the core aspects of the story; that computers were taking too much responsibility out of people's hands.

Despite the fact that the script had dropped the central idea of Falken being a brilliant but doomed scientist, the character still featured. Lasker later stated during an interview with Wired that Falken had been based loosely on Stephen Hawking – especially during the initial stages. The idea that a man could hold all this knowledge and might never get the chance to pass it on, intrigued him. In his mind, Lasker pictured John Lennon playing the character, and at one point received word from music producer David Geffen that Lennon was interested in the role. Sadly, while working on the second draft (in which Falken was now an astrophysicist), the scriptwriter received a phone call informing him that Lennon had been shot and killed.

As the script transformed from a drama to a thriller, its scale altered to match. The screen version of the NORAD control centre had Universal voice concerns about its construction costs. Further complicating the matter was the fact that the studio executives didn't understand the script or much of its terminology – a fear they thought the general public would share. Universal opted to pass, and the project stalled until United Artists stepped in to pick up the reigns. By now, WarGames was a fully-fleshed out and ready-to-shoot script, and UA wasted no time in attaching Martin Brest to direct the picture.

Brest was an interesting choice as director. He had won some acclaim for a short he made during his film school days – *Hot Dogs for Gauguin*, which starred Danny DeVito and Rhea Perlman (making her movie debut). The film told the tale of a photographer determined to catch that one amazing shot – and in an effort to achieve this, planned to blow up the Statue of Liberty. Brest's work on *Gauguin* secured him his first major directing gig – that of the George Burns caper, *Going in Style*. This raised his profile higher, and bought him to the attention of United Artists, who were now getting ready to move forward on WarGames.

Brest got straight to work and is said to have had a major hand in the design of the NORAD control room, which would end up being the most expensive set built up to that point at a cost of one million dollars (WarGames overall budget was $12M). Interestingly, because the production team wasn't allowed access to the actual war room, they had to create their own interpretation of what it might look like. It wasn't until several years later that it was revealed that the movie's NORAD set was far more elaborate than the real thing and visitors to the place would often ask to see the 'modern computer rooms'.

With set construction underway, work got started on casting the lead roles of David Lightman and Jennifer Mack. For Lightman, the producers opted for Matthew Broderick, a newcomer with only a single film credit to his name. Despite the lack of screen work, Broderick was no stranger to theatre and had recently won acclaim for his work in *Torch Song Trilogy*. A favourable review of the play by veteran critic Mel Gussow got the young actor Broadway's attention. He went on to win further positive notices for Neil Simon's *Eugene Trilogy* and would make his screen debut in *Max Dugan Returns*, another project penned by Simon.

Ally Sheedy, who would play Jennifer, came to acting from a different direction. Although she performed with the American Ballet Theatre from age six to fourteen, she found herself thrust into the public eye when she wrote a best-selling children's book, *She was Nice to Mice*, when aged just twelve. Having dabbled in acting during her summers off, Sheedy switched to the profession full-time when she discovered she would need to stay on a starvation diet if she was to continue with ballet.

In the meantime, her book gained her the attention of The Village Voice and the New York Times, both of whom wanted her to write for them. She ended up taking on another writing assignment, and it was while promoting it on *The Mike Douglas Show* that she was spotted by an agent and signed up almost immediately. She initially worked on commercials, off-Broadway plays and after-school specials. Once she hit 18, Sheedy headed for Hollywood and appeared in a number of one-off dramas, along with a short recurring role on *Hill Street Blues*. This work led her to be cast opposite Sean Penn in *Bad Boys* and secured her role in WarGames.

Even though the character of Steven Falken had started out as the lead role, by the time WarGames had a shooting script, he was relegated to a shadowy figure who had designed the system than Lightman hacks in to. It was Martin Brest who decided Falken should be altered. He felt a wheelchair bound man arriving at NORAD would feel too much like *Dr. Strangelove.* For the role of Falken, John Wood was cast. The English actor was well revered for his work in theatre, particularly his interpretation of Shakespeare's characters. Wood was joined by Dabney Coleman as system engineer Dr. John McKittrick and Barry Corbin as General Jack Beringer (a role highly influenced by NORAD commander James Hartinger).

Despite the many drafts the script went through and the picture being dropped by its original studio, everything looked to finally be in place. Shooting began on Goose Island for a sequence that would feature in the last third of the film. But there was trouble as soon as the first dailies were screened. The studio clashed with Brest over the dark tone he was taking. There's much speculation over what happened next, but the outcome was the same – Brest was fired after 10-12 days of shooting. Such was the fallout that the director was essentially blackballed in Hollywood for nearly two years. United Artists acted quickly to ensure the production wasn't delayed and hired John Badham to take over the job.

In stark contrast to Brest, Badham was a seasoned veteran of both TV and movie directing, having received his first credit back in 1971. Initially cutting his teeth on various television shows, he made his feature debut on *The Bingo Long Traveling All-Stars & Motor Kings*. However, it was his work on the 1977 smash hit, *Saturday Night Fever*, which thrust him well into the limelight. Badham followed that up with an adaptation of *Dracula* (featuring Frank Langella and Laurence Olivier) and the drama *Whose Life is it Anyway*, with Richard Dreyfuss. When the director received the call for WarGames, he was also in production on futuristic helicopter flick, *Blue Thunder* (the two films would be released within weeks of one another).

Badham was puzzled by what Brest had completed on WarGames before being fired. While some of it worked, (Indeed, some scenes which Brest shot remain in the finished movie), much of it felt stilted. Part of the issue was that both Broderick and Sheedy were convinced they were next to be fired, a fear that obviously fed into their performances. Having managed to convince them otherwise, Badham realised the problems on-screen were simply that the characters weren't having any fun. Hacking into the school's computer system and altering grades should have been a prank, something David did to impress Jennifer. Instead, it felt like two spies on a deadly serious mission.

All concerned set about loosening things up a little, having a bit more fun with the characters and their actions. Broderick's Lightman became less edgy and had a few of the lone-hacker traits removed or toned back. To ensure authenticity, Badham had a number of hackers visit the set, but learned that he would need to tread a fine line between realism and entertainment – erring more on the latter. The process of hacking into a computer system, he discovered, was too long winded and complicated for a movie, and needed to be stripped back to keep the story flowing. The idea to give the computer a voice also meant there was less need to have half of the movie play out on a green screen monitor. Even with many of the technical aspects removed, most hackers believe its portrayal of their kind is still one of the more accurate ones Hollywood has produced.

With shooting back on track, things progressed smoothly. Not even an on-set jeep accident could derail proceedings – a quick decision meant the crash was actually included in a scene, with an extra sequence shot to explain the aftermath. As the film entered post-production, United Artists looked towards marketing as the proposed June 3rd release date began to loom large.

Reviews for WarGames were exceptionally strong, and the film holds a 92% approval rating at Rotten Tomatoes. Roger Ebert awarded it four stars, and many other critics praised the all too realistic nature of the movie as one of its main strengths. The summer of 1983 was a busy one. The weeks leading up to

WarGames' June 3rd release had seen *Spacehunter: Adventures in the Forbidden Zone*, *Breathless* and John Badham's other picture, *Blue Thunder*. There were also re-issues of *Rocky III*, *Porky's* and *Poltergeist*. The real heavy hitter of 1983, *Return of the Jedi*, had opened the week before and took in over $30M. WarGames would also face competition on the same weekend from *The Man With Two Brains* and *Psycho II*, whilst *Octopussy* and *Trading Places* were waiting in the wings.

A solid start saw the picture open to $6.2M on that first weekend, good enough for a third place finish behind *Jedi* and *Psycho II*. Signs that WarGames was in it for the long haul appeared a week later when it lost only 22% of its business up against the new releases. By day nine, it had already recouped back its production budget. As word-of-mouth spread, its weekend takings actually increased and by the end of its first month on general release the picture had made almost $30M.

In all, WarGames managed nine straight weeks in the top ten, and never dropped lower than thirteenth place throughout its entire theatrical run (it re-entered the top ten in weekend eleven, fourteen and fifteen). The biggest weekend to weekend fall it endured was only 27%. Come the end of 1983, it was the fifth most successful film of the year, making an astounding $79.5M and finishing above *Octopussy*, *Sudden Impact* and the *Saturday Night Fever* sequel, *Staying Alive*. (*Blue Thunder* made $42M). Given its $12M investment, United Artists had been well rewarded. The picture was even nominated for three Academy Awards the following year, for cinematography, sound and for Lasker and Parkes' script.

As a result of WarGames' success, the U.S government created and updated the Computer Fraud and Abuse Act of 1984, screening footage from the film before proceedings began. Hackers and their actions came under far more scrutiny too, with their skills being blown somewhat out of proportion based on what Lightman achieved in the movie. Convicted hacker Kevin Mitnick learned this the hard way when a prosecutor convinced a federal judge that Mitnick could order a nuclear strike if allowed access to a phone. As result, he found himself in solitary confinement for a year.

WarGames did have positive effects on the hacking community too and they were in turn influenced by the film. Bulletin boards and the like saw a sharp rise in user numbers in the following months and years, and while the Internet did exist at this point, the influx of people began to shape it into the more recognisable form we know today. A yearly hacking convention took on the name DEFCON in tribute and a year after WarGames' release, the quarterly hacker magazine, 2600, made its debut.

The principal cast and crew all went on to bigger, brighter things, at least during the 1980s. Matthew Broderick followed the movie with a role in fantasy drama *Ladyhawke*, but it was his next role, as the titular character in *Ferris Bueller's Day Off*, that he is most famously remembered for to this day. He also reprised two of his early theatrical roles on the silver screen, first in *Biloxi Blues* and again in *Torch Song Trilogy*. In recent years he has preferred the stage, and won much acclaim for his work opposite Nathan Lane in *The Producers* and again in *The Odd Couple*.

Ally Sheedy became a member of The Brat Pack when she starred in *The Breakfast Club* and *St. Elmo's Fire*, both in 1985. She also re-teamed with John Badham on *Short Circuit* in 1986. However, by the turn of the decade, roles in *Heart of Dixie* and *Betsy's Wedding* saw her nominated for a Golden Raspberry award two years running. She spent much of the 1990s on smaller movie projects and TV roles, and won much acclaim for her part in the indie drama *High Art*.

John Badham had a misstep with 1985's *American Flyers*, but then had a run of hits well into the 1990s, including the aforementioned *Short Circuit, Stakeout, Bird on a Wire* and *The Hard Way*. He went on to direct a number of TV movies, before switching back to episodic TV in 2003, a place where he continues to work to this day. Lawrence Lasker and Walter Parkes worked together again on *Project X*, another picture to star Matthew Broderick. They also revisited hackers with their 1992 thriller, *Sneakers*. Parkes would go on to become president of Steven Spielberg's Amblin Entertainment and was a key player in setting up Dreamworks SKG.

As for Martin Brest, it would seem getting almost thrown out of Hollywood was the best thing that could have happened to him – at least to begin with. After being in the wilderness for a year, he bounced back with *Beverly Hills Cop*, a hugely popular (and financially successful) Eddie Murphy vehicle. He followed that up with *Midnight Run, Scent of a Woman* and *Meet Joe Black*. However, the outright disaster (both critically and financially) of 2003's *Gigli* destroyed his career, and he has not had a single credit since.

WarGames itself spawned a belated straight to DVD sequel in 2008 – *WarGames: The Dead Code*. It featured a hacker and a new computer system known as RIPLEY. WOPR and Steven Falken would also appear, though John Wood was absent from the role, as were any other original cast members. In recent years, there has been talk of a WarGames remake, and in 2009, it was rumoured that Leonardo DiCaprio was looking to produce one. In 2011, Seth Gordon signed on to direct a new version but the project didn't move forward. As of summer 2014, director Dean Israelite is attached and a new script is being worked on.

Unlike many movies that feature computers, WarGames has aged quite well, mainly due to the fact that the creators didn't go overboard with their interpretation of what the technology could do or how it appeared. The computerised voice of Joshua and

Lightman's green screen monitor stand up much better than other computer-based pictures such as *Hackers* and *The Net*. The film remains grounded and can still offer a thrilling and tense ride.

'Wouldn't you prefer a nice game of chess?'

If you enjoyed WarGames, try one of these...

Tron

Absolutely ground-breaking at the time due to its use of computer-generated images, Tron was the brainchild of writer/director Steven Lisberger. The film features Jeff Bridges as Flynn, a computer programmer who finds himself digitised into The Grid, a mainframe cyberspace where he must battle other computer programs. Teaming up with Tron and Ram, Flynn attempts to destroy the MCP system, an artificial intelligence that is seeking global domination.

While the story may be a bit convoluted, Tron is still unlike anything produced since, save for the belated sequel in 2010. The scenes inside the MCP, which make up a good two-thirds of the movie, are still a sight to behold, with the light cycle race being a particular highlight. Along with *The Last Starfighter*, Tron began a computer-generated revolution.

Trivia: The term 'computer virus' was coined by Fred Cohen after a real world analysis of system vulnerabilities highlighted in the movie.

Short Circuit

This tale of a military robot that's struck by lightning and ends up becoming human-like in the process was a hit back in 1986. Led by Steve Guttenberg and Ally Sheedy, Short Circuit gained a lot of its charm (and laughs) from the Tim Blaney-voiced Johnny 5. The robot was the most expensive part of the production, and several versions were created for use in different scenes, depending on what was required.

The picture still retains much of its charm and thanks to Johnny 5 being a mechanical creation and has aged a bit more gracefully than other films of the time. Sheedy and Guttenberg have good chemistry, and they're ably backed up by Fisher Stevens, who went on to lead the sequel. Short Circuit came midway through a great run for director John Badham, who saw box office success with *WarGames* and *Blue Thunder*, then *Stakeout* and *Bird on a Wire*.

Trivia: Fisher Stevens was fired and replaced by Bronson Pinchot, who was then fired and replaced by Stevens.

D.A.R.Y.L

A slightly more advanced take on ideas that would be raised in *Short Circuit*, regarding a machine becoming more human. In D.A.R.Y.L (Data-Analysing Robot Youth Lifeform), Barret Oliver plays what appears to be an ordinary ten-year old boy. However, he's actually the result of a military experiment to create a super soldier and has a head full of microprocessors along with super-human abilities.

When D.A.R.Y.L is released by a scientist, he's taken to an orphanage and ends up adopted by the Richardsons. In living with the family, his human traits begin to develop, but the military aren't far behind, and the last thing they want is a super-soldier with feelings. The picture was a minor hit in 1985 and while dismissed by critics at the time, remains solid family entertainment.

Trivia: The film was renamed T.O.D for its Russian release, which did not take place until 1990.

Romancing the Stone

She's a girl from the big city. He's a reckless soldier of fortune. For a fabulous treasure, they share an adventure no one could imagine... or survive.

Studio: 20th Century Fox
Release Date: 30th March 1984
Director: Robert Zemeckis
Starring: Michael Douglas, Kathleen Turner
Budget: $10M – 2015 Equivalent: $23M
U.S Box Office: $76.5M – 2015 Equivalent: $175.9M

Joan Wilder is a timid, lonely romance novelist, but a panicked phone call thrusts her into a deadly South American adventure. Teaming up with smuggler Jack T. Colton, she has to contend with all manner of dangers while trying to recover a fabled jewel and save her sister. She'll have the story of a lifetime, if she lives long enough to tell the tale.

A director being fired from a movie is a rare occurrence. One being fired from a future project because their current one is so bad, that's something of a one-off. Yet that's exactly what happened to Robert Zemeckis while working on action-adventure Romancing the Stone. The film was a gamble for all involved, but for Zemeckis, it was make or break; failure would signify the end of his short Hollywood career. In the latter half of 1983, the situation wasn't looking good.

Romancing the Stone was written by Diane Thomas, a would-be screenwriter who was working as a waitress to make ends. In true Hollywood fashion, the tale goes that Michael Douglas came into her place of work to eat and Thomas pitched the idea to him. Impressed, Douglas is said to have about purchased the script for $250,000. In reality, Thomas completed the script and sent it to her agent, who sold it to the actor some time later. Despite the comparisons Romancing the Stone would face with *Raiders of the Lost Ark*, the script actually pre-dates Spielberg's classic by two years.

At that point, Michael Douglas had a production deal with Columbia Pictures and planned to produce the film with them, as well as taking on the lead role. The studio was against the idea and wanted a much bigger name, such as Sylvester Stallone or Christopher Reeve. It's worth noting that back in the early 1980s Michael Douglas wasn't seen as movie star material. The son of famed actor Kirk, Michael had got his first break in a CBS TV playhouse production in 1969. In that same year, he appeared in the movie *Hail, Hero!* for which he was nominated for a Golden Globe in the category of Best Male Newcomer. Other film roles followed, but his next big break came via TV, when he took on the part of Steve Keller in police drama *The Streets of San Francisco.* He would stay with the show for four years, departing in 1976.

It was during this time that Kirk handed Michael the rights to *One Flew Over the Cuckoo's Nest.* Douglas Snr. had secured them back in the earlier 1960s and had appeared opposite Gene Wilder in a stage adaptation that ran for six months, to mostly negative reviews. Michael teamed up with producer Saul Zaentz with a view to bringing the book to the big screen. Kirk Douglas hoped to reprise the role of Randle McMurphy but was deemed too old for the role by his son. Instead, Jack Nicholson took on the lead, and the $4.4M picture became a sensation, making almost $300M during its lifetime. It was the seventh most successful movie ever made at the time and ended up being nominated for nine Academy Awards, winning the 'big five' – Best Film, Director, Actor, Actress and Screenplay.

While the financial success and award wins were impressive, Michael struggled as an actor once he departed *The Streets of San Francisco.* He appeared in Michael Crichton's *Coma* in 1978, and played a supporting role a year later in *The China Syndrome,* a movie which he also produced. Still, Columbia weren't interested in making Romancing the Stone with Douglas as the lead – though they appeared to have no issue with him acting as producer. When he moved his production deal to 20th Century Fox, the script came with him. Much to his annoyance one assumes, Fox didn't want Douglas as the lead either and offered the role to both Clint Eastwood and Burt Reynolds, neither of whom were interested. Eventually the studio relented, and Romancing the Stone found its Jack Colton.

Diane Thomas' screenplay still needed some work and at least three unnamed script doctors helped knock it into shape. In the meantime, she had completed a new script entitled *Blonde Hurricane*, and rumour has it, was working on a draft of *Indiana Jones and the Temple of Doom*. Meanwhile, Fox set aside a budget of $10M for Romancing the Stone and, like everyone in Hollywood at the time, hoped they'd found their own *'Raiders'*. However, even at that early stage, the knives were out and many studio executives had the movie pegged as flop material. Douglas pushed on and set about hiring a director and female lead, both of which would end up being very interesting choices.

Douglas was initially interested in Debra Winger for the role of Joan Wilder. Views differ on why Winger wasn't cast, with the studio line being that she wasn't glamorous or athletic enough. The actress was already gaining a reputation for being somewhat difficult to work with – she'd refused to promote *An Officer and a Gentleman* (a role which arguably put her on the map) and had been dismissive of directors and actors with whom she had worked. A further, more bizarre reason emerged in 2008, when Kathleen Turner stated in her memoirs that Winger had lost the role when she bit Michael Douglas during a dinner the actor had organised to discuss the part. For whatever reason it ended up being, Debra Winger was off the list. The studio favoured newcomer Kathleen Turner, who had burnt up the screen with her first major role, that of Matty Tyler Walker in the 1981 noir thriller, *Body Heat*. She also gained notice for her work opposite Steve Martin in *The Man with Two Brains*. Turner and Douglas would prove to have a ready chemistry, which legend has it, spilled over into real life during the film's production.

For what was essentially the film's only other major role, that of the kidnapper Ralph, Douglas chose to cast Danny DeVito, someone who he had known for many years, and had lived with when the pair were struggling actors in the 1960s. DeVito had played Martini in the stage adaptation of *One Flew Over the Cuckoo's Nest*, a role he reprised in the film adaptation. While the actor had appeared on screen before, it was his part in *Cuckoo's Nest* that brought him attention. The recurring role of Louie De Palma in the sitcom *Taxi* made him a household name in the early 1980s. The remainder of the cast included Manuel Ojeda as the villainous Zolo and Zack Norman as Ralph's partner, Ira. Directing the picture, which would shoot on location in Mexico after real-life kidnappings became prevalent in Columbia, was Robert Zemeckis.

Robert Zemeckis got his start in film like many other directors –
making 8mm movies with his parents' camera. He wasn't even aware
that film schools existed until he heard one mentioned on an episode
of *The Tonight Show*. His desire to make movies grew further after
seeing *Bonnie & Clyde* and he set about applying to the University
of Southern California's School of Cinematic Arts. Submitting an
entrance essay and a music video based on a Beatles record,
Zemeckis was disheartened to discover his average grades had
gotten him rejected. Determined not to give up, he made a promise
to attend summer school and work on improving if USC would
accept him, which they eventually did.

It was while attending film school that he met writer Bob Gale. Like
the wannabe director, Gale was more interested in working on
mainstream movies as opposed to the art house fare that many of
their contemporaries favoured. Remaining true to his word,
Zemeckis worked and studied hard, and graduated USC in 1973,
winning a Student Academy Award for *A Field of Honour*. At
around the same time, Zemeckis met Steven Spielberg when the
latter screened *Sugarland Express* for USC students. Approaching
the director afterwards, Zemeckis urged him to watch *A Field of
Honour*, and set up a screening at Universal for him to do so.
Spielberg was impressed with what he saw, and the two stayed in
touch. Later, John Milius would approach Zemeckis and Gale, with a
view to them writing *1941*. When the script was complete, Spielberg

committed to direct and the duo visited the set of *Close Encounters of the Third Kind*, spending the evenings re-writing *1941*'s screenplay. In the meantime, Spielberg offered to executively produce Zemeckis' first major picture, a story he had co-written with Bob Gale entitled *I Wanna Hold Your Hand*.

Universal put up a budget of $2.8M, on the proviso that if Zemeckis looked to be making a mess of things, Spielberg himself would step in to take over. *I Wanna Hold Your Hand* was a fictionalised account of the day The Beatles appeared on the Ed Sullivan show and while critics and preview audiences were impressed, the general public gave it a wide berth. As a result, the film failed to recoup its budget. Spielberg moved forward on *1941* and as is well-documented, it became his first major failure, though it wasn't the flop that history would lead one to believe. Coming off back-to-back hits with *Jaws* and *Close Encounters*, the studio had simply expected a much bigger return on *1941*. Zemeckis and Gale worked on their next script, *Used Cars*, a comedy that would end up starring Kurt Russell. Spielberg and John Milius executively produced the picture but like *I Wanna Hold Your Hand*, it reviewed well yet failed at the box office.

Zemeckis was now two for nought and was gaining a reputation as a great writer whose work didn't translate to the screen. The writing duo began work on a new screenplay, a time travel tale about a high school student who finds himself transported back to 1955. Every major studio rejected it, including Columbia Pictures, who felt the story wasn't sexual enough – something that the current spate of teen comedies had in abundance. Zemeckis was offered other similar work, but none of it interested him, and by 1983, he began adapting David Saperstein's book *Cocoon*, with a view to directing it himself.

When Michael Douglas named Robert Zemeckis as the man he wanted to direct Romancing the Stone, 20th Century Fox baulked, arguing that the director had already made two flops and they didn't intend to fund a third (this despite the fact they were entertaining the idea of him directing *Cocoon* for them). But Douglas stuck to his guns; he'd seen a style in *I Wanna Hold Your Hand* that he wanted on Romancing the Stone. Douglas also played up the fact that Zemeckis hadn't been responsible for the script, like he had been on his previous two failures. And so it was, that Robert Zemeckis signed up for Romancing the Stone purely as a director-for-hire.

Shooting got underway in Mexico, and while all appeared to go smoothly, Turner would later confess to clashing terribly with Zemeckis, who she saw as a typical film school graduate – more concerned with cameras and angles as opposed to what the actors had to do to make the shots work. For his part, the director felt the script contained a number of good elements, but that the story didn't bear them out, and it would be up to him to pull it together to make the climax work. He was also instrumental in casting Alfonso Arau as Juan, having worked with the actor on *Used Cars*. In the background, Zemeckis continued work on *Cocoon*. With Fox still jittery, a rough cut was hastily assembled once shooting was completed and a screening arranged.

It was a disaster. The studio, which had never been sure of the picture or its director in the first place, hated it and prepared for the worst come its release. So bad did the screening go that Fox fired Zemeckis from *Cocoon*, despite him having spent a year developing it. With the power of hindsight, it was the best thing that ever happened to his career, but at that point, he must have assumed his time in Hollywood was truly over. The concerned director worked towards finishing up the picture in time for its March 1984 release. In an interesting aside, the film's temporary soundtrack, composed by Alan Silvestri, so impressed Zemeckis that he opted to keep it in the film. Silvestri went on to score every picture the director has made since.

20th Century Fox decided to open the film at the end of March, keeping it clear of much of the summer's competition, which would include *Indiana Jones and The Temple of Doom, Star Trek III: The Search for Spock* and *Ghostbusters*. The first sign that things weren't as bad as suspected came with the reviews, which were surprisingly positive, citing Douglas and Turner's on-screen chemistry as one of the film's many strong points. While some were quick to dismiss it as yet another *Raiders* knock-off, the good reviews easily outweighed the bad. The picture currently holds an 87% approval rating on Rotten Tomatoes. March 30th would see Romancing the

Stone open opposite *Greystoke: The Legend of Tarzan*, while having to contend with *Police Academy*, which had already made over $8M during its first three days. *Splash* and *Footloose*, while looking a little long-in-the-tooth, would also still offer very real competition.

Opening at just over 800 locations, Romancing the Stone got off to a solid enough start, making $5.1M over its first three days. While it had to settle for fourth place, that first weekend was encouraging and allowed both the studio and Zemeckis a small sigh of relief. A week later the film actually moved up the chart and increased its weekend to weekend takings by 9% – recouping its budget in the process. Before the start of its third frame on release, it had already made more than Zemeckis' previous two films combined. Fox were no longer concerned with failure; rather they wondered how high the picture could go. By now it was out to over 1,000 locations, and word-of-mouth was white hot. By the end of its fifth weekend, it had made more than $34M.

Romancing the Stone would remain in the top ten for an astonishing eleven weeks, never seeing a bigger fall in weekend to weekend takings than 30% (and that was due more to it giving up screens to newer releases). It would face down the aforementioned summer blockbusters, and many more besides. All up, the film remained in theatres for 16 weeks, closing with an incredible $76.5M. It went on to become the eighth most successful film of 1984, and also made a number of 'best of' lists. It enjoyed great success on the burgeoning home video market too. In something of surprise, Turner won a Golden Globe for her work on the film (she would go on to win another for *Prizzi's Honor*).

Fox immediately set about commissioning a sequel, *The Jewel in the Nile*, tentatively planning its release for the winter of 1985. Despite Romancing the Stone's huge success, not everyone was interested in making a follow up. With the attention and acclaim the film had bought him, Robert Zemeckis was able to move forward on his time travel script, which would become known as *Back to the Future*. All three lead actors were contractually obligated to return for the sequel, though Douglas and Turner felt they should quit while they were ahead. Turner attempted to back out of the film during pre-production, but Fox threatened to sue her for $25M if she proceeded. In the director's chair for the sequel was Lewis Teague, best known at that point for directing the Stephen King adaptation, *Cujo*.

The *Jewel of the Nile* would go on to be almost as successful as its predecessor (it made $75M at the domestic box office) though it didn't score as favourably with critics. In a sad note, Romancing the Stone writer Diane Thomas was killed in a car crash just months before *Jewel*'s release. While she didn't contribute to the script (apart from the creation of the original characters) the film is dedicated to her memory.

A second sequel was said to be in development, but work on *The Crimson Eagle* didn't progress far. It was rumoured to take place a number of years after *Jewel*, and would see Joan and Jack in Thailand with their teenage children, forced to recover a priceless statue. In the mid-2000s, Michael Douglas began developing a new sequel, said to be titled Racing the Moon, but little has been heard of the project since 2007.

After Romancing the Stone and *The Jewel of the Nile*, the three leads would reunite in 1989 for the unrelated movie, *The War of the Roses*. Danny DeVito would both direct and co-star, while Turner and Douglas played a warring, divorce-bound couple. The picture was a huge success, taking over $160M at the global box office. Prior to *Roses*, Douglas would give a legendary (and Oscar-winning) turn as Gordon Gecko in Oliver Stone's *Wall Street*. He also saw major success with *Fatal Attraction* and *Basic Instinct*. He continues to produce movies and act across many genres to this day.

Aside from *Prizzi's Honor*, Kathleen Turner starred opposite Nicolas Cage in *Peggy Sue Got Married* in 1986 for which she was nominated for an Academy Award. She later re-teamed with Zemeckis to provide the sultry voice of Jessica Rabbit in the 1988 smash hit, *Who Framed Roger Rabbit?* Some poor career choices (turning down *Ghost* and *The Bridges of Madison County*) and notable failures (*V.I Warshawski*) stalled her career in the early 1990s. The onset of rheumatoid arthritis confined her to a wheelchair for some time and made working difficult. However, thanks to medical advances in the latter part of the decade, she went into remission and began to slowly rebuild both her health and career. In recent years, she has favoured the stage over the screen, and also gave a memorable turn as Chandler's father in the TV sitcom, *Friends*.

Danny DeVito appeared in a series of very successful comedies during the remainder of the 1980s, including *Ruthless People* and *Twins*. He'd made his directorial debut on the 1984 TV movie *The Ratings Game*, and returned to the chair for *Throw Momma from the Train* (1987), *The War of the Roses* (1989) and *Hoffa* (1992). He would continue to take on acting and directing work throughout the 1990s and into the 2000s, winning acclaim for his work on *Matilda* (as director and actor) and *L.A Confidential*. He can currently be seen in the hugely successful sitcom, *It's Always Sunny In Philadelphia*.

As for Robert Zemeckis, getting fired from *Cocoon* did indeed turn out to be the best thing that could have possibly happened. He would go on to see massive success with the *Back to the Future* trilogy, along with the stunning technical achievement that was *Who Framed Roger Rabbit*. He would win an Academy Award for his work on *Forrest Gump* in 1994, and continued to have major mainstream success for the rest of the decade and well into the next. After three ground-breaking motion capture films (*Polar Express, Beowulf* and

A Christmas Carol) Zemeckis returned to live action with 2012's *Flight*. With an impressive body of work, Robert Zemeckis is the fourth biggest director in cinematic history, whose films have grossed over 4 billion dollars.

Romancing the Stone is still a great action comedy, mainly due to the strength and chemistry of its leads. Because the film didn't concentrate on special effects, it has aged remarkably well, and while considered by some to a poorer, somewhat forgotten cousin to Indiana Jones, it still stands up as an enjoyable thrill ride.

If you enjoyed Romancing the Stone, you might like these…

Raiders of the Lost Ark

For some, the best movie of the decade, if not all time. Harrison Ford plays archaeologist/adventurer Indiana Jones on a quest to beat the Nazis in finding the fabled Ark of the Covenant. Aided by the feisty Marion Ravenwood, Jones faces off against the German army, rival archaeologist Belloq and ultimately, the Ark itself.

A rip-roaring adventure in the traditional Saturday morning matinee-sense, Raiders never puts a foot wrong and barely stops for a breath. The story, stunts and effects stand up well and the rousing John Williams score is one of his best. A true classic that still retains the ability to impress, with ease.

Trivia: After the difficult and costly shoot on 1941, director Steven Spielberg brought Raiders of the Lost Ark in under budget and ahead of schedule.

King Solomon's Mines

Cannon Films' answer to *Raiders* and *Romancing the Stone* sees Richard Chamberlain as Henry Rider Haggard's hero, Allan Quatermain on an adventure to find the fabled King's mines. Hired by Jesse Huston (played by Sharon Stone) to help track down her father, Quatermain, his partner Umbopo (with Huston in tow) set off together but soon run foul of Herbert Lom and John Rhys-Davies.

One of a number of shameless cash-ins, King Solomon's Mines still has some fun with the over-the-top villains and general scrapes the leads find themselves in. Amongst fans of the action adventure genre, it is all but forgotten, but holds just enough charm to make it worth a watch.

Trivia: Sequel *Allan Quatermain and The Lost City of Gold*, released in 1986, was shot back-to-back with King Solomon's Mines.

The War of the Roses

A dark comedy featuring the cast of *Romancing the Stone* and *The Jewel of the Nile* – but this is far from a sequel or a happy-ever-after. Danny DeVito directs Michael Douglas and Kathleen Turner as husband and wife, Oliver and Barbara Rose, a couple who appear to have everything. As time goes by, cracks begin to appear in their relationship, culminating in them deciding to divorce.

This quickly turns into a bitter battle over the house and their possessions, leading to humiliation and attempted murder as neither side backs down. Having seen Douglas and Turner work so well together previously makes their descent into mutual hatred all the funnier. Director (and co-star) DeVito doesn't hold back either, ensuring the couple is fighting to the bitter end.

Trivia: The War of the Roses actually out-grossed both *Romancing the Stone* and *The Jewel of the Nile* at the domestic box office. The guy being told the story by Danny DeVito is Dan Castellaneta, the voice of Homer Simpson.

Mannequin

When she comes to life, anything can happen!

Studio: Fox

Release Date: 13th February 1987

Director: Mike Gottlieb

Starring: Andrew McCarthy, Kim Cattrall

Budget: $7.9M – 2015 Equivalent: $16.6M

U.S Box Office: $42.7M – 2015 Equivalent: $90M

In one of his many jobs, failed artist Jonathan Switcher creates the perfect mannequin. Fired yet again, he later sees his creation in a shop window and sets about getting a job at the store. Much to Jonathan's amazement, he discovers that when he is alone with the mannequin, she comes to life. But the path of true love is never a smooth one, and soon the duo are dealing with an obsessed night watchman, a hostile takeover and Jonathan's colleagues, who are getting concerned with him talking to a shop dummy....

On the surface, Mannequin seems like any other romantic comedy, albeit with a somewhat original start point for the central couple. However, if one delved a little deeper, they'd find that the movie was cleverly constructed with the help of one of the most powerful men in Hollywood. He wasn't a studio head or a hot-shot producer, in fact Mannequin was the first feature he'd ever put his name to, and all but the last, yet his influence could not be underestimated. Loved by executives but loathed by directors, that man was Joseph Farrell.

According to director Mike Gottlieb (brother of *Jaws* screenwriter Carl), he got the idea for the film when he was walking past a shop window and a trick of the light made it look as though a store dummy had moved. Inspired by this, he teamed up with Edward Rugoff to write the first draft on what would become known as Mannequin. A number of observers have also noted the film's similarity to the 1948 Ava Gardener picture *One Touch of Venus*. Gottlieb had started his career as an assistant on film and photo shoots, before becoming a successful fashion photographer in his own right. From there, he graduated to creating Clio award-winning commercials for the likes of Xerox and Coca-Cola. It was only a short step to becoming a feature director.

Gottlieb's idea was a simple one – have a down-on-his-luck guy fall in love with a store mannequin who comes to life whenever he (and only he) is around. Originally the lead role was written as a much older character who would be the store caretaker. The duo had in mind Dudley Moore for the role, but that would change in the next draft of the script. Work continued with Gottlieb planning to make Mannequin his feature directorial debut. This would be 1986 and around the time Joseph Farrell became involved. As already mentioned, Farrell had no experience in film or film production, but his knowledge was sought by many a studio during the 1980s and 90s.

Joseph Farrell was born in New York on September 11th 1935. He studied sculpture at the University of Notre Dame and graduated from Harvard with a law degree. He continued to work in both law and the arts throughout the early part of his career, holding a number of positions including chief operating officer of the American Council of Arts. In 1976, he was hired by polling firm Lewis Harris to open an office on the west coast and it was there he began to apply research practices from other areas, to the movie industry. Two years later, with business partner Catherina Paura he founded NRG – the National Research Group. Initially, the pair conducted research themselves, polling cinema-goers in car parks as they emerged from screenings and even going so far as to bribe children with ice cream to get their thoughts on the feature they'd just seen.

Over time, the company built up its research database and refined its processes. While NRG didn't invent the pre-release screening process, they did extensively re-shape it, and the use of focus groups.

They began to provide studios with invaluable demographic studies and tracking analysis, which in turn helped them decide how and to whom they would promote their movies. As budgets rose, Hollywood began to rely more and more on Farrell and NRG, going so far as to allow them to dictate trailer content and placement, release dates and advertising campaigns. The company even found a way of dividing up audiences into 'demographic quadrants' – men and women under and over twenty-five years-of-age. A film that appealed to all groups became known as a four quadrant movie, seen by many as the closest thing to a sure-fire hit.

Studios by and large loved Farrell and NRG. Paramount Pictures directly credit him for helping *Fatal Attraction* become a smash hit in the autumn of 1987. When test audiences disliked the original ending in which Glenn Close takes her own life, Farrell convinced the studio to re-shoot the finale that would see the character get her just desserts. The result was a $320M global hit. He stated, rightly it would seem in this case, that no matter how good a movie was, if the audience hated the ending, it was that that they would take away with them – and tell their friends about. Directors argued that by giving the audience exactly what they had asked for, they lost the ability to confound them, and in the long term it would make pictures too similar and predictable. Hollywood didn't seem to care about that aspect, especially when budgets began to approach upwards of $50M – they'd take safety, predictability and success over risk.

It is unclear why Farrell decided to become involved in Mannequin, though some speculate it was a case of putting his money where his mouth was. If he was so good at advising studios how to market their movies, could they yield bigger success by having him enter the frame earlier? On Mannequin, they would find out. Gottlieb and Rugoff's script was now all but finished, with the central character remaining as the older caretaker figure. Farrell worked out that a younger man in a similar role would better appeal to the female target demographic. However, he also realised that the budget couldn't sustain a major actor being cast. For this reason, the production opted for a recognisable actor, but one who was arguably not a star – someone whose name alone could not open a film.

For the lead role of Jonathan Switcher, Andrew McCarthy was cast. McCarthy made his movie debut opposite Rob Lowe in the 1983 college comedy, *Class*. The picture was a minor hit and led to the young actor being cast, again with Lowe, in the 1985 Brat Pack comedy-drama, *St Elmo's Fire*. McCarthy then starred opposite Molly Ringwald in John Hughes' *Pretty in Pink* – cementing his status as the good-guy boyfriend. Prior to McCarthy's casting, Farrell held a number of test screenings and proved the actor appealed strongly to the primary target audience. He was a recognisable and dependable safe bet for the lead role in Mannequin. As for the role of Emmy, that went to Kim Cattrall, an actress whose first role was in Otto Preminger's *Rosebud* in 1975. For the next few years she'd dabbled mainly in TV, and then appeared as part of the ensemble cast of adult comedy *Porky's*, a smash hit in 1982. She scored another hit with *Police Academy* and starred opposite Timothy Hutton in comedy-drama, *Turk 182!* When the role of Emmy came up, she was working on John Carpenter's *Big Trouble in Little China*.

Like McCarthy, Cattrall was cast because she was a popular actress who had a broad appeal – without breaking the bank. She'd proved she could handle comedy and was seen as someone who would attract the male demographic. Farrell knew that getting in the female audience was a good start, but if he could get them to bring their boyfriends and husbands, he'd have a hit on his hands. Estelle Getty, who was riding high on the success of TV show *The Golden Girls*, would play store owner Claire Timkin – giving the picture another recognisable face. As antagonists, Kim Cattrall's *Police Academy* co-star G.W Bailey was cast, alongside James Spader, who McCarthy had worked with on *Pretty in Pink* (The duo would team up again in the same year for *Less Than Zero*). Two further notable roles went to Carole Davis as Switcher's ex-girlfriend Roxie, and Meshach Taylor as the flamboyant (and memorable) Hollywood Montrose.

With a budget of $7.9M in place, filming commenced in the summer of 1986, with the production shooting in actual stores in Philadelphia and Pennsylvania. Things went smoothly enough, and Farrell soon began to plan out the advertising campaign, along with a proposed release date that would give the film maximum exposure with the minimum of competition. In hindsight, the summer of 1987 wasn't actually that busy, but the studio were taking no chances and opted for the most obvious release date for a romantic comedy – Valentine's weekend. Reviews were poor to say the least. Siskel & Ebert gave it two thumbs down; Leonard Maltin savaged it while Washington Post's Rita Kempley described the picture as being "made by, for, and about dummies." Farrell and the studio weren't after critical favour or awards, they wanted box office.

The film would go head-to-head with *Over the Top*, which was expected to be Sylvester Stallone's fourth hit in a row after *Rambo: First Blood Part 2, Rocky IV* and *Cobra*. Comedy *Outrageous Fortune* was still riding high too, having opened well two weeks previously. *Platoon* would be expanding, and was expected to keep tight hold on the no.1 spot. Oliver Stone's Vietnam War epic had opened back in December 1986 and slowly crept up the charts as more and more screens were added and word-of-mouth spread.

Opening on February 13th at 938 locations, Mannequin got off to a great start, recouping most of its budget within its first three days. While it had to settle for third place, it beat out *Over the Top* by almost one million dollars and was only $300K shy of besting *Outrageous Fortune*. The picture added $1M during the week and had moved up into second place by the following weekend, when it made another $5M (a drop of just 16% on its opening frame). It seemed that Farrell's calculations were paying off. In weekend three, it faced fresh competition in the guise of romantic drama *Some Kind of Wonderful*, but still managed to clear $4M. At the end of its first full month on general release, Mannequin had surpassed the $20M mark and was showing little sign of slowing down. Thanks to MTV's heavy rotation of the Starship track, *Nothing's Gonna Stop Us Now* (which played over the end sequence), the film was kept firmly in the public eye.

As time wore on, the new releases managed to push the picture down to ninth place, but a week later it moved back up the chart, and spent a further fortnight in the top ten. All told, Mannequin earned $42.7M at the domestic box office against a budget of $7.9M. It may not have been one of the biggest hits of 1987, but it was easily one of the most profitable. *Nothing's Gonna Stop Us Now* became a smash hit on both sides of the Atlantic and was nominated for an Academy Award the following year. The film went on to enjoy a healthy run on video too and gained something of a following over the years.

A sequel, *Mannequin Two: On the Move* was released in 1991. The story would begin with a princess being turned into a wooden mannequin. A thousand years later, her curse is lifted by shop assistant Jason Williamson (himself a reincarnation of the princess' original love). The picture was written by David Isaacs and Ken Levine, who'd carried out uncredited work on the first movie. Of the original cast, only Meshach Taylor's Hollywood Montrose would return. *Mannequin Two* failed to make an impact at the box office, earning only $4M against a budget of $13M.

Joseph Farrell and NRG continued to supply Hollywood with all manner of information. As film became an even bigger business during the 1990s, his work, and that of similar companies, became even more valuable to studios. It was rumoured that for a period of time, there wasn't a Disney release that he hadn't had an influence on. The rise of the internet allowed many more people to be surveyed on their thoughts and awareness of a particular movie, and opened up new windows of opportunity. Farrell sold NRG in 2003 and with his original business partner, Catherine Paura, set up his own production company. He passed away in 2011, a year before the release of their first feature, *Joyful Noise*.

Andrew McCarthy enjoyed further success in the 1980s with *Weekend at Bernie's* but like other Brat Pack members, moved away from the mainstream in the next decade. He would work consistently on smaller films and TV, going on to become an award winning travel writer, as well as a successful TV director on shows such as *Orange is the New Black* and *Gossip Girls*. Kim Cattrall would appear in a number of features over the years, including *Star Trek: The Undiscovered Country* in 1991. However, it was the role of Samantha Jones in the long-running TV show *Sex and the City* that brought her global fame. She would reprise the character for two hugely successful films, first in 2008 and again in 2010.

Mannequin still retains a certain charm, though its highlight on fashion ages the film more than many of its contemporaries. McCarthy and Cattrall's chemistry works well, with the supporting cast adding their own unique touches. It is debatable how much of the film's success was down to Joseph Farrell, but his influence on the picture (and many others) cannot be denied. While his methods may have been condemned by some, they also shaped many of Hollywood's biggest hits and continue to do so to this day.

Further viewing if you enjoyed Mannequin

Electric Dreams

An 80s rom-com with a modern technology twist. On a quest to design an earthquake-proof brick, Miles buys a computer. Before long, the machine is not only helping with the design but it's also running the devices in his home. When it overheats while downloading data, Miles panics and pours champagne over the keyboard, causing the machine to develop a mind of its own.

Before long Edgar (as it identifies itself) is attempting to woo Miles' new neighbour, with whom he has become friends. The bizarre triangle takes a dangerous turn when Edgar realise the couple are falling in love and sets about trying to destroy Miles' life. A fairly lightweight movie with a memorable theme (and soundtrack), Electric Dreams makes a perfect double bill with the equally wacky *Mannequin*.

Trivia: The movie is dedicated to the UNIVAC I, the first commercially available computer in the United States.

Pretty in Pink

The third of three movies John Hughes made with Molly Ringwald. After playing the spoilt rich girl in *The Breakfast Club*, the actress was on the other side of the tracks here, as the daughter of an unemployed man still struggling to get over the divorce of his wife. When she falls for a rich-kid, played by Andrew McCarthy, no one seems happy for her – least of all her best friend Duckie.

With themes of class, money, love and loss, Pretty in Pink is much closer to drama than comedy, and along with *The Breakfast Club*, is Hughes' most mature film. The leads are ably supported by the likes of Jon Cryer, Harry Dean Stanton and James Spader, as McCarthy's manipulative friend, Steff. A film of its time, but one whose message is as apt now as it was then.

Trivia: After test audiences disapproved of the original ending, it was re-shot. As a result, Orchestral Manoeuvres in the Dark had just two days write a new song that worked better with the new version.

The Princess Bride

A classic tale of love and adventure, The Princess Bride is seen by many as the ultimate love story. The beautiful Buttercup falls for the handsome farm boy Westley, who goes off to seek his fortune so that they may marry. Fate sees him caught by the Dread Pirate Roberts and presumed dead, leaving Buttercup to mourn for five years before finally agreeing to marry Prince Humperdinck.

But before the wedding can take place, Buttercup is kidnapped by a Sicilian, a giant and a great fencer. Prince Humperdinck mounts a search, but a mysterious man in black is also in pursuit. A perfectly cast and played movie, with so many great moments and quotable lines, The Princess Bride is little short of a modern classic.

Trivia: In the 1970s, when the film was initially set to be made, a then-unknown Arnold Schwarzenegger was considered for the role of Fezzik as writer William Goldman's first choice, Andre the Giant, refused to read for the part.

The Last Starfighter

He's got one extraordinary chance at the dream of a lifetime

Studio: Universal
Release Date: 13th July 1984
Director: Nick Castle
Starring: Lance Guest, Robert Preston
Budget: $15M – 2015 Equivalent: $34.5M
U.S Box Office: $28.7M – 2015 Equivalent: $66M

When trailer park resident Alex Rogan breaks the high score on a Starfighter arcade machine, he doesn't realise he has just proved his worthiness to be a real Starfighter pilot. Visited by the mysterious Centauri, Alex soon finds himself in the middle of an intergalactic war that'll require more than just his skills to survive.

Like a number of 1980s movies The Last Starfighter is often forgotten, yet for those who saw it in cinemas, or more likely on video, it remains a much loved gem. Released in July 1984, it broke ground for its revolutionary use of computer graphics but actually owes its inspiration to one of the oldest of legends, that of the sword in the stone. With the popularity of the video arcade still on the rise, writer Jonathan Betuel sought to combine the classical adventure with a modern one, and thus The Last Starfighter was born.

Betuel was working at an ad agency in the very early 80s and during time between client meetings, found himself in an arcade watching a young kid playing a game. He pictured the game as a test, and the young Arthur being someone who achieved the highest score. From that vision, Betuel was able to craft a script in which the machine acted as a recruitment tool – when the high score was broken the machine would beam out a message to a distant civilisation, who would know this person was worthy of being a Starfighter. He continued to work on the script and before long it gained the attention of Gary Adelson. The Last Starfighter would be the first movie Adelson would produce and he met with a number of directors before being bound over by the enthusiasm of one Nick Castle, a fledgling director looking for his next major feature.

Born the son of famed cinematographer, Nicholas Charles Castle, Nick got into acting as a young boy, appearing as an extra in a number of films on which his father worked. It was while studying film at the USC School of Cinematic Arts that he met and became friends with fellow student John Carpenter. The duo worked together on the award winning live action short, *The Resurrection of Broncho Billy*. With two credits already under his belt (*Broncho Billy* and the earlier short *Captain Voyeur*) Carpenter dropped out of USC to work on his first feature, *Dark Star*, a sci-fi black comedy he had co-written with another classmate, Dan O'Bannon (future writer of *Alien*). Nick ended up with an uncredited role in Dark Star, which became a cult success thanks to it playing at numerous film festivals throughout the mid-1970s.

A few years later, while looking for someone to play The Shape (AKA Michael Myers) in *Halloween*, Carpenter called up Nick, paying him $25 a day to portray the infamous killer. The duo would collaborate again, this time on paper, on the script for Kurt Russell classic, *Escape from New York*. When he met with Gary Adelson about The Last Starfighter, Castle knew he could bring it to the screen. At the time, he was working on his directorial debut, action thriller *Tag: The Assassination Game*, which would star Robert Carradine and a young Linda Hamilton. Castle set to work with Jonathan Betuel to shape the script further, but they soon became painfully aware of the influence George Lucas and Steven Spielberg had had on cinema in recent times. In order to limit comparisons, Castle claimed that each time they found themselves veering into Lucas/Spielberg territory, he pushed the story in the opposite direction, but even then the influence could be felt.

In one example, the original script for The Last Starfighter had hero Alex Rogan living in a suburb, but this felt too much like where *E.T.* or *Poltergeist* had been set. The location was changed to a trailer park to add to Rogan's feeling of isolation. This gave the writers a chance to concentrate on the fellow residents, some of whom became an extension of Alex's family. Betuel had a few actors in mind for some of the characters and that too would influence the script. With *Star Wars* and its sequel being such big hits, science fiction was everywhere and all the studios wanted their own vehicle. The Last Starfighter went a step further – not only did it have the science fiction angle covered, but videogames, which were becoming more popular by the minute, featured prominently. With a $21M budget attached courtesy of Lorimar Productions, Castle could begin pre-production and casting.

There were four central roles to cast in the picture, Alex Rogan and his girlfriend Maggie, along with Centauri, the game's inventor and Grig, a Starfighter navigator. Once again, it would be John Carpenter's influence that would help cast at least two of those roles. Acting as producer on *Halloween 2*, Carpenter was in the editing suite when Castle dropped by and noticed a young Lance Guest on screen. Being impressed by what he saw, he made sure Guest tested for the role. The *Halloween* sequel was Guest's first major screen role, having made his acting debut earlier the same year with a bit-part in *Dallas*. He followed this up with an after-school special (*Please Don't Hit me, Mom*) and a spot on the TV show *Lou Grant*, a spin-off for a character who had appeared on *The Mary Tyler Moore Show*. He went on to play the role of Jimmy in the *Halloween* sequel.

As for Maggie, that went to Catherine Mary Stewart a dancer-turned-actress who made her debut in sci-fi musical, *The Apple*, while studying in London. After returning to the United States, she won a recurring role on daytime soap, *Days of Our Lives*, a stint which would last two years. Screen-testing for the position of Maggie, she found herself paired with Lance Guest, with whom all concerned felt she had a ready chemistry. That, combined with her girl-next-door qualities meant she won the role over other actresses, which included Ally Sheedy and Jennifer Jason Leigh (Guest was said to have beaten Eric Stoltz to the role of Alex).

Back when he was still writing the script, Betuel had an actor in mind for the key role of Centauri, the inventor of the Starfighter arcade machine and someone who had the qualities and mannerisms of a fast-talking conman. When he mentioned Robert Preston, Nick Castle was instantly on-board with the idea and set about making it happen. By the time of The Last Starfighter, Robert Preston had long been a veteran of stage and screen, having made his debut in *King of Alcatraz* in 1938. He went on to work consistently throughout the next two decades, but it was his role in Meredith Wilson's *The Music Man* for which he became famous. The actor had originated the role on stage in 1957 to great acclaim (and a Tony award), and when it was adapted for the screen, Wilson insisted Preston reprise the role, much to the annoyance of Jack Warner who'd favoured Frank Sinatra. *The Music Man* character of 'Professor' Harold Hill, a con-man who tricks a town into thinking he will equip and train a marching band, had many of the traits that Betuel saw in Centauri. So perfect was he for the role that when he officially signed on-board, the screenplay was refined further to highlight his performance. Post-Last Starfighter, Nick Castle would refer to it as 'one of the greatest castings of the 80s'.

Finally, the role of navigator Grig went to Dan O'Herlihy, another screen veteran whose career stretched back almost as far as Robert Preston's. O'Herlihy began acting in the mid-1940s, and earned an Academy Award nomination for his role in Luis Buñuel's *Robinson Crusoe* (1954). Over the years he worked on many film and TV shows, including recurring characters in *The Man from U.N.C.L.E*, *Dr Kildare* and *Colditz*. He too would have a link to John Carpenter, appearing in the third *Halloween* movie, *Season of the Witch*. As Grig, he would be buried under layers of prosthetics, limiting his normal acting abilities. As production got underway, there would be one more Carpenter-alumni to join the fray.

Despite the leaps and bounds movie model-making had seen over the last few years, the team behind The Last Starfighter wanted to try something different. It would be production designer Ron Cobb, working with the newly formed Digital Productions, who would offer up the idea of computer-generated effects over conventional model making. Cobb had gotten his first break working on Disney's *Sleeping Beauty*. After the film was completed, he found himself without a job and took on a number of non-film related positions before being drafted into the army. After being discharged some three years later, he became a freelance artist and cartoonist.

He also went on to create album covers and contributed some design work to John Carpenter's *Dark Star*. This in turn led him to working on *Star Wars* (Uncredited creature concepts), *Alien* and *Raiders of the Lost Ark*. He also had a hand in the first, darker version of *E.T The Extra Terrestrial* and was even offered the chance to direct the picture by Steven Spielberg. However, commitments to the production design on *Conan the Barbarian* saw him turn the offer down, allowing the famed director to extensively re-work the script and opt to helm the picture himself.

Back in 1981, Cobb met John Whitney Jnr and Gary Demos, who were working on making photo-realistic computer-generated imagery, a reality. So impressed was he by what he saw, Cobb joined their company, Digital Productions, and approached Nick Castle with idea of creating all of the Last Starfighter's effects (aside from explosions and make-up) on a computer. The director liked the idea and could see that if done well, it would not only be a great selling point but would impact film for years to come. Furthermore, without the need for costly model work, the production could reduce the budget from \$21M to \$15M. As design work and visual testing got underway, the final touches were made to the shooting script.

Given the amount of work required to encompass the make-up, pre-visual effects and day-to-day shooting, it is somewhat surprising that The Last Starfighter completed shooting in just 40 days. There seems to have been little in the way of issues, though acting against things that would be added in later, proved an interesting exercise for all concerned. To aid this, real life props were built that would help the cast and crew visualise where things would be. As mentioned, Dan O'Herlihy was buried under layers of prosthetics, which limited his abilities. To counter this, the actor exaggerated his movements, which ended up enhancing his performance in the finished movie. For Guest, it was almost like working on two different pictures due to a subplot that saw his earth-bound character replaced by Beta, a robot (also played by Guest) while the real Alex travelled into space.

Work on the computer-generated sequences was also well underway, with Ron Cobb supplying Digital Productions with detailed sketches of the Gunstar, the experimental fighter craft that Alex Rogan pilots in the movie. Because this was one of the first films to make extensive use of computer graphics (*Tron* aside), there was a real seat-of-the-pants element about it all. Early on, visual effects coordinator Jeffrey Okun sat down with Cobb, Whitney and Demos and discussed the time frames involved in getting the computer work done. They explained how they'd be creating the shots and how long it would take to render each frame. Okun worked out it would take 17 months to complete all the sequences. They had just six.

Knowing that if the effects weren't finished in time, they had no movie, Okun approached producer Gary Adelson and explained the time frame issue. He told Aldeson that he had three model companies standing by who could complete the work on time, and on budget – all the producer needed to do was fire Digital Productions. To Adelson's credit, he refused, and chastised Okun for making the suggestion. But there was no getting around the issue, there simply wasn't enough time to complete all the effects to meet the film's summer 1984 release date. A compromise was eventually reached – Digital Productions would reduce the number of polygons per frame. While this would all but remove the chance of photo realism, it also meant the picture could be finished on schedule. However, it left no room for error – if a scene didn't render correctly, they either had to scrap it or use it – there was no time to begin again. This goes some way to explaining why some sequences don't look as impressive as others.

Over time, the company perfected quicker code and found a number of shortcuts. They also discovered that the compromise in polygons could be disguised somewhat when they began to add colour to the surfaces of the wire frame models they had created. With over 70 billion colours to choose from, they could create shadows, dents and blemishes, giving the effects a worldlier, realistic feel. They worked day-and-night, often sleeping around the Cray X-MP super computer that was producing the final shots. The finished version of the Gunstar, whose data took three months to put into the computer, was made up of over 750,000 polygons and is arguably the highlight of the film's impressive computer-generated imagery.

Back in the real world, Nick Castle had quickly assembled a rough cut of the movie to screen for preview audiences. The reaction was very positive, especially to the Earth-bound Beta unit sequences, which added some much needed comic relief. The studio was pleased enough to allow Castle to re-assemble the cast and crew and shoot some additional Beta scenes. The problem was that since production had ended some four months ago, Lance Guest had had his curly hair cut, resulting in the actor having to wear an ill-fitting wig in the new footage. He was also under-the-weather when filming took place, requiring a lot of make-up to ensure he looked like the character in the original scenes. As fans of the film can attest, the wig and make-up didn't always convince.

As the race to the finish line picked up pace, production company Lorimar became involved with Atari, with a view to create an arcade machine based on the one seen in the film, along with home versions for their console and computer range. Promotional work got underway too, with the standard trailer highlighting the film's impressive effects work. Lance Guest, Catherine Mary Stewart and Nick Castle all hit the promotional trail as the release date approached. Reviews for The Last Starfighter were positive enough, and it sits with a 76% approval rating on Rotten Tomatoes. Roger Ebert awarded it two and half stars, while Gene Siskel described it as a *'Star Wars* rip off, but the best one'.

In terms of summer releases, 1984 contained some of the biggest of the entire decade. Just a casual look reveals such classics as *Indiana Jones and the Temple of Doom, Gremlins, Ghostbusters, The Karate Kid* and *Star Trek III*. Even though The Last Starfighter would open against only one new release (*Muppets Take Manhattan*), the earlier summer movies were still a very real threat – *Ghostbusters* and *Gremlins* had ruled the top two places for the previous five weekends and showed little sign of cracking. While it had the visuals, it didn't have the major stars to promote the movie on talk shows and the like, setting it at something of a disadvantage.

Sadly, The Last Starfighter never really got the chance to shine. Despite a decent enough opening weekend of $6M, it couldn't cope with the existing competition. *Ghostbusters* and *Gremlins* clocked up their sixth weekend in first and second place respectively. A week later, *Best Defence* and *The NeverEnding Story* opened, pushing The Last Starfighter down to sixth place. By weekend three, it was gone from the top ten altogether, having made $16.5M in total. The studio had quickly decided to cut its losses, slashing more than 400 screens in that third weekend. A fortnight later it had cleared $21M, and would end up making $28M by the end of its theatrical run. Not a failure as such given its $15M budget, but some way short of what Universal (and Lorimar) had hoped to see. Talk of a sequel quickly evaporated.

Like many films of the time, The Last Starfighter came into its own on video, where it enjoyed a long and successful run, becoming one of the many cult hits of the 1980s. The Atari-made arcade machine never came to fruition due to the fact it would have needed to sell at $10,000 per unit to break even – a figure deemed too high at the time. Similarly, the console game never materialised, though the home computer version did appear some time later, retooled as Star Raiders II. Bizarrely, a version for the Nintendo Entertainment System appeared in 1990, but this ended up being a modified version of the Commodore 64 classic, Uridium.

Lance Guest would go on to appear in *Jaws: The Revenge*, before moving back to TV with *Knots Landing* and *Life Goes On*. He continued to act in both mediums throughout the 1990s. Of late he has made a name for himself portraying Johnny Cash in the long running stage production of *Million Dollar Quartet*. Catherine Mary Stewart followed up the film with another science fiction tale, *Night of the Comet*. She also saw success in the late 80s opposite Andrew McCarthy in *Weekend at Bernie's*. Stewart would appear in a number of TV shows and TV movies over the years, but pulled back from acting in the 1990s to concentrate on raising a family.

Sadly, The Last Starfighter marked the final theatrical appearance for Robert Preston, who passed away in 1987. He left behind a huge body of work and his performance in the movie is still cited by many as a highlight. Dan O'Herlihy worked throughout the 80s and well into the late 1990s, and gave a memorable turn as 'the old man' in *Robocop*. As for Nick Castle, he continued to work as both a director and screenplay writer. He directed the adaptation of *Dennis the Menace*, along with *Major Payne* and *Mr. Wrong*, while supplying the screenplay for Steven Spielberg's *Hook*. He also contributed to the soundtrack of the John Carpenter picture, *Big Trouble in Little China*.

The legacy of The Last Starfighter didn't end with the film's release. A novel and comic book adaptation were also produced, as was a 2004 off-Broadway musical. Over the years, news of a sequel would surface with regularity. In a 2012 interview with website Popcultureaddict, Lance Guest said he'd talked with the studio about a sequel not long after the original's release, but they viewed its performance as a disappointment and didn't pursue it any further. In 2008 GPA Entertainment added 'Starfighter' to its list of upcoming projects, describing it as 'The sequel to the classic motion picture Last Starfighter'. Little progress appears to have been made beyond that point.

Yet stories of a remake persist. The picture was once again in the news in November 2014 when movie website /film posted a link to a re-edited version of the trailer. Things took an almost incredulous turn shortly after when it was revealed by the website's Peter Sciretta that he had heard Seth Rogen had been pursuing the sequel/remake rights for years, to no avail. Rogen himself entered into the conversation and confessed that not even Steven Spielberg had been able to secure the rights – something the director had apparently tried to do after hearing about the problems the actor had ran into. In the aftermath of this story, it came to light that Jonathan Betuel still retained the rights to the movie (and presumably any sequel/remake) and flat out refused to sell them to anyone. At the time of writing there are rumours of a Last Starfighter TV show, though little progress seems to have been made.

Looking back on the film, it is easy to see why so many people took it to heart. Its theme of a lonely, isolated teenager finding success via videogames resonated with many at the time – and still does. The leads have great chemistry and the space battles are nicely contrasted with the comedic sequences of the Beta unit attempting to pass itself off as Alex. It is something of an oddity in that it rarely gets mentioned in the same breath as other 80s classics, yet remains a much loved film by those who know it. While its visual effects haven't quite stood the test of time, one can see why they were viewed as being ground-breaking upon the film's release – *Tron* aside, there was simply nothing like it anywhere else. It proved that computer-generated effects could work and created a path that many, many others would follow. It may be one of the lesser movies of the

1980s, but The Last Starfighter can easily be counted amongst the best of them.

After watching The Last Starfighter, why not try one of these?

Starman

A change of pace for director John Carpenter after the likes of *Halloween*, *The Thing* and *Escape from New York*. When an alien craft responding to Voyager 2's invitation to Earth is shot down, a floating ball of light emerges. It soon finds the home of Widow Jenny Hayden and clones itself into the image of her deceased husband. Fearful, Jenny is coerced into helping the Starman reach a rendezvous point.

As they travel, Jenny becomes impressed by the visitor's abilities and begins to warm to him. However, the army are on their trail and the Starman is running out of time. Jeff Bridge and Karen Allen make engaging leads, turning what could have been a run of the mill sci-fi flick into a touching love story. A box office disappointment upon release, it's a film worthy of finding an audience.

Trivia: Jeff Bridges' performance marks the only time a John Carpenter movie has received an Academy Award nomination.

Flight of the Navigator

A wonderful science fiction feature from Disney about a young boy named David who is abducted by aliens. When he's returned to Earth, he discovers that while only hours have passed for him, eight years have gone by for his family. At the same time, NASA discovers a crashed spaceship, which begins to communicate telepathically with David who, it has been discovered, has a head full of star charts and maps.

The ship's artificial intelligence, Max, convinces David to escape and join him, but while retrieving the star maps from David's mind, it also transfers some of his emotional attributes. Some great special effects are offset perfectly by Paul Reubens as the voice of the now emotionally-equipped Max. Overshadowed by the likes *of E.T the Extra Terrestrial*, Flight of the Navigator is a cracking little family adventure.

Trivia: After *The Black Hole*, Flight of the Navigator was only the second Disney movie to contain profanity.

Battle Beyond the Stars

Essentially *The Magnificent Seven* in space, the Roger Corman-produced Battle Beyond the Stars has much to offer and enjoy. Richard Thomas, better known at the time as John-Boy Walton, plays Shad, an inhabitant of the plant Akir which is threatened with destruction by John Saxon's villainous Sador.

Travelling into space, he manages to round up a motley crew of rogues, including Robert Vaughn and George Peppard, to help defend Akir for when Sador's army returns. A step above Corman's usual fare, at the time it was the most expensive picture he'd produced (and the footage would be reused in other productions). Battle Beyond the Stars is a minor entry in the science fiction genre but remains an enjoyable one.

Trivia: James Cameron was the art director on the movie and is also credited for some visual effects work.

Gremlins

Cute. Clever. Mischievous. Intelligent. Dangerous

Studio: Warner Brothers

Release Date: 8th June 1984

Director: Joe Dante

Starring: Zach Galligan, Phoebe Cates

Budget: $11M – 2015 Equivalent: $25.3M

U.S Box Office: $148.1M – 2015 Equivalent: $347.3M

Billy's new pet, a mogwai, comes with three simple rules. Never expose it to bright light, never get it wet and most importantly of all, never, ever feed it after midnight. But when all three rules are inadvertently broken, it's down to Billy, Kate and Gizmo to save the picturesque town of Kingston Falls from the chaos unleashed by Gremlins.

If things had worked out as planned, Gremlins would never have been produced. The script was written purely as an exercise by Chris Columbus to show studio executives that he could write screenplays. The young author had no idea at the time that his story would be made, and go on to be one of the biggest blockbusters of the year – not to mention spawn a wave of merchandising and bring about a change to the film classification system. But Gremlins, released in the summer of 1984, did all that and more.

Chris Columbus was born in Ohio in 1958 and after graduating, went on to attend the Tisch School of the Arts. Hoping to find a way into Hollywood, he started work on the script for Gremlins. The idea of a gremlin in the works was first conceived during the Second World War when aircraft suffered seemingly unexplained mechanical failures. This was elaborated on by author Roald Dahl in his 1943 book, The Gremlins, a title which was written as a precursor to a Disney movie that was never made. Columbus' primary inspiration came from listening to what seemed to be an army of mice scuttling around his loft late at night. From that starting point, he began work on the spec script that would become Gremlins. [A spec script is a non-commissioned, unsolicited screenplay that a writer hopes will be picked up by a studio]. At some point, the manuscript ended up on the desk of Steven Spielberg, who would later describe it as 'one of the most original things I've come across in many years'.

Spielberg opted to produce the film through his Amblin Entertainment production company along with studio Warner Bros. The script still needed some work, primarily to remove a number of the much darker elements. In the original screenplay, Billy's mother is killed during her encounter with the Gremlins and her head thrown down the stairs when Billy rushes into the house. Another scene saw Billy's dog get eaten and hordes of gremlins attacking patrons at a fast food restaurant. All these were either cut or rewritten. Another major change would be the roles of Gizmo the mogwai and Stripe, but that would not come until the picture was six weeks away from shooting. Even with Spielberg's huge success on *Jaws, E.T* and *Raiders of the Lost Ark*, Warner Bros. were still cautious of the project. However, they also wanted to work with the famed director so pushed ahead despite reservations. Just to be sure of reducing the risks, the studio put up a budget of less than $10M, which would rise to $11M during post-production.

The search was now on for someone to helm the picture. Spielberg himself was knee deep in a number of projects, along with directing the second Indiana Jones film, *Temple of Doom*, so he was out of contention (if indeed, he had ever been). However, a young animator-turned-director was making waves with his short film *Frankenweenie*. Spielberg considered Tim Burton for some time, but ultimately passed on the idea due to Burton's lack of feature experience (he would go on to make *PeeWee's Big Adventure* his feature debut in 1985). Instead, Spielberg turned his thoughts to Joe

Dante, a director he had recently worked with while shooting his segment on *Twilight Zone: The Movie*. The anthology, based on the cult TV show, consisted of four short films, with Spielberg and Dante helming two, while John Landis and George Miller directed the others.

Joe Dante, like a number of directors of the time, had got his break in the industry thanks to Roger Corman. His first actual directing credit was on the 1968 flick, *The Movie Orgy*, a seven-hour compilation of old movie clips, adverts and film trailers that he cut together while still a college student. His editing skills caught the attention of Corman despite *The Movie Orgy* not getting a showing beyond colleges and repertory theatres. For his actual feature debut, Dante co-directed *Hollywood Boulevard* with Allan Arkush. The picture was the result of a bet that Roger Corman had with fellow producer Jon Davison, who claimed he could make a film for less money than Corman had done previously. Taking him up on the bet, Corman gave the production just $60,000 and a ten-day shooting schedule. To get around budget (and time) constraints, Dante and Arkush created a movie that would feature footage from previously produced Corman flicks, linked by the story of a girl coming to Hollywood to find fame and fortune.

While it didn't set the world alight, it put Joe Dante on the map. His next film, *Piranha*, written by John Sayles, elevated his status further and showed his keen skill for combining horror and comedy.

The film was a shameless cash-in/parody of *Jaws*, but thanks to a smart script and direction, managed to rise above the other similar movies of the time. It also caught the eye of Steven Spielberg who called it "the best of the *Jaws* rip-offs" and convinced Universal Pictures not to take out an injunction against it. Dante would re-team with Sayles on the 1980 werewolf horror *The Howling*, again adding a darkly humorous streak. Reviews for that film were generally positive and it received notable mentions for its impressive special effects work (courtesy of Rob Bottin, who took over the job when Rick Baker left to work on *An American Werewolf in London*). Despite the success, Dante struggled to find further feature directing work and instead worked on episodes of *Police Squad*. When Spielberg began assembling a crew for *The Twilight Zone*, Joe Dante got a call. He would turn in segment 3, the tale of a teacher and an omnipotent boy, a remake of the episode *It's a Good Life*. While Landis and Spielberg's sections disappointed critics, Dante and Miller's won much acclaim.

Being able to blend horror and comedy so well, Dante was the perfect match for Gremlins, which would tread a very fine line between the two genres. Steven Spielberg would co-produce the picture via Amblin and Warner Bros, with Michael Finnell acting as overall producer (a role he had also occupied on *The Howling*). Pre-production work could now begin and while decisions over how to portray the gremlins were on-going, Dante set about casting the lead and supporting characters. For the role of Billy Peltzer, Zach

Galligan was cast despite having just two minor credits to his name – an after school special and a TV movie. However, his chemistry with Phoebe Cates during the audition phase convinced Spielberg to rally for him to get the part. On the other hand, Cates was almost passed over for the role of Billy's girlfriend Kate Beringer due to the risqué nature of her previous work. The young actress had made her debut in the 1982 feature *Paradise* and then gave a memorable turn in Amy Heckerling's *Fast Times at Ridgemont High* and the teen sex comedy, *Private Lessons*.

The supporting cast would be made up of more experienced actors, starting with Dick Miller, who had already worked with Joe Dante on *Piranha*, *The Howling* and his segment of the *Twilight Zone* movie. He'd be cast as Billy's neighbour, World War 2 veteran Murray Futterman. Country singer Hoyt Axton would take on the role of inventor Rand Peltzer (Billy's father) thanks to his turn in the 1979 picture *The Black Stallion*. According to the director, Axton had always been the number one choice for Rand, but he still screen-tested a number of other actors including Pat Hingle and Michael Gough. There is some conjecture over who actually gave the best performance. According to one source, Hingle was too good, and it was feared his character would dominate the picture if he were cast. Dante himself claimed on the DVD commentary that Michael Gough tested the strongest, but that the tone of his performance didn't gel with what they were looking for. Axton's role was further expanded to that of narrator when an introductory scene was scrapped.

Polly Holliday would provide a memorable turn as the dastardly Mrs Deagle, the old woman hell bent on making the townsfolk's lives miserable. At the time Holliday was seen as something of a casting coup, being that she was a popular TV star thanks to her role in the sitcom *Alice*. Rounding out the cast would be veteran actor Keye Luke as Mr. Wing, along with Judge Reinhold and Edward Andrews, who would play Billy's superiors at the bank in which he works. Finally, child star turned movie actor Corey Feldman took on the part of Pete Fountaine. With casting complete, two things were about to affect proceedings – one of which would have a lasting effect on the film's on-going success.

Steven Spielberg came up with what would be a game changer, not only for the film but also its merchandising prospects. In Columbus' original script, Gizmo and Stripe were one and the same – after the rules are broken, Gizmo turns into Stripe, and proceeds to terrorise Billy and the townspeople. But going over the script again, Spielberg could see that the audience would take to Gizmo, sympathise and root for him. He'd also make a great sidekick for the leads. The decision was made to rework the story that would see Stripe spawn from Gizmo when water was spilt on him. While this gave the puppet and effects crew extra work, all felt the pay-off would be worth it.

The other big change wasn't to the film's content, rather its release date. It's often puzzled people why Gremlins, which is set at Christmas time, wasn't released in December. In reality that was the plan; with Warner Bros. hoping it would be their big festive hit. However, when they discovered they had no major releases for the summer of 1984 – when Universal had *Temple of Doom* and Columbia had *Ghostbusters* – they pulled the film's release forward into the middle of the year. That meant the production team had around six months less in which to complete the picture, and put a sense of urgency onto getting shooting completed so the extensive effects work could get under way. None of this helped solve the biggest issue the film faced – how to bring Gizmo and the gremlins to life.

CGI was still very much in its infancy – and what was available simply wasn't capable of creating living, breathing creatures with any level of believability. Joe Dante turned to Chris Walas, a special effects guy with whom he'd worked on *Piranha*. Walas would later state that he had had no idea how they were going to make it all work, and took the job on out of desperation more than anything else. Initially they opted for stop-frame animation, but this was quickly dismissed due to the incredible amount of time it took to do even the simplest of scenes. Next, in what was surely a moment of panic (or insanity) they tried putting a gremlin-style mask on a monkey to see if that would work. It was a disaster, with the animal bouncing around the room in pure terror.

In the end, they opted to create full and partial models of the gremlins, along with numerous ones of Gizmo, including a larger version of his head that could be used for close ups. The animatronic creatures weren't cheap to produce, costing around $30-40,000 each. This led to security guards being posted on the set to ensure that all the models were returned at the end of the day's shooting. Even with two months of puppet work set aside after the main shoot was complete, filming was still arduous. Gizmo in particular caused the crew a number of headaches and required up to twelve people to control, depending on the scene and what was required. Small internal parts meant it was often breaking down, resulting in many long hours on set while scenes were re-shot. According to Dante, the scene in which the gremlins pin Gizmo and throw darts at him was created at the behest of the puppeteers, who wanted some small revenge for the hours of difficult work they had endured. But no one could deny, the character worked incredibly well and proved Spielberg's idea was a great one – the public would love Gizmo.

The fictitious town of Kingston Falls, where the film is set, was actually created on the Universal back lot, and would be used again for *Back to the Future*. Other sequences, such as the *Chinatown* opening, were shot on the Warner Bros. lot. Having begun shooting in April of 1983, principal photography was finally completed in August. By this stage, Chris Walas was already burnt out from the long days (and nights) on set and still had another two months of puppet work to complete. Further partial models were created, enlarged gremlin ears, legs and hands, along with over-sized food to be used in scenes showing the creatures eating and drinking. An enlarged Gizmo was required for the shots in which he multiplies after water is spilt on him – the pulsating mogwai fur balls being created via the use of fur-covered balloons. By the time the puppet work was completed, Walas was on crutches, suffered kidney stones and had spent weeks surviving on three hours sleep a night. He would later say it was the most horrendous film experience of his career, yet bizarrely, because of how close-knit the cast and crew were, it was also one of his happiest.

Work continued apace to meet the summer release date. The score for the picture was provided by Jerry Goldsmith, who would win a Saturn award for his efforts. Goldsmith would go on to score two further Dante-directed pictures (*The 'Burbs* and *Small Soldiers*). The 'voice' of Gizmo was provided by comedian Howie Mandel, while noted voice actor Frank Welker supplied the few words Stripe speaks. He, along with *Police Academy's* Michael Winslow and Mark Dodson, would give voice to the remainder of the gremlins, whose sounds and dialogue were largely improvised. At Spielberg's suggestion, the ending of the movie was also re-shot. Originally Billy was the clear hero of the finale, but in the new ending, Gizmo in his pink Barbie car saves the day. Actor Zach Galligan had no idea of the change until he sat down to watch the completed picture for the first time. Judge Reinhold and Edward Andrews saw their roles reduced as Dante attempted to get the film's edit down from two hours and forty minutes. The movie's title sequence would mark the debut of the Amblin logo, and also featured the Warner Bros. shield for the first time in years. [If one looks very closely at the poster, you can also see the Amblin logo on the button of Billy's jeans].

Ultimately, Gremlins original low budget swelled to $11M. Despite the fact the film would only need a couple of good weekends to break even, Warner Bros. were still unsure of its chances, with executives especially concerned about its dark tone. Even Steven Spielberg wasn't sure how the film would play, and one scene in particular – where Kate relates the death of her father, led him to believe it would polarise audiences. He talked at some length with Dante about the possibility of removing it, but the director refused and Spielberg let it be. What they were sure about was the merchandising potential of Gremlins. If they could get people to fall in love with Gizmo, the sky was the limit – dolls, lunchboxes, games – anything that could carry a picture of Gizmo (or Stripe) was a potential money-spinner. As was becoming the normal practice, Atari had already started work on a videogame adaptation, while Topps had a line of trading cards readied for release.

Critical reception for Gremlins was largely positive, with one notable exception. Roger Ebert loved its sly, satirical humour but Leonard Maltin famously savaged the film, noting its picture postcard setting felt at odds with the chaos and violence that befell it. But whether critics liked or loathed the picture, many noted that its graphic violence felt at odds with its PG rating. The issue would have long term effects and before the end of the summer, set changes in motion.

As has been mentioned before, the summer of 1984 was a big one. There wasn't a glut of new releases, but many that were released, struck gold. In a move that seems inexplicable to the modern box office reporter, Gremlins opened on the same weekend as *Ghostbusters*. It's hard to figure out the reason for this, considering both films would have surely eaten into the other's audience. If Gremlins failed, Warner Bros. would at least have *Ghostbusters* to blame rather than the quality of their own movie. In terms of other competition, the summer had already seen success with *Indiana Jones and the Temple of Doom* and *Star Trek III: The Search for Spock* – two films that would still be relatively new by the time of Gremlin's release. Older hits such as *Police Academy, Romancing the Stone* and *Footloose* were still in theatres. However, there wouldn't be much to trouble the picture in the weeks ahead.

If the weekend of June 8th 1984 proved anything, it was that you could release two pictures with similar target audiences, and have two smash hits regardless of their final chart position. Gremlins may have had to settle for second place, but with a $12.5M opening total, it was anything but the loser. Interestingly, the film played stronger in New York than *Ghostbusters* did. In an interview for Empire magazine in the summer of 2014, Dante stated that this was because the filming of *Ghostbusters* had caused so much annoyance and disruption to New York that the natives stayed away – at least initially. Within only three days, Gremlins had earned back its production budget and the character of Gizmo was already winning fans. This was something the studio, and Spielberg in particular had banked on. The merchandising stepped up.

A week later there was no change for the two top spots, and incredibly, both films saw an 11% increase in takings over the previous weekend. While *Ghostbusters* widened its lead, there was little cause for concern. Weekend three told a similar story, even with *Rhinestone*, *The Karate Kid* and *Top Secret* thrown into the mix. By this point Gremlins had recouped its budget some five times over and the studio was already looking at Gizmo (and Stripe) dolls being major sellers in the coming holiday season. In all, the two films occupied first and second place for six straight weeks, at the end of which Gremlins had made $95M. Only in weekend seven did it slip one place with the release of the Dudley Moore/Eddie Murphy comedy, *Best Defence*. Summer came and almost went, and the film was still in the top ten. While the gap between its takings and that of *Ghostbusters* had widened substantially, Gremlins was still clearing anywhere between $1-3M each weekend.

Records show it remained in the top ten for sixteen weeks in total, making an impressive $148M. The merchandise continued to fly off shelves while new opportunities were explored and exploited. Gizmo even got his own back story courtesy of a novelisation written by George Gipe (who never actually got to see the film). The picture also cleaned up on VHS too, making a further $79.5M in rentals. Warner Bros. put the film back into theatres in August 1985, adding another $5M to its total. It became the fourth biggest hit of 1984 behind *Beverly Hills Cop*, *Ghostbusters and Temple of Doom* and while figures aren't available, it is safe to assume the merchandising was equally, if not more successful. In its wake, other studios tried to jump on the bandwagon, and a number of knock-offs were quick to emerge including *Critters, Ghoulies* and *Munchies*. Of those three, *Critters* was the most successful and spawned three further sequels. Its director, Stephen Herek, also maintains that it was written before Gremlins and the script rewritten later to distance itself.

But one downside did continue to raise its head throughout the theatrical run – that of the film's PG rating and its graphic violence. A similar thing had been raised against *Indiana Jones and the Temple of Doom*. There were reports of parents walking out of screenings with their young children and Joe Dante himself sympathised with them. Despite its cute character and Christmas setting, Gremlins wasn't a film for young children. It was Steven Spielberg who suggested to the MPAA that an intermediate rating between PG and R was what was needed. This would inform parents that a film was unsuitable for young children, without alienating the slightly older market (or their parents). The introduction of the new rating came very quickly, and the first film to carry the PG-13 moniker, John Milius' *Red Dawn*, was released just two months after Gremlins debut. For a while, it opened up a new market to studios and movie makers – it meant they could craft more violent, edgier films with losing the all-important teen market by being hit with an R-rating.

Having seen how much the film and its related merchandise had made the company, Warner Bros. wanted a sequel as soon as possible and asked Joe Dante to begin work almost immediately. The director wasn't interested, saying that Gremlins worked well as a single picture – it had a beginning, middle and logical ending. Furthermore, working to such a tight deadline and budget, along with all the headaches the puppets had provided, had left him burnt out. The studio pressed ahead anyway, approaching numerous writers and directors to get the project moving while the characters were still fresh in the public's eye. A number of ideas were entertained – the gremlins invading Las Vegas or travelling to Mars being just two of them, but nothing stuck. Eventually Warner Bros. returned to Joe Dante and offered him triple the budget and full creative control to do whatever he wanted. A number of years had passed since the original and the director wasn't even sure the characters were relevant anymore, but the promise of full control convinced him to sign up.

The setting for *Gremlins 2: The New Batch* would be New York, and both Zach Galligan and Phoebe Cates would return, along with Dick Miller's Murray Futterman (Miller has appeared in almost every single film Dante has directed). Christopher Lee would play a genetics scientist while John Glover gave a memorable turn as CEO Daniel Clamp. Someone who didn't return was Chris Walas, and so creature design fell to Rick Baker, who initially turned the job down for fear of being too constrained by what came before. When Dante told him that he too had free reign to create whatever he wanted, he signed on-board. The plot would allow for all manner of gremlins this time around, including a super intelligent one with the ability to talk (and voiced by Tony Randall). Unlike the first film, where the merchandising developed as its success increased, *Gremlins 2* hit the ground running with numerous tie-ins and the like. Sadly, critics weren't as impressed with the sequel, and despite a $9M opening weekend, it made only $41M in total. But at least the gremlins got to have their revenge on critic Leonard Maltin in one scene.

Between the two movies, Joe Dante directed *Explorers, The 'Burbs* and *Innerspace*. He'd go on to make *Matinee, Small Soldiers* and *Looney Tunes Back in Action*, amongst others, but none were ever as successful as Gremlins. *The Hole* (2009) was well-received but criminally under-seen thanks to being barely publicised or released. As we have seen a number of times already with 80s actors, Zach Galligan struggled to find work outside of the Gremlins franchise.

He appeared in *Waxwork* and its sequel and now divides his time between TV, movie and theatre work. Phoebe Cates would appear opposite Michael J. Fox in *Bright Lights, Big City* (1988) and with Rik Mayall in the 1991 comedy, *Drop Dead Fred*, before retiring from acting in 1994 to raise her family. Since that time she has appeared on screen just once, as a favour to friend Jennifer Jason Leigh in the 2001 comedy drama *The Anniversary Party*.

Over the years there has been much talk of a reboot or remake and the characters themselves continue to remain popular. Speaking in 2012, Chris Columbus stated that he couldn't see how a remake would work in today's CGI obsessed environment. However, by 2014 he had changed his mind was said to be co-producing the remake through his 1492 production company. In April that same year, a number of websites reported that Warner Bros. were planning to fast-track a new Gremlins film (along with the long-gestating *Goonies* sequel). A few months later, Film Divider reported that Morgan Jurgenson and Alex Ankeles had pitched an idea that went down a storm with 1492 and they were now awaiting approval from Steven Spielberg before moving forward on the script. At the time of writing, there is no further update on their remake.

Gremlins still plays incredibly strong today, its deeply dark streak coming off well against the Christmas setting. The puppets may be showing their age, but there's no denying the charm of Gizmo and mischievousness of Stripe & Co. The violence, particularly in the kitchen sequence, is still strong enough to shock, as is the graphic finale. The creatures offer up a real sense of danger, but Dante manages to perfectly tread that fine line between hilarious and horrifying. It still makes essential viewing for a cold festive evening.

Looking for something like Gremlins? Try these...

Ghostbusters

Along with *Back to the Future*, arguably one of the best and quintessential movies of the entire decade. Dan Aykroyd, Bill Murray and Harold Ramis take on all manner of supernatural beings across New York. Investigating spooky goings-on in the apartment of Sigourney Weaver, the gang discover the end of the world might just be about to take place – and that isn't happening on their watch.

An absolutely brilliant comedy, with endlessly quotable dialogue, great special effects and an infectious theme tune. Ernie Hudson, Annie Potts, Rick Moranis and William Atherton provide solid support too, as does the city of New York itself. A massive hit for Columbia Pictures in the summer of 1984 that went on to spawn a sequel, animated shows and in 2016, an all-female reboot.

Trivia: The part of Peter Venkman was originally written for John Belushi. When the comedy actor died, Bill Murray was offered the part, but only agreed on the proviso that the studio would greenlight a remake of *The Razor's Edge*.

Little Shop of Horrors

This bizarre musical comedy began life as low budget Roger Corman feature, before being adapted into a Broadway musical. Things came full circle with Frank Oz's film version of the stage show. Starring Rick Moranis and Ellen Greene, the picture also featured a host of cameos from the likes of John Candy, Bill Murray and Steve Martin, as a sadistic dentist.

However, the real star of the piece is Audrey II, a huge man-eating plant with a thirst for human blood that convinces Moranis' Seymour to feed him victims. Audrey II came in six different sizes and getting her to move (and talk) convincingly took the crew many days to figure out. In the end, scenes with the character were shot at 12-16 frames a second, and then played back at normal speed. Little Shop of Horrors is something of a curio and unlike almost anything else released in the decade. For this reason alone, it's worth a watch.

Trivia: Test audiences reacted so negatively to the 23-minute finale that it was scrapped and the entire thing rewritten and re-shot.

Beetlejuice

Tim Burton's darkly comic tale of the afterlife featured Geena Davis and Alec Baldwin as a recently deceased couple trying to get the new residents out of what was their home. Only a young Winona Ryder takes any real notice, but things soon get out-of-hand when Davis and Baldwin employ the services of Michael Keaton's manic bio-exorcist Betelgeuse.

The comedian steals every scene he's in, but the make-up, sets and costumes also go a long way to making this one of Burton's most striking and best features – an astounding achievement given the visual effects budget was only $1M. A strong supporting cast featuring Jeffrey Jones, Glen Shadix and a shrieking performance from Catherine O'Hara all helped make this a huge critical and box office hit back in 1988.

Trivia: Tim Burton originally wanted Sammy Davis Jnr to player Betelgeuse, but was convinced by producer David Geffen to audition Michael Keaton for the role.

Heathers

Best Friends, Social Trends and Occasional Murder

Studio: New World Pictures

Release Date: 31st March 1989

Director: Michael Lehmann

Starring: Winona Ryder, Christian Slater

Budget: $3M – 2015 Equivalent: $5.8M

U.S Box Office: $1.1M – 2015 Equivalent: $2.1M

Veronica Sawyer is a reluctant member of the most powerful clique in her high school. Heather Duke, Heather Chandler and Heather McNamara are unrelenting in their judgement of others. But when loner J.D. joins the school, Veronica may have just found her ticket out of the popularity game, even if it means murder.

Heathers is a 1989 black comedy that was once described as the 'Anti-John Hughes' movie. Told through the eyes of student

Veronica Sawyer, it takes a number of teen-flick clichés and turns them squarely on their head. Yet even with its subversive nature, it's hard to believe that writer Daniel Waters created the script with the idea of getting Stanley Kubrick to direct.

Daniel Waters was born in Cleveland, Ohio in 1962 and secured his first writing work on the school newspaper. His contribution, entitled Troubled Waters, consisted of a fictitious story that featured real students. The column became popular and led to Waters embarking on a career in screenwriting. His first credit would be on the Monty Python-esque ensemble *Beyond Our Control* in the early to mid-1980s. Waters then set about writing what would become Heathers, working on the assumption that Stanley Kubrick would be the only person who could get a three-hour high school movie made. At this stage, the script was far more ambitious and covered the entire teenage years of the students. He even took cues from Kubrick's *Full Metal Jacket* for the opening cafeteria sequence.

The admittedly arrogant writer tried and failed a number of times to get the script out to Kubrick and soon realised the futility of the exercise. In the meantime, it was being passed amongst Water's fellow students at USC and one in particular, Michael Lehmann, took more than a passing interest in it. However, the two didn't initially hit it off and in a recent interview given to the Topless Robot website, Waters stated that Lehmann managed to annoy him before the two had even met by supplying notes and proposed changes to the screenplay. At the time, Lehman hadn't directed a commercial feature but had gained some notoriety for this short film, *Beaver Gets a Boner*. With Kubrick obviously not interested (it is highly unlikely the director even received the script), Waters partnered up with Lehmann, who took the project to producer Denise Di Novi (the three, Di Novi, Lehmann and Waters would go on to share the same theatrical agent – though some articles state they already did, and it was the agent who put the three of them together).

Denise Di Novi began her career as a copy editor for the National Observer, before taking up a job as publicist on the film, *Final Assignment* (1980). This led to her joining production company Film Plan, where she worked on *Videodrome* and *Visiting Hours*, amongst others. When Film Plan was sold, she took on the role of executive vice president for New World Pictures, a production company originally founded by Roger Corman. After a time in that role, she managed to secure an independent production deal within the company. Heathers would be her first full producer credit – but it wasn't plain sailing. The executives holding the purse strings didn't get the story at all and had concerns about many of its themes. Di Novi persevered and eventually managed to secure a $3M production budget.

In the meantime, Waters (with Lehmann's help) began cutting back the script to a workable length, as well as lightening up the tone a little. As the pieces began to fall into place, work began on casting.

However, it quickly became apparent that the dark nature of the script turned off a lot of potential actors – if the manuscript managed to get past their agents in the first place. Both Jennifer Connelly and Justine Bateman were sought to play Veronica Sawyer, but rejected the role. Drew Barrymore auditioned and during an initial read through, Dana Delaney read for the part too. Ultimately, Lehmann went with his third choice, Winona Ryder, who would go against her agent's advice in accepting the role.

Ryder had made her screen debut in the 1986 picture, Lucas, but it was her part in Tim Burton's *Beetlejuice* that brought her to the public's attention. Daniel Waters wasn't convinced that Ryder was attractive enough for the part. While she tested very well, it was a hastily organised makeover at a local mall that convinced the doubters that she had the looks to play the role (at the time of the audition, Ryder still looked very much like her gothic *Beetlejuice* character). Any remaining doubts were quickly erased once filming started. In the original script, Veronica's morals were little better than J.D.'s, but thanks to Ryder's sympathetic portrayal the script was retooled to show her as a more concerned/less willing participant in the schemes.

Christian Slater won the part of the rebellious J.D., beating out, the then unknown, Brad Pitt. Pitt had impressed during the read through with Dana Delaney, but had been deemed too nice for the role. On the other hand, Slater felt he'd blown his audition and tossed the script as soon as he was out of the building. The actor began his career at seven years of age, appearing in soap opera *The Edge of Night*, before making his Broadway debut in 1980 alongside Dick Van Dyke in a revival of *The Music Man*. Further theatre roles followed and Slater made his film debut in *The Legend of Billie Jean*. The picture had been expected to be a hit, but sank quickly upon release. Slater followed this up with more soap opera work before appearing opposite Sean Connery in an adaptation of Umberto Eco's *The Name of the Rose*. The role of J.D., for which he channelled a young Jack Nicholson, would help him become one of the most popular actors of the late 80s/early 90s.

Like the casting of Veronica, the search for the three Heathers – Chandler, McNamara and Duke, would bring its own set of issues. Lehmann stated he was blown away by how good an audition Heather Graham gave as Heather Chandler, and quickly offered her the role. The actress initially accepted but due to being under 18 at the time, needed her parents' permission. Unfortunately, they found the script offensive and forbade the actress from taking on the role. Even after Lehmann met with them personally, they still refused. At the casting director's suggestion, they met with Kim Walker, who at the time was Slater's girlfriend. Despite a lack of experience, Walker won the role and went on to give a memorable turn as the lead Heather.

Way before she got the role of Heather McNamara, Lisanne Falk was a hugely successful child (and later teenage) model, having worked with Brooke Shields at the Ford Modelling agency. By 1979, she found herself the subject of a book – *Lisanne: A Young Model*, which followed her day-to-day life. She also appeared on the cover of the 1980 Foreigner album, *Head Games*. When she auditioned for the role, she lowered her age to 18 (she was in fact 23). Only after being officially cast, did she let slip her real age over a celebratory dinner with the cast and crew – much to their surprise.

The final Heather – Duke, was played by Shannon Doherty. Out of the main female cast, Doherty had the most experience in front of cameras. She'd begun her career at a young age, appearing in minor roles on *Father Murphy* and *Voyagers!* before landing the role of Jenny Wilder in *Little House on the Prairie*. She stayed with the show up to its cancellation in 1983. Other roles followed, including voice work on *The Secret of Nimh* and the teen movie, *Girls Just Wanna Have Fun*, with Helen Hunt and Sarah Jessica Parker. Her next major break, and the show she was starring in when she got the Heather's call, was *Our House*, a drama that ran for two years. Doherty was interested in Heathers, but wanted the role of Veronica Sawyer, even though Winona Ryder was cast by the time she auditioned. Originally the casting team had envisioned Doherty as Heather Chandler, but after reading the script she asked to try out for the role of Heather Duke.

Even at this relatively early stage in her adult career, the actress was gaining a reputation. Prior to her audition, the casting agent warned Lehmann that Doherty was coming in for the part of Veronica Sawyer – she knew the role was taken but had hoped to impress them enough that they'd recast it. Lehmann said she gave a spirited audition but Ryder was already in place, and so Doherty settled for the role of Heather Duke. [In a 2014 look back at the film, Doherty denied she wanted Ryder's job]. The remainder of cast came together, with Lance Fenton and Patrick Labyorteaux playing jocks Kurt and Ram respectively. Renee Estevez, daughter of Martin Sheen, got the role of Veronica's friend Betty Finn (Daniel Water's purposely gave Veronica and Betty their surnames – seeing them as having a Huckleberry Finn/Tom Sawyer-like friendship). Finally, Carrie Lynn was cast as Martha 'Dumptruck' Dunnstock – a role which was a struggle to fill according to Lehmann, given how casting agents only sent 'cute, slightly plump' girls to audition. Lynn was a 400lb loner – the role of Martha was essentially her playing herself, she would later state.

The film shot in the first half of 1988 on a 32-day schedule. Filming took place at a number of locations, with actual working schools standing in for Westerburg High (named after Paul Westerburg, lead singer of Ryder's favourite band, The Replacements). Corvales High School was used for some of the interior shots, with external scenes taking place at John Adams Middle School. The gymnasium at John Adams also housed several sets including Veronica's bedroom. In a further cost-saving measure, the kitchen set for both Heather Duke and Heather Chandler's house was one and the same – it was dressed and lit differently for each respective scene.

The high school setting and cliques led to many of the same groups hanging out together when not shooting. Slater immersed himself in his character to such a degree that he barely to spoke any of the other cast members, save for Winona Ryder. The Jocks Fenton and Labyorteaux spent their downtime sending suggestive notes to the Heathers – and getting far worse back in return. Ryder spent much of her time at Lisanne Falk's place, but also had to find time to study and attend the premiere of *Beetlejuice* (which took place the same night as the filming of the J.D./Veronica croquet sequence).

The shoot itself wasn't without its issues. There were restrictions on the amount of hours Ryder was allowed to work each day, given she was 15 at the time (she would turn 16 during filming). Further conditions were placed on the times of day she could shoot, which would result in at least one proposed night time sequence being re-written to take place at dawn (it was shot late afternoon). If Ryder ran out of filming hours for the day, Lehmann would shoot her double walking down corridors or from the knees down. The actress would then add in her dialogue later.

Doherty also gave Lehmann a few headaches and proved to be a bit of a handful – as did her mother who would often mention how

"Shannon is the star of a TV show" when filming issues arose. The actress wasn't used to profanity either, and sometimes struggled to get through dialogue if she was required to swear or say something shocking. The character of Heather Duke is seen throughout the film reading *Moby Dick*. Originally it was meant to be *Catcher in the Rye* (which made more sense) but the production was unable to get permission to use the book. Similarly, companies such as 7-11 refused to allow their brands to be used. For his part, Christian Slater kept things mostly professional, but the director recalls at least a couple of times when they had to rouse him from his trailer.

Lehmann began assembling his edit to meet the March 1989 release date. In the meantime, the production team were in talks with representatives of Doris Day, hoping to license her version of *Que Sera, Sera* for use in the opening and closing sequences of the picture. Producer Denise Di Novi had a link to Doris Day – her musician father Gene had worked with the actress/singer in the 1950s. However, the request was refused as Day wouldn't allow the track to be used in any show or film that featured profanity (Gene Di Novi mentioned at the time that Day even organised a swear jar for her recording team when she was working). In the final version of the film, two different versions of the song are heard, one by Syd Straw, the other by Sly and the Family Stone.

Sometime after production had ended, Ryder and the Heathers were reassembled to shoot the opening croquet game sequence.

Unfortunately, by this point Lisanne Falk had cut her hair, and had to wear a wig while filming. The studio still weren't sure what they had with the finished film, but gave little feedback to Lehmann other than to say Slater's character didn't seem evil enough by the end of picture. New World had actually taken issue during the initial funding stage because of the original ending. A much darker finale would see both J.D. and Veronica dying, and reuniting in heaven where cliques no longer existed and everyone mingled happily. Daniel Waters claimed the ending went even further, and saw the happy group drinking punch spiked with drain cleaner. New World had refused to fund the film if it wasn't altered, fearing it was simply too dark for audiences to take. [At least one other ending existed, in which Martha stabs Veronica, who then lies bleeding, repeating the phrase "My name's not Heather"]

As finishing touches were applied, the production received news that New World were on their last legs, and wouldn't be able to promote the film to any great level – if at all. The good news was that critics were impressed with Heathers, and it currently sits on a 95% approval rating at Rotten Tomatoes. The box office of March 1989 was dominated by *Rain Man*, as it had been in January and February. *Fletch Lives* had knocked it off the top spot earlier in the month but by the time of Heather's release on March 31st, the Dustin Hoffman/Tom Cruise drama was back at number one. While there were no other major releases that weekend, it would have made little difference if there had been – Heathers debuted at just 35 theatres.

Either due to a lack of confidence or funds (perhaps both), New World couldn't get the initial theatre count any higher. It earned $177K during its first three days, and while it had one of the highest screen-to-taking averages of the top 15, it was of little consolation. A week later and things were worse – Denise Di Novi had to use $1800 of her own money to take out an advert for the film in the LA Times. The picture shed nine of its screens and made $123K; and while word-of-mouth was strong, not enough of it was reaching the general public. Even if they wanted to see Heathers, there was little chance of them finding a screening outside of Los Angeles. The film expanded to 54 locations during its third weekend and made almost $245K, but the writing was more than on the wall. By the end of its theatrical run three weeks later, Heathers had earned $1.1M.

It would be a long time before anyone made money off the film. Writer Daniel Waters joked that he made more money from an unproduced treatment for *The Parent Trap 3* than he did off Heathers. But like so many misses of the 1980s, the home video market saved it. The picture quickly developed a cult following, and for a time its dialogue and terminology was adopted by a generation of film fans (and high school students). It arguably paved the way for similar movies such as *Clueless, Jawbreaker* and *Mean Girls*. If the latter film shares more in common with Heathers than most, it is because it was directed by Daniel Waters' brother, Mark.

Lehmann followed up Heathers with *Meet the Applegates*, a movie about a group of giant praying mantis who disguise themselves as humans and move to Los Angeles. It actually made less money than his debut theatrical feature. His next project would see him re-teaming with Daniel Waters (who in the interim had written the Andrew Dice Clay vehicle, *The Adventures of Ford Fairlane*) on what was expected to be one of the biggest blockbusters of the summer of 1991. *Hudson Hawk* was famously known for being Bruce Willis' vanity project and had a very troubled and messy production. It became one of the biggest failures of the time and all but killed Willis' career until the critical success of *Pulp Fiction* and the financial smash of *Die Hard with a Vengeance* in 1994 and 1995 respectively.

Lehmann didn't direct another feature until *Airheads* in 1994. He went on to direct *40 Days, 40 Nights, The Truth about Cats and Dogs* and *Because I Said So*, before moving to direct almost exclusively for television. In recent years, he's worked on *True Blood, Nurse Jackie* and *Californication*. Despite having worked on three back-to-back failures, Daniel Waters secured the job to provide the screenplay for Tim Burton's *Batman Returns*. He followed this up with the script for the Sylvester Stallone picture, *Demolition Man*. In 2001, he made his directorial debut with *Happy Campers* and reunited with Winona Ryder on 2007's *Sex and Death 101*. In more recent times, he provided the screenplay for *Vampire Academy* (directed by his brother) and is currently at work on a *Sabrina the Teenage Witch* reboot.

Despite the bumpy start to her producing career, Denise Di Novi went from strength-to-strength. She worked again with Michael Lehmann on *Meet The Applegates* before going on to produce Tim Burton's next three features, including *Batman Returns* (she also produced *The Nightmare Before Christmas* and *James and the Giant Peach*). She teamed up again with Winona Ryder on *Little Women*, after which she began to focus almost exclusively on romantic comedy/dramas, including *Message in a Bottle, Life as We Know It* and *Crazy, Stupid, Love.*

Winona Ryder saw great success during the 1990s, though admitted that the role of Veronica Sawyer did initially see her passed over for a number of projects. Post-Heathers she went on to star opposite Cher in *Mermaids*, worked with Tim Burton again on *Edward Scissorhands* and joined the impressive cast of both *Dracula* (for Francis Ford Coppola) and *The Age of Innocence* (for Martin Scorsese). Further acclaim followed with *Little Women, The Crucible* and *Girl, Interrupted* (opposite Angelina Jolie) but her career stalled after a bizarre shoplifting incident in 2001. The actress was given community service and ordered to pay $10,000, but the damage to her career was long-lasting. After a brief hiatus, she took on roles in smaller projects, and received critical acclaim for her work on 2010's *Black Swan*. She also reunited with Tim Burton on the animated feature, *Frankenweenie*.

Similarly, Christian Slater saw notable success in the 1990s with *Robin Hood: Prince of Thieves, Young Guns 2* and arguably his finest role, as Clarence Worley in *True Romance*. Turns in *Interview with the Vampire* (replacing River Phoenix), *Broken Arrow* and *Hard Rain* all bought him varying degrees of success. But a 1997 arrest for the assault of his then girlfriend, Michelle Jonas, saw him spend time in rehab and jail. His career took years to recover fully and while he has worked consistently in TV, film and theatre since, he has been unable to recapture that earlier success.

Shannon Doherty initially went on to bigger things after Heathers, taking on the role of Brenda Walsh in the hugely successful TV show, *Beverly Hills 90210*. After leaving in 1994, she worked on a number of TV movies, but appearances in *Playboy*, brushes with the law and her on-set reputation all hampered her career. She returned to success in the Aaron Spelling show, *Charmed*. In recent years, she has hosted or appeared on a number of reality TV shows. She also reprised the role of Brenda in the new version of *Beverly Hills 90210*.

Lisanne Falk took on a number of smaller roles throughout the 1990s, notably in *Night on Earth* (which also featured Winona Ryder in one segment) and *Suicide Kings*. She retired from acting in 2002.

Despite her villainous performance, Kim Walker took on few roles after Heathers, mainly in TV movies or one-off episodes. She died of a brain tumour in 2001, aged just 32.

It's little surprise that Heathers never got a sequel, despite Winona Ryder pleading with Daniel Waters every few years to write another. At one point, there was talk of a follow-up being set in the world of politics that would see Veronica Sawyer murdering her way to the top – egged on by the ghost of J.D. The actress even managed to get Meryl Streep interested while the two worked on *The House of Spirits*. Two unrelated TV shows were also proposed, in 2009 and again in 2012, but neither developed past the pilot stage. A musical based on the film was produced in 2010 and played a number of small venues. It has continued to be performed in the intervening years and appeared at Off Broadway's New World Stages in March 2014.

Even though Heathers wasn't one of the most memorable films of the 1980s, many of its themes still resonate today – perhaps more so than at the time of its release. The picture's darkly comic, cynical tone seems more in line with the modern portrayal of high school life than the movies of John Hughes. Given its late 80s release date, its music and fashion is less jarring than most, and the picture retains the ability to shock – Winona Ryder still finds the film to be incredibly dark and subversive, particularly the closing seconds of the cow-tipping sequence in which you can glimpse in the background, Heather McNamara being date-raped by one of the jocks. One imagines if it were remade today, the comedy would be jettisoned in favour of gritty realism, yet it is that comedic edge that allowed the film to get away so with much. They might say war is hell, but then so is high school.

Did you enjoy Heathers? Try one of these...

Fast Times at Ridgemont High

Based on a Cameron Crowe book, which he researched by going undercover at a high school, Fast Times is an interesting coming-of-age comedy, which takes the time to cover some bigger, more serious issues. The central plot revolves around a group of friends but the film plays as more of an ensemble piece, covering the events of a single year in their lives.

It marked early screen roles for Forest Whitaker, Eric Stoltz, and Nicolas Cage (credited at Nicolas Coppola) along with a very memorable turn from Sean Penn as surfer/stoner Jeff Spicoli. The film was also the directorial debut of Amy Heckerling, who would tackle teens in school again in 1995's *Clueless*. A lot less explicit than other teen comedies of the time, Fast Times at Ridgemont High is an important entry in the genre and paved the way for such movies as *The Breakfast Club* and *Heathers*.

Trivia: The principal of the high school in which Cameron Crowe did his research only agreed to the project after discovering he'd interviewed Kris Kristofferson of which he was a huge fan.

River's Edge

A dark and controversial drama, River's Edge is the story of a group of teenagers and the murder of a young girl by one of their own. When Samson discusses what he's done with his friends and offers to show them the body, apathy seems to be the main response. Layne wants to hide the body and smuggle Samson out of the state, while Matt is traumatised. But deep down, it's hard to tell if anyone really cares at all.

Tim Hunter's picture contains some incredible performances, Crispin Glover and Dennis Hopper's, in particular, and is as far from *The Breakfast Club* and *Ferris Bueller's Day Off* as it is possible to be. A cautionary tale of sadness, hopelessness and foreshadowing with themes that still resonate today.

Trivia: The story is based on Marcy Renee Conrad, whose boyfriend killed her before bragging about it to friends. Despite thirteen people seeing the corpse, it was two days before anyone reported the crime.

Footloose

City boy Ren McCormack moves to a small town and discovers they have a ban on dancing and rock music. Making friends (and making waves), Ren pleads with the city council to revoke the ban, even citing Bible verses which mention dancing and rejoicing, but it all seems for nought. Yet he refuses to give up and continues to push toward the ban being revoked and the high school kids being allowed to hold a prom.

Footloose was directed by Herbert Ross, who took the reins from Michael Cimino after his demands got out of control. The public ignored the distinctly average reviews and turned the picture into a $80M smash hit. The soundtrack proved incredibly popular too, selling in excess of nine million copies. One of the great feel-good movies of the 1980s.

Trivia: The film was loosely based on events which took place in Elmore City, where a group of teens challenged a 90-year ban on dancing.

Fletch

Meet the only guy who changes his identity more often than his underwear.

Studio: Universal Release
Date: 31st May 1985
Director: Michael Ritchie
Starring: Chevy Chase
Budget: $8M – 2015 Equivalent: $17.7M
U.S Box Office: $50.8M – 2015 Equivalent: $111.9M

Posing as a beach bum while investigating the local drug trade, journalist Irwin 'Fletch' Fletcher is approached by a well-dressed man with a proposal. All Fletch has to do is show up at the man's house, shoot him dead and he'll be rewarded handsomely. Intrigued, and with his drug story stalled, he agrees to the deal and begins to investigate, little suspecting the danger he's about to put himself into. He'll have the story of his career, all he has to do is live long enough to write it.

Irwin Maurice Fletcher, or Fletch, was created by author Gregory McDonald and made his debut in a 1974 novel. McDonald was a Harvard graduate who had put himself through college by operating yachts. After graduating, he worked as a teacher and then a journalist, whilst writing his first book, *Running Scared* (1964). He left his job at the Boston Globe to concentrate on writing full-time and in 1974, released the first book to feature investigative journalist, Fletch. It was a huge success and won an Edgar Allen Poe award for best paperback original. McDonald has stated that he never intended to write a sequel but the success of the first book was overwhelming. Before long, he was back writing and in 1976, released *Confess, Fletch*. This too sold in great numbers and earned the author another writing award – the only time in history that a book and its sequel have won back-to-back Edgars.

Hollywood soon came knocking and the rights to Fletch were snapped up by Universal Pictures. However, McDonald wisely had a clause written into the contract that gave him veto over who could play Fletch. Anyone who was anyone wanted the role and the author passed on, amongst others, Mick Jagger and Burt Reynolds, who was arguably one of the biggest stars at the time. The studio then put forward the name of Chevy Chase and despite never really seeing him in anything previously, McDonald agreed on his casting as Fletch. This wasn't the first time the *Saturday Night Live* star had been considered for the part – according to movie legend, years earlier Chase's manager had urged him to read the novels with a view to him playing the role. At the time, the actor was balancing a number of projects and wasn't interested. However, when producer Alan Greisman became involved, along with screenplay writer Andrew Bergman, Chase came on-board.

By the time he took on the role of Fletch, Chevy Chase was already a popular TV star, with a budding film career. He was born in 1943, to parents Edward and Cathalene Chase, a prominent book editor and concert pianist respectively. He grew up in New York (the family are native New Yorkers in every sense of the phrase, being able to trace back their ancestry in the city some fourteen generations) and attended Riverdale Country School before being expelled. He eventually wound up at Haverford College, where he quickly gained a reputation for slapstick, and created a long-running urban legend – that he was expelled again for keeping a cow in his room (Chase would perpetuate this myth for many years despite his roommate revealing in 2003 that the actor left of his own accord, for academic reasons).

Chase graduated in 1967 but did not go on to study medicine as he had planned at one point. By not continuing his education, he ran the risk of being drafted, but managed to dodge the situation by implying he had homosexual tendencies. Chase got his first break into comedy that same year by co-founding the ensemble Channel

One. He would go on to contribute to MAD magazine and provide jokes and sketches for the Smothers Brothers, before taking up comedy full-time.

He appeared on *National Lampoon's Radio Hour* alongside John Belushi, Gilda Radner and Bill Murray, who would all go on to feature on the *Saturday Night Live* precursor, NBC Saturday Night. He made his feature film debut in *The Groove Tube* (1974), a low budget comedy that satirised commercial television, directed by Channel One co-founder Ken Shapiro. In October 1975, when *Saturday Night Live* launched, he was part of the cast, and had the honour of opening all but one show of that first season with the immortal line "Live from New York, It's Saturday Night!" He soon became known for his sketches, particularly the Weekend Report, to which he contributed material. Curiously, Chase was never actually meant to be part of the cast of SNL, he was contracted for a year as a sketch writer. He only became a cast member during rehearsals for the premiere.

The actor proved incredibly popular and went on to win two Emmy awards, and a Golden Globe. It was therefore something of a surprise when he opted to leave the show at the end of his contract. Some attributed it to the film offers that were now pouring in, but in reality Chase's girlfriend didn't want to remain in New York and the pair ended up moving to Los Angeles and marrying. For season 2 of *SNL*, Chase would be replaced by Bill Murray. The role of Eric

'Otter' Stratton in *National Lampoon's Animal House* was written with Chase in mind, but he turned down the role to play opposite Goldie Hawn in *Foul Play* (Tim Matheson, who would co-star in Fletch, wound up playing Otter). He then appeared in Harold Ramis' *Caddyshack* and worked again with Goldie Hawn on *Seems Like Old Times*. In 1983 he appeared in the role for which he is most commonly known, that of Clark Griswold in *National Lampoon's Vacation*.

The film, written by John Hughes and based on his short story, *Vacation '58*, was a smash hit in the latter half of the summer of 1983, making $61M on a budget of only $15M. It was also a critical success too, with almost all the reviews being positive. Yet, despite being on top of the world, Chase was using cocaine on a daily basis and had been for a number of years. His increased usage was making him paranoid and difficult to work with and was said to be the reason for the break-up of at least one of his marriages. By the time Fletch came around, the actor had sought help for his cocaine (and alcohol) usage, but Universal still weren't sure he could be relied upon. To go some way to ensure Chase stayed on the straight and narrow, they employed veteran director Michael Ritchie to helm the project. Ritchie also had to contend with author Gregory McDonald, who hated the script and what they had done to his story and characters.

Screenwriter Andrew Bergman had made a name for himself writing comedy – his first script, *Tex X*, became the basis for Mel Brooks' *Blazing Saddles*. He produced the first draft for Fletch in just four weeks, which was, to all intents and purposes, a very loose adaptation (The shooting script would receive another pass by Phil Alden Robinson). Gone was Fletch's military background, along with a number of other changes that author McDonald objected to, including one imagines, the increase in comedy. He went through the script and highlighted his every grievance to the studio. Wanting to keep him on side, Ritchie invited McDonald onto the set to see filming taking place. Afterwards, over dinner, the director went through every single issue the author had with the screenplay and explained why he was wrong.

When he took on the job of directing Fletch, Michael Ritchie already had more than 25 years directing experience behind him. In his final years at Harvard, he had produced a version of Kopit's play, *'Oh Dad, Poor Dad, Mamma's Hung You in the Closet and I'm Feelin' So Sad'*. This bought him the attention of producer Robert Saudek, who offered him the chance to direct an episode of Omnibus, entitled *Saint Joan*. From there he went on to direct episodes for a number of popular TV shows of the time, including *Dr. Kildare, The Man from U.N.C.L.E* and *Run For Your Life*. He made his feature directorial debut on the 1969 picture *Downhill Racer*, the first of a number of sport-themed movies he would make. He re-teamed with Robert Redford (star of *Downhill Racer*) on the 1972 satire, *The Candidate*, before having a smash hit with *The Bad News Bears*. Despite a few misses over the years, Ritchie was seen as a reliable and experienced director. Fletch would be the eleventh movie of his career (discounting an uncredited role on *Student Bodies*).

In addition to Chevy Chase, who would feature in almost every scene of the film, Tim Matheson would play Alan Stanwyk, Joe Don Baker took on the role of Chief Jerry Karlin and newcomer Dana Wheeler-Nicholson appeared as Stanwyk's wife, Gail. As previously mentioned, Tim Matheson took on the role in *Animal House* intended for Chevy Chase, yet by that point (1978) he had been acting for almost 18 years in all kinds of roles across numerous genres, including voice-over work on *Jonny Quest* and *Sinbad Jr*. Joe Don Baker was similar, and found himself in the public eye thanks to the unexpected hit, *Walking Tall*, based on the life of sheriff Buford Pusser. In stark contrast, Dana Wheeler-Nicholson had had just two minor roles prior to appearing in Fletch. The remainder of the cast was filled out by George Wendt, Richard Libertini and Geena Davis.

With a May 1985 release date in place and an $8M budget to work with, Ritchie got production underway in and around Los Angeles. He was more than aware that he had to keep Chevy Chase occupied, and allowed the actor to improvise many of his lines. In an interview given to the A.V Club in 2009, Tim Matheson stated that Ritchie would shoot two takes for most scenes – the first would be as scripted, while on the second he would allow Chase free reign to do or say as he pleased, within reason. This had the effect of not only keeping the actors on their toes, but creating some of the best lines and reactions in the movie. Chase would later claim he 'winged' most of the shoot, seeing Bergman's script as little more than a guide to the plot and action. He stated that much of the dialogue was unscripted and he would often make up names or directions on the spot.

With little in the way of action sequences, shooting went smoothly enough and work soon began on assembling the finished movie. The director had to sift through a great deal of footage thanks to the improvised nature of the shoot, deciding what played best for any given sequence. The initial cut ran far too long and had to be edited down to a tight 95 minutes (without end credits). This meant a second dream sequence was removed (Fletch being called to pitch for the Dodgers) and a voiceover track was added to help the audience keep track of the plot now that some of the exposition had been removed.

Very late into post-production, composer Tom Scott was replaced by Harold Faltermeyer. There is scant evidence as to why this took place, other than Scott's work seemed very jazz noir, which may not have fit with what Michael Ritchie was after for the film. Harold Faltermeyer, a one-time protégé of Giorgio Moroder, had seen huge success with his work on the *Beverly Hills Cop* soundtrack, which in turn spawned the hit single, Axel F. He bought his distinctive sound to Fletch, but revealed in October 2014 that things could have ended up quite differently had it not been for Billy Idol. Around the time of Fletch, Faltermeyer was already at work on the *Top Gun* soundtrack (it would be a rare instance where a soundtrack was all but completed before a film was shot). He'd created a piece of music that would be used as Fletch's theme, but friend Billy Idol, who was recording close by, convinced Faltermeyer to use the song on *Top Gun* instead. The composer agreed, and crafted a new piece of music for Fletch. 'Fletch's theme' went on to become one of *Top Gun*'s memorable anthems. As mentioned, the change in composer came very late in the film's production – Tom Scott's name was still listed as composer on the initial posters and trailer.

Reviews for the movie were generally positive, though more than one critic mentioned how Chase's performance was so casual and knowing, that at times it took you out of the picture. Roger Ebert, in his two and half star review summed the film up as needing 'an actor more interested in playing the character than in playing himself.' At the time of writing it holds a 75% approval rating on Rotten Tomatoes. Fletch was scheduled for an early summer release. While Chevy Chase was now a major star, the picture wasn't expected to be a runaway success – and with an $8M budget attached, it didn't need to be. There would be competition, both direct and indirect, on all sides. The Richard Pryor comedy *Brewster's Millions* had opened the week before to the tune of $9.8M, while the second *Police Academy* film, *Their First Assignment*, was still going strong after two months on general release. Inexplicably, *Beverly Hills Cop* was also a very real threat despite having opened some six months previous, in the December of 1984. The Eddie Murphy vehicle had been at number one for thirteen straight weeks, and while it had fallen to the lower rungs in March and April, it was back in the top five come May. There was also the second weekend of *Rambo: First Blood Part 2* and *A View to a Kill* to contend with.

In true Fletch style, the picture hit the ground running, making a solid $7M from its 1,225 screen count during its opening weekend. By the middle of that first week, it had already recouped its production budget and was bracing itself for the release of *The Goonies* and *Perfect*. While the former knocked Fletch down a place, the latter barely had an impact. Even with the increased competition, the picture held exceptionally well during that second frame, taking a further $6.3M (a fall of just 10% on the previous weekend). The film continued to play well and by the end of its fourth week on general release, had made over $30M. Even up against *Back to the Future*, which opened on Fletch's sixth weekend of release, the picture managed to earn $2.3M and fell 22% on its previous frame.

All up, Fletch made $50.6M in North America and a further $9M overseas, against that budget of $8M. It was the 12th biggest film of 1985, beating out the likes of *Commando, Teen Wolf* and *Brewster's Millions*. Chase had two other hits in 1985 – *Spies Like Us* (which would become the tenth biggest film of the year) *and National Lampoon's European Vacation* (which made just over $50M). Along with Sylvester Stallone and Michael J. Fox, Chevy Chase was one of the biggest stars of the year. The film performed strong on video, earning over $24M in rentals. Universal knew a good thing when they saw one and with more books to adapt, hoped they had the making of a franchise. However, it would be four years before Fletch returned to the big screen.

In the interim, Chase's career had begun to flounder. *The Three Amigos*, with Steve Martin and Martin Short didn't clear $40M, *Funny Farm* made $25M and the ill-fated *Caddyshack* sequel crashed to $11.8M. Universal managed to convince both Chase and director Michael Ritchie to return for 1989's *Fletch Lives*. By that point there were eight other Fletch books that could have been adapted for screen, but the studio opted to create an original story instead, written by Leon Capetanos (*Down and Out in Beverly Hills, Moscow on the Hudson* and *Moon Over Parador*). The story would see Fletch inheriting a mansion in Louisiana and quitting his newspaper job to live the life of luxury. But when he arrives he discovers the place is completely run-down, finds himself framed for murder and suddenly offered a huge sum of money for his apparently worthless piece of land. Reviews were mixed, but the film debuted at the top of the chart upon its release. While history has largely forgotten *Fletch Lives*, it actually did OK at the box office, making $40M (again, against a budget of $8M).

Chase would hit the big time again in December 1989 with *Christmas Vacation*, but three back-to-back failures (*Nothing but Trouble, Memoirs of an Invisible Man* and *Cops & Robbersons*) saw him cast into the wilderness for many years. A failed chat show did little to help matters and his reputation for falling out with co-stars and production staff was as bad as it had ever been. He would continue to work fairly consistently and even returned to the role of Clark Griswold for *Vegas Vacation* in 1997, but it would not be until 2009, and his appearance in the sitcom *Community*, that the actor was again back in the limelight. While he would leave the show in 2012 amid disagreements with creator Dan Harmon, it gave him the break he needed. At the time of writing, he has returned to the role of Clark Griswold for a new *Vacation* movie that will see Ed Helms as his son, Rusty, taking his own family on the holiday of a lifetime.

Post-Fletch, Michael Ritchie re-teamed with Chase on *Cops & Robbersons*, before directing *The Scout, Fantasticks* and *A Simple Wish*. He died from prostate cancer in 2001. Actor Tim Matheson continued to work at an incredible pace, moving between film and TV. In recent years he has had recurring roles in *The West Wing, Burn Notice* and *Hart of Dixie*. Dana Wheeler-Nicholson appeared in a number of one-off TV episodes, along with turns in *Tombstone* and *Fast Food Nation*. Finally, writer Andrew Bergman continued to produce comedy scripts, and turned his hand to directing with *The Freshman, It Could Happen to You* and *Striptease*, amongst others.

While no second sequel was forthcoming, a reboot of sorts has been talked about for at least 20 years. During his time working with the Universal Pictures subsidiary Gramercy, Kevin Smith (who had made *Mallrats* and *Chasing Amy* for the studio) talked about writing a third Fletch feature, which would once again star Chevy Chase. While the duo did meet to discuss the possibility, little movement was actually made. The actor would later go on to state that Smith had talked up the role over a dinner they had had, but never contacted him again. Smith tells it differently, and states that while they did meet for dinner, his Fletch movie was at least a year away due to him commencing work on *Dogma*. The director claims the dinner was a disaster, with Chase taking credit for all and sundry. He would take pot shots at Smith in the press for years to come.

In 2000, it was announced that Smith would direct a new Fletch movie for Miramax, who had gained the rights after they had reverted from Universal. He opted to adapt *Fletch Won*, a later book of McDonald's that chronologically, was the first story in the series. It would see Fletch as a junior reporter just making a name for himself. Both Jason Lee and Ben Affleck were said to be in mind for the role. In the August of 2003, the studio announced that Smith was set to begin shooting in January of the following year. The director lobbied for Jason Lee but Miramax baulked, claiming the actor was not box office material. By the time Lee was a household name thanks to *My Name is Earl*, Miramax deemed him too old for the role.

A number of other actors were considered, and at one point, Smith looked to be moving forward with Scrubs star Zach Braff, but nothing came of it. He left the project shortly after and returned to the Viewaskew universe with *Clerks 2*. In 2006, *Scrubs* creator Bill Lawrence had taken on the job of directing *Fletch Won* (and an untitled sequel). In January of the following year, Zach Braff announced that Lawrence saw him as a young Fletch, but no deal was in place and the script was still being written. Three month later, the actor ruled himself out of the running, opting to concentrate on directing *Open Hearts* (a remake of a Danish film) instead. Lawrence himself would leave the project in June 2007, to be replaced by Steve Pink. Little more was heard of a Fletch remake until 2011, when Warner Bros. gained the rights. They set a number of writers to work on separate drafts but all were deemed unsuitable. In 2013, writer David List, who represents Gregory McDonald's estate, submitted his own draft. This new script was good enough to attract the attention of Jason Sudekis, who signed on-board. The studio has apparently signed off on the script but as of January 2015, is still looking for a director.

Fletch is still a terrific comedy-thriller. Chevy Chase claims it is his favourite role because it allowed him to improvise and utilise props and physical comedy. The character is never caught off guard, and has a line (or lie) for every situation he finds himself in – not dissimilar to Eddie Murphy's Axel Foley. The film moves at a cracking pace, and while the plot does seem a little convoluted, Chase's performance holds it all together, easily covering any cracks that may appear. It also stands up well to repeat viewings, allowing the character's subtleties and wisecracks to shine.

"By the way, I charged the entire vacation to Mr. Underhill's American Express Card. Want the number?"

If you enjoyed Fletch, try one of these…

Beverly Hills Cop

Detroit cop Axel Foley sets off to Beverly Hills to investigate the murder of an old friend. Before too long he's run foul of the police and a local businessman he suspects of arranging the killing. A superb fish-out-of-water story, with Foley always one step ahead of everyone else, with a line or a lie for any situation. The supporting cast, featuring Judge Reinhold, John Ashton and Ronny Cox, are also well placed, even if they are the butt of many of Foley's jokes and schemes.

The film is still one of the biggest R-rated comedies of all time, even adjusted for inflation. This, *48 Hrs* and *Trading Places* put star Eddie Murphy firmly on the map, making him one the most bankable stars of the 1980s. The sequels didn't work quite as well, especially the third, but the original remains a stone-cold classic of the genre and almost certainly the best action comedy of the decade.

Trivia: Beverly Hills Cop was the first ever movie to open at more than 2,000 cinemas and along with *Tootsie*, held the record for the most consecutive weeks at the top of the box office until the release of *Titanic*.

Trading Places

John Landis directs Eddie Murphy and Dan Aykroyd in this hilarious comedy that sees the lives of two people swapped on a bet. Randolph and Mortimer Duke disagree about whether it's circumstance or money that makes the man. They decide to put this to the test and destroy the life of the well-to-do Louis Winthorpe III, while elevating the life of homeless bum, Billy Ray Valentine to that of an executive.

There's not a weak member of the entire cast, with the leads both giving near-career best performances. They're matched by Jamie Lee Curtis and a brilliant Denholm Elliott, along with another memorable turn from Paul Gleason as Clarence Beeks. With so many great lines and sequences, Trading Places rightly takes its place as one of the best pictures of the decade. A true gem and a great festive treat too.

Trivia: In 2010, a new law was put into place that banned the use of insider information to corner a particular market. Inspired by events at the end of the movie, it is unofficially known as 'The Eddie Murphy Rule'.

Real Genius

Mitch Taylor is a teenage wunderkind who wins a scholarship to the illustrious Pacific Tech, where he'll be working with the equally-talented Chris Knight. Despite discovering that Knight is a slacker, more concern with fun than work, the duo works well together and manages to create a brand new type of laser. However, when they discover it's actually an assassination tool for the CIA, they decide to take matter into their own hands to stop the agency getting it.

Val Kilmer is superb as Chris Knight in this seriously underrated comedy, directed by Martha Coolidge and also starring the best 80s A-hole, William Atherton. The one-liners come at a rat-a-tat pace and the scientific backdrop makes for some great set pieces. The fashions and technology may have aged but Real Genius is still a great deal of fun and well worth discovering.

Trivia: The popcorn used in the climax of the movie took three months to produce and the film's climax was even the subject of an episode of *Mythbusters*.

The Lost Boys

Sleep all day. Party all night. Never grow old. Never die. It's fun to be a vampire

Studio: Warner Bros.

Release Date: 31st July 1987

Director: Joel Schumacher

Starring: Jason Patric, Keifer Sutherland

Budget: $8.5M – 2015 Equivalent: $17.9M

U.S Box Office: $32.2M – 2015 Equivalent: $67.4M

When Michael and Sam move to Santa Carla with their mother, they're all hoping for a new start. But when Michael falls in with a bad crowd who have a taste for blood, it'll be left to Sam and the Frog Brothers to battle the creatures of the night and save Michael's soul before it is too late…

Back in the 1980s, vampires weren't cool. Horror films had taken a decidedly nasty turn and while cannibals, zombies and werewolves were now the go-to villains, the vampire was relegated to bit-player status, reserved for the art house (*The Hunger*) or for laughs (*Love at First Bite*). Films such as *Lifeforce* and *Vamp* put their own spin on the genre but they couldn't grab an audience. If blood suckers were going to survive the 80s, they needed a re-invention. In a vampire spin on *Peter Pan* and his lost boys, director Richard Donner was convinced he'd found it.

By the mid-1980s, Richard Donner was a hugely successful director. He'd begun his career some thirty years earlier, initially as an actor before moving swiftly on to directing TV commercials. Like many veteran directors, he cut his teeth on episodic television, working on a number of major shows including *The Man from U.N.C.L.E*, *Gilligan's Island* and *The Wild Wild West*. His first feature credit was on the Charles Bronson-Mary Tyler Moore picture, *X-51* (1961). It would be more than seven years before he would direct another movie; this time, the comedy caper *Salt and Pepper*, which was followed up by *Lola*, a romantic drama again featuring Charles Bronson and Susan George. However, it was his next picture, *The Omen*, which put him firmly on the map.

The terrifying story of a demonic child, *The Omen* was a financial and critical success, making over $60M off a budget of only $2.8M. Donner then moved onto *Superman the Movie*, arguably the first modern-day take on the genre; setting up a template which almost every other superhero movie would follow. Despite having already shot a lot of footage, Donner was replaced by Richard Lester on *Superman II* (The story behind which would fill, and has filled, many column inches). Instead, he would direct *Inside Moves* and the Richard Pryor comedy, *The Toy*, the former being largely forgotten and the latter being a hit in 1982. Three years later, he was back with not one but two new movies, passion project *Ladyhawke* (which he had tried and failed to get off the ground a number of times) and 80s favourite, *The Goonies*. While *Ladyhawke* didn't recoup its budget, *The Goonies* was a smash hit, becoming the ninth most successful movie of the year.

When he read the script for The Lost Boys, it seemed a natural progression – essentially being *The Goonies* as vampires and the Frog Brothers as eight-year-old boy scouts. *Psycho II* director Richard Franklin had already passed on the project, but Donner could see the potential and suggested making the characters older to open up further opportunities. Scriptwriter James Jeremias had been influenced initially by Anne Rice's *Interview with the Vampire*, in particular the tale of ageless child vampire, Claudia. Teaming up with friend Janis Fletcher, the duo was further taken by J M Barrie and envisaged the story as a reinterpretation of his classic, *Peter Pan*. They argued that Peter never aged, could fly and only appeared to Wendy at night – it wasn't much of a stretch to believe he and his fellow lost boys were vampires. The first draft of the script even referred to them by names Barrie had used in his story – David was originally called Peter, and the names of John and Michael (Wendy's siblings) also appeared as fellow lost boys/vampires. Donner was interested in the project but another script had also caught his eye – Shane Black's *Lethal Weapon*.

In the end, Donner would pass on The Lost Boys due to the slow pace at which progress was being made. He may also have been weary of working with kids again so soon after *The Goonies* (The director has stated a number of times that keeping the cast under control was harder than directing the picture itself). For whatever reason, The Lost Boys was now without someone at the helm – though Donner would stay on as producer while moving forward with *Lethal Weapon*. The studio was still keen on making the picture and hired newcomer Mary Lambert to take over the picture. Like many directors of the time, Lambert made her name on music videos, working with the likes of Janet Jackson, Mick Jagger and Madonna, for whom she shot *Like a Virgin, La Isla Bonita* and *Material Girl* (she would later create the controversial *Like a Prayer* video). It didn't take long for her to exit the project, citing creative differences. Richard Donner now looked to Joel Schumacher, a costume designer-turned-director he had met through his then-girlfriend Lauren Shuler, who'd produced his hit, *St. Elmo's Fire*.

Joel Schumacher was born in Long Island in 1939. Losing his father at a young age, and with a mother working more than she was at home, the young Schumacher led a very lonely life. Cinema was his primary escape, to such a degree that he would skip school to watch (or re-watch) whatever was showing at the theatre behind their apartment. He initially studied fashion but soon realised that film directing was what he wanted to do. Moving out to Los Angeles, he secured work as a costume designer on *Play it as it Lays*. This in turn led to him working with Woody Allen on *Sleeper* and *Interiors*, while also writing the scripts for *Car Wash, The Wiz* and *Sparkle* (which was remade in 2012). His directing career began with two TV movies – *Virginia Hill* and *Amateur Night at the Dixie Bar and Grill*, while his first theatrical feature would be the Lily Tomlin vehicle, *The Incredible Shrinking Woman*.

After helming the Mr. T comedy, *D.C Cab*, Schumacher turned his attention to writing (and later directing) *St. Elmo's Fire*, which launched or furthered the careers of a number of young actors, including Rob Lowe, Ally Sheedy and Andrew McCarthy. Despite being something of a critical failure, the picture made good box office and the core group of actors became known as The Brat Pack, a phrase coined in a New York magazine article by David Blum. [The piece was seen by the group as being very negative and the attention it brought led them to stop socialising with each other. Long term, it would have a detrimental effect on their careers].

When Donner called Schumacher, he agreed to read the script. His first impression wasn't good and he almost turned it down, but he too could see the potential if the characters could be rewritten as young adults. Aiming for the same market that had made *St Elmo's Fire* a hit, Schumacher agreed to direct if he could get someone to re-write the script more in line with his vision. Schumacher hired Jeffrey Boam, who had written *The Dead Zone* and *Innerspace*, as well as being an in-demand script doctor for Warner Bros. The duo upped the horror content and turned the character of Star into a girl (she was a young boy in the original version), thereby introducing a sexual element too. Boam was also responsible for creating the grandfather character, along with supplying the names of Edgar and Alan for the Frog Brothers (after fabled horror writer, Edgar Allan Poe). Together, Schumacher and Boam managed to take The Lost Boys from a family-friendly caper to an R-rated tongue-in-cheek horror. The studio weren't quite sold on the project, but with an $8.5M budget attached, felt it was a risk worth taking and greenlit the movie for production.

The director felt the budgetary restraints before shooting had even commenced, something reflected in the largely unknown cast. Bizarre as it may seem to a modern audience, Corey Feldman was actually the biggest name attached to the picture prior to its release. The child actor had made the successful jump to teenage star with turns in *Gremlins, The Goonies* and *Stand by Me*. He would sign on-board to play Edgar Frog – but only after convincing Schumacher he was right for the role by turning up to his audition with long hair. In what proved to be fateful casting, the role of Sam Emerson went to

Corey Haim, another young actor whose first screen role was in the TV show, *The Edison Twins*. He made his feature debut shortly after, opposite Robert Downey Jnr, Sarah Jessica Parker and Peter Weller in *Firstborn* (the disintegration of Haim's parents' marriage led to him living with Downey and Parker at one point). He appeared in Stephen King adaptation *Silver Bullet*, along with other smaller parts, and went on to win a Young Artist Award for his work opposite Liza Minnelli in *A Time to Live*.

It would be his performance in the coming-of-age drama, *Lucas*, which really brought him the attention of Hollywood and curiously, set his career on a very different path. Haim had read for a part in *Stand by Me* – and was offered the role on the same day that he was offered the part in Lucas. He chose the latter and River Phoenix ended up in *Stand by Me* instead. Haim would later state that had he had the time again, he would still have made the same decision. Newcomer Jamison Newlander would take the part of the other Frog brother, Alan.

That left three major parts to cast – Michael, Star and leader of the vampire gang, David. Schumacher cast Kiefer Sutherland after seeing his work in *At Close Range* – this was a few months prior to the release of *Stand by Me*, in which the Canadian actor played a menacing bully (it was also his first US film). Equally as much of a newcomer was Jason Patric, who would take on the role of Michael, Sam's older brother. The actor had done just one TV movie

(*Toughlove* with Bruce Dern and Lee Remick) and one feature film (*Solarbabies*) before landing The Lost Boys gig. Schumacher stated that it took him six weeks to convince Patric to take on the role and only then would he do it on the promise that he would not be required to wear vampire make-up (A promise the director always knew he would have to break).

For the final part of the triangle, the role of Star, Jami Gertz was cast, thanks in some part to Jason Patric's recommendation (the two had appeared in *Solarbabies*). The actress had been working in film since 1981 and already appeared in *Endless Love, Sixteen Candles* and the Ralph Macchio flick, *Crossroads*. She would be one of the few female cast members, but proved to be more than a match for the boys. Dianne Wiest, who was coming off an Academy Award win for her part in *Hannah and Her Sisters*, would play Sam and Michael's mother Lucy, while Edward Herrmann took on the part of Max, the mysterious new man in her life. One final role, that of Grandpa ended up involving three different actors. Keenan Wynn was initially cast, but passed away before shooting commenced. Next in line, John Carradine was too ill to work at the time, leaving Barnard Hughes to put his own memorable spin on the character. [It's worth noting that while Wynn was said to have passed away before shooting took place, he actually died in October 1986, after filming was all but complete. Given his death from pancreatic cancer, he may have been too ill to take on the role].

An interesting (yet largely ignored) addition to the back room team was the return of Director of Photography Michael Chapman. A legend in almost every sense of the word, Chapman had been cameraman *on The Godfather* and *Jaws*, before graduating to Director of Photography on *The Last Detail*. He worked with Martin Scorsese on *Taxi Driver, The Last Waltz* and *Raging Bull*, along with Paul Schrader (*Hardcore*), Philip Kaufman (*Invasion of the Body Snatchers*) and on the Carl Reiner comedies, *Dead Men Don't Wear Plaid* and *The Man With Two Brains*. He made the jump to directing with the Tom Cruise feature, *All the Right Moves*, before making the near dialogue-free flop *The Clan of the Cave Bear* with Daryl Hannah. He directed one more film, TV movie *Annihilator*, before returning (almost permanently) to cinematography on The Lost Boys.

The movie was set to shoot in Santa Cruz, but local authorities keen to uphold their family-friendly reputation of the area refused them permits to film on the boardwalk, unless the name of the town used in finished film was changed. This is the reason for The Lost Boys being set in the fictional town of Santa Carla. The shoot itself, which took place in the summer of 1986, was a fairly chaotic one thanks to its relatively young cast. Not long after work began, Sutherland broke his wrist while showing off on his motorbike. Knowing they would be unable to film around the injury, the actor got a surf shop to create a thin polyurethane cast that immobilised his wrist and allowed him to put on black leather gloves (the character is rarely seen out of them for this reason).

He and his fellow vampires, who included future *Bill and Ted* star Alex Winter, supposedly went the method acting route, staying nocturnal for much of the shoot. Corey Feldman used cocaine for the first time during the production, and ended up so obviously out of it that Schumacher fired him, temporarily at least. The Lost Boys would also see the start of Corey Haim's descent into drugs, which would plague him for years to come. While it was a fairly wild shoot, there was also much camaraderie, and many of the cast spent time together when they weren't filming; Patric took Haim under his wing and the two became like brothers both on-set and off.

There were also issues with the special effects to contend with, which resulted in Greg Cannom joining the picture midway through shooting. That gave him precious little time to pull everything together. He, along with Schumacher and make-up artist Ve Neill came up with the concept of the 'vamp out'. Instead of having David and Co. look like traditional vampires, they made them appear as normal people, with the ability to transform into something horrific at a glance. This idea would go on to influence other vampire features, along with Joss Whedon's *Buffy the Vampire Slayer* and *Angel* TV shows. When Warner Bros. saw the first dailies, they were concerned. The tone of the picture made little sense to them and when they asked Schumacher if he was making a horror or a comedy, he simply replied, 'Yes'. To their credit, the director would later state, they did accept a lot without much fuss – the mainly unknown cast he'd chosen, the way the picture was shaping up and its level of violence.

As the elements began to come together and Schumacher commenced editing, his thoughts also turned to the soundtrack. The haunting *'Cry Little Sister'* was written by Gerard McMann and Michael Mainieri (McMann, actually a pseudonym for Gerard McMahon, would also perform it). Roger Daltrey and Echo and The Bunnymen covered Elton John and Doors tracks respectively. Lou Gramm of Foreigner recorded *'Lost in the Shadows'* and Jimmy Barnes & INXS supplied two tracks – *'Good Times'* and *'Laying Down the Law'*. The only issue was that the Lost Boys' budget didn't stretch to cover all this music. Rather than lose the tracks by INXS and Gramm, the director cut a deal with the artists – if they'd allow him to use their songs, he'd direct a music video for each of them in the following year. Both agreed, and while Gramm never took up the offer, INXS had Schumacher direct the video for *Devil Inside*.

The Lost Boys was something of a difficult sell for Warner Bros. The trailer had to play up both the horror and comedy elements, without alienating the respective fans of each genre. Music taken from the soundtrack helped get the film noticed via MTV, and a tie-in novelisation was also readied to coincide with picture's release. On the flip side, the R-rating meant that a large part of the potential audience would be barred from seeing the film – or would need to drag along their parents. There was also the fact that there were no major stars on which to hang the picture. But as Schumacher had told the studio when they voiced their concerns during the shoot – they were only in it for $8.5M. A couple of decent weekends would see that figure covered.

The Lost Boys was set to debut at the very end of July 1987. The summer had already seen the major releases *Beverly Hills Cop 2, Predator, Robocop, Dragnet* and *The Untouchables,* many of which were still in theatres. Furthermore, it would open up against *The Living Daylights*, the long awaited return of James Bond, played for the first time by Timothy Dalton. In the weeks ahead there'd be *Stakeout, Masters of the Universe* and *Can't Buy Me Love* all to contend with. Reviews for the vampire flick were quite positive, with Roger Ebert awarding it two and a half stars and praising the cast and cinematography. Others felt it was more style over substance, and the general consensus at Rotten Tomatoes (where it holds a 72% approval rating) is that the film is 'Flawed but eminently watchable'.

The Lost Boys opened at 1,027 locations on July 31st, making an OK $5.2M. It missed out on the top spot thanks to *The Living Daylights*, which to be fair, had the built-in appeal, safer rating and almost 700 extra screens. A week on, Bond was still at the top and The Lost Boys slipped down to fifth place thanks largely to the new releases. The good news was that it lost only 23% of its business from the previous weekend. That meant that within its first week, The Lost Boys had already recouped its production budget. In weekend three, it fell down to ninth place but again, its weekend-to-weekend fall wasn't too bad (*The Monster Squad*, which was released that week, had little impact and didn't break the top ten). It managed to recover a place in the next frame as it crossed the $20M point, helped by a 247 screen expansion.

However, a week on and it had slipped out of the top ten, never to return. It managed one more weekend before beginning its exit from theatres. In North America, it ended its theatrical run with $32.2M, a decent enough return for an R-rated horror with no major stars. Schumacher and Warner Bros.' gamble had paid off and things were about to get even better. Debuting on video in January 1988, The Lost Boys went on to be one of the most popular rentals that the studio had ever seen – ultimately far out-grossing its theatrical takings. It also became a popular movie on HBO and Showtime, where it played on rotation for many years. Talk of a sequel quickly began to circulate, and Schumacher pitched *The Lost Girls* to WB, that would see David return (the character being the only one who isn't shown exploding or dissolving, implying that he wasn't dead) to lead a group of female vampires. The studio opted not to move forward with the idea and while other scripts were pitched over the years (with and without Schumacher's support), none made it very far.

It would be almost twenty years before The Lost Boys got its sequel. *The Tribe* began life as a werewolf movie, but Warner Bros. executives rejected it due to it similarity to The Lost Boys. When they decided to move forward with a sequel (spurred on by the renewed interest in the vampire genre thanks to the *Twilight* series) they hired *The Tribe* scriptwriter Hans Rodionoff to re-tool the story as a Lost Boys sequel. Many rumours circulated as to who would return for the film and at one point, both Jason Patric and Kiefer Sutherland were said to be considering roles, though nothing would come of it and it may have been more a way to stir up press interest than anything else. Angus Sutherland, Kiefer's brother, would step in to play a new vampire leader. Corey Feldman, who was initially reluctant to return, changed his mind when the studio further developed the script that would see his character, Edgar Frog, have a similar level of prominence to what he had in the original movie. Corey Haim, who wasn't initially involved, would return for a short end credit scene (he would also feature in the two alternate endings included as extras).

The film was released on the studio's straight-to-DVD label, Warner Premiere, which was set up to release cheap sequels to older movies in their catalogue (at one point *Goonies* and *Gremlins* sequels were said to be in development by the label). Despite the very poor reviews, the film was a big success on DVD, recouping its $5M budget in only three weeks. It became the label's best-selling release of 2008, and by 2011 has sold in excess of 1.25 million copies. A second sequel, *The Thirst*, was soon put into production. Feldman would again return, to be joined this time by fellow Frog brother, Jamison Newlander. Haim ruled himself out but stated he hoped to return if a further sequel was produced. In a case of once bitten, twice shy, the public by-and-large passed on *The Thirst*, signalling a close to The Lost Boys franchise. In recent years, the vampire genre has seen a major resurgence across most forms of media thanks to *Twilight, The Vampire Diaries* and similar, with vampires now seen as tragic romantic figures rather than the subject of horror.

Post-Lost Boys, the two Coreys became teen-sensations and starred in a string of movies together including *License to Drive, Dream a Little Dream* and *Blown Away*. But substance abuse, arrests and money issues saw both their careers dwindle as quickly as they'd risen. Things came to a head in 1996, when Feldman was forced to fire Haim from *Busted*, a movie he was directing and co-starring in, due to Haim's refusal to curtail his drug use. While he continued to work, Haim struggled with his addictions, spending time getting clean only to relapse again and again. Feldman's public battle with drugs saw him clean himself up and while his fame never rose to those earlier levels, he appeared content with the movie and voiceover work he was doing and branched out into music. In 2007, the two would reunite on the reality TV show *The Two Coreys*. It would see an unemployed Haim moving in with Feldman and his then-wife, Susie Sprague. The show, initially partly scripted, took on a much darker edge when it was revealed Haim was back to using drugs. This led to a six-month hiatus, and Feldman refused to promote the show because of Haim's relapse. The show ended up being cancelled midway through its second season.

The duo planned to team up again on *Lost Boys: The Tribe*, but Haim was devastated when he discovered there was no role for him. He would end up filming a cameo, but the influence of drugs was evident and he struggled to remember his few lines. In 2010, the actor moved back in with mother to help support her during her battle with breast cancer. He died on March 10th 2010 from complication with pneumonia. Despite using prescriptions drugs, the autopsy revealed there were no such substances in his blood at the time of his death. Feldman revealed later that the two had actually reconciled and had begun developing a sequel, *License to Fly*. Feldman continues to work in all areas of media, including film, animation and reality TV. He released his memoir, *Coreyography*, in October 2013.

Jason Patric won acclaim for his work on *Rush*, opposite Jennifer Jason Leigh, and again for *Sleepers*, but his only foray into blockbuster territory with *Speed 2: Cruise Control*, proved a disaster. He went on to co-star and produce *Your Friends and Neighbours* and starred opposite Ray Liotta in the well-received *Narc*. His recent work includes *The Outsider, Cavemen* and *The Prince*, opposite Bruce Willis. Jami Gertz followed up The Lost

Boys with a role in the Brett Easton Ellis adaptation, *Less Than Zero*. She'd appear again with Sutherland in the 1989 action flick, *Renegades*, before moving onto the comedies *Sibling Rivalry* and *Don't Tell Her It's Me*. She returned to the big time after a four-year hiatus working in Paris, with a role in *Twister*. Since that time, she has favoured TV work, with parts in *ER, Ally McBeal* and *Still Standing*. Her recent sitcom, *The Neighbours*, was cancelled in 2014 at the end of its second season.

Of all the cast, Kiefer Sutherland went on to have the biggest career. He followed up The Lost Boys with turns in *Bright Light, Big City, Young Guns* (and its sequel), *The Three Musketeers* and *A Few Good Men*. He also worked again with Joel Schumacher on *Flatliners*, *A Time to Kill* and *Phone Booth*. In 2001, he appeared as CTU Agent Jack Bauer in the TV show *24*, a role that made him a global star. It would run for eight seasons as well as a 12-episode event entitled *24: Live Another Day* in 2014. He has continued to work in film, as well as lending his voice to *Monsters Vs. Aliens*, *Marmaduke* and *The Wild*.

Despite The Lost Boy's success, scriptwriters James Jeramias and Jan Fischer would never produce another screenplay. Jeffrey Boam, who re-wrote the picture, scripted *Funny Farm* for Chevy Chase and *Lethal Weapon 2* and *3*, as well as supplying the script for *Indiana Jones and the Last Crusade*. He also co-created the TV shows *The Witches of Eastwick* and *The Adventures of Brisco County Jr. The*

Phantom, starring Billy Zane, was his last produced script prior to his death in 2000. Cinematographer Michael Chapman worked with Bill Murray on *Ghostbusters 2, Scrooged* and *Quick Change* in 1990. Throughout the next decade, he would rarely be away from film, acting as DoP on *Kindergarten Cop, The Fugitive, Rising Sun, Space Jam* and *Primal Fear*. He retired in 2007 after shooing *Bridge to Terabithia*. Producer Richard Donner made four *Lethal Weapon* films, as well as *Conspiracy Theory, Maverick* and *Timeline*. His version of *Superman II* also saw the light of day in 2006. He remains married to producer Lauren Shuler.

Joel Schumacher went from strength-to-strength, following up The Lost Boys with *Flatliners, Dying Young, Falling Down, A Time to Kill* and *Batman Forever*. By 1997, he was one of the most successful directors working in Hollywood, but the critical failure and fallout of *Batman and Robin* saw his career falter. He continued to work consistently, turning out *8mm, Phone Booth* and *Phantom of the Opera*, but his career never again saw the same heights it did in the early 1990s. His most recent work includes the barely seen Nic Cage-Nicole Kidman film, *Trespass*, and episodes of the Kevin Spacey show, *House of Cards*.

Looking back at The Lost Boys, it is easy to see why it was a success. Its mix of comedy and scares, along with the attractive cast proved to be a perfect box office combination. There are many neat touches, including Edgar Frog discussing how no two vampires die the same way, foreshadowing the order and method in which the vampires die later in the film. Its dialogue, violence and soundtrack also added to its success and helped guarantee repeat viewings. In a world where the vampire has again become something to mock, The Lost Boys still retains a decent amount of blood (and bite).

Similar to The Lost Boys...

The Goonies

A wonderful kids-own adventure that sees The Goonies embark on an adventure to find the treasure of One-Eyed Willie and save their homestead in the process. Pursued by convict family, The Fratellis, The Goonies face danger (and booby traps) at every turn. Adventure, laughs and even some soul searching are brought together by director Richard Donner and executive producer Steven Spielberg.

Easily one of the most enjoyable and re-watchable movies of the entire decade, The Goonies never talked down to its target audience. With a pitch perfect cast featuring the likes of Sean Astin, Corey Feldman and Josh Brolin, it's a slice of pure 80s nostalgia up there with *Back to the Future*. Always worth seeing again, and definitely one to introduce your kids to.

Trivia: The pirate ship set was hidden from the cast so that the first time they saw it their reactions would be genuine (and used in the film). However, because Josh Brolin swore during the reveal, the scene had to be re-shot and the reactions faked.

Big Trouble in Little China

John Carpenter's inspired mash-up of supernatural, action and Chinese ghost story works thanks to great characters, special effects and truly bizarre plot. Kurt Russell plays Jack Burton, a trucker who can talk the talk, but not necessarily walk the walk, and gets caught up in a kidnap and rescue plot relating to his friend's fiancée and reporter Gracie Law – both of whom have green eyes.

Villain Lo-Pan needs the girls to complete a ritual and he's aided by the three demigods, Thunder, Rain and Lightning. Burton, with friend Wang Chi and sorcerer Egg-Shen launch a rescue attempt that threatens to shake the pillars of Heaven. Off-the-wall, but exceptionally good, Big Trouble in Little China continued Russell and Carpenter's partnership to a tee. Like *The Goonies*, it still stands as one of the most enjoyable movies of the decade despite being a failure upon its initial release

Trivia: The script was originally written as a Western, with Jack Burton being a cowboy who rides into town – and all manner of mystical trouble.

The Monster Squad

Written by Shane Black and its director Fred Dekker, The Monster Squad is essentially *The Goonies* meets the Universal Monsters. The squad love the classic monsters but things take a darker turn when Sean, the gang's leader is given a diary belonging to famed vampire slayer, Van Helsing. The book details an amulet comprised of 'concentrated good' – and the one day a century when it can be destroyed.

Knowing the day is soon to come Dracula seeks to find and destroy the amulet once and for all, and enlists The Mummy, The Wolfman and more, to help achieve his goal. But he didn't count on having to deal with The Monster Squad. The film was a flop on release in 1987 but gained a cult following in the intervening years that's resulted in cast reunion screenings and fan-demanded special DVD and Blu-Ray editions. While overshadowed by the likes of *The Goonies*, The Monster Squad is a solid little movie that doesn't talk down to its audience. Well worth seeking out.

Trivia: Mary Ellen Trainor played the mother role in both The Monster Squad and *The Goonies*. She was also a regular in a number of Joel Silver movies, going so far as to play the same writer/reporter in the seemingly unrelated *Die Hard* and *Ricochet*.

The Secret of My Success

There's no such thing as an overnight success. Brantley Foster took two weeks.

Studio: Universal Pictures

Release Date: 8th April 1987

Director: Herbert Ross

Starring: Michael J. Fox, Helen Slater

Budget: $12-18M – 2015 Equivalent: $25.4 – 38.2M

U.S Box Office: $66.9M – 2015 Equivalent: $142.1M

Brantley Foster has dreams of making it big in the world of business. Coming to New York, he gets a rude awakening and ends up having to call upon a distant relative for a job. But starting in the mail room might not be such a bad thing, especially when he starts leading a double life as executive Carlton Whitfield. If he can survive the advances of his aunt, the corporate sharks and his suspicious boss, he might just make it to the top.

If one type of person summed up the 1980s, it would be the yuppie. Young businessmen and women, dressed for success and earning thousands in the corporate world. Their money-making matched only by their extravagance; the yuppie was equally lauded and despised, yet was a true product of the decade of excess. Hollywood took notice and the smartly dressed businessman and his multi-million-dollar empire became the new villain, and just occasionally, the hero. This is probably nowhere more evident than in Oliver Stone's *Wall Street*, yet it would be another 1987 picture set in the same world, that would make big money at the box office.

The Secret of My Success took the age-old rags-to-riches story and gave it an 80s twist. At the helm would be Herbert Ross, taking on what would be his 18th feature. The veteran director had actually started his career as a dramatic actor, before moving into the role of choreographer for the American Ballet Theatre. This, in turn, led to choreography work on Otto Preminger's *Carmen Jones* and the Cliff Richard pictures *The Young Ones* and *Summer Holiday*. By 1968, he'd moved up to director of musical numbers on the Barbra Streisand flick, *Funny Girl* and a year later made his feature directorial debut on *Goodbye, Mr. Chips* (for which Peter O'Toole would be Oscar nominated). He would reteam with Streisand on the 1975 picture, *Funny Lady* (for which the actress won an Academy Award) and also worked with Woody Allen on *Play It Again, Sam*. He directed Richard Dreyfuss to an Oscar for his work on *The*

Goodbye Girl, and with writer Neil Simon made *The Sunshine Boys* and ensemble *California Suite.*

Ross didn't abandon his theatrical work either, though it did take a backseat as he became more in demand as a feature director. He managed to combine the two in the critically-acclaimed picture, *The Turning Point*, a dramatic tale set in the ballet world. Yet despite 11 Oscar nominations, Ross and the film came away empty-handed. While he may not have seen such high praise again in his career, he did become a very profitable director. One of his most successful pictures, the 1984 musical drama *Footloose*, set him up to take on The Secret of My Success. *Footloose* starred a young Kevin Bacon, moving to a town where rock music has been banned, and clashing head on with the local minister, played by John Lithgow. The $8.2M production was a smash hit, making over $80M in North American cinemas. Its soundtrack was also a major seller, spawning a number of hit singles. Ross would direct one more picture, the Goldie Hawn vehicle *Protocol*, before signing on-board The Secret of My Success – a script Universal Studios had been developing.

At the time of writing the story, AJ Carothers was already a successful screenwriter for both film and TV, having begun his career in the 1940s working as story editor on the show *Studio One*. He soon graduated to scriptwriting and became close friends with Walt Disney when he worked as a contract writer for the company during the 1960s. He turned out a number of projects, notably the script for *The Happy Millionaire* and *Never a Dull Moment* (starring Fred MacMurray and Dick Van Dyke respectively). Carothers continued to write, creating the 1970 show, *Nanny and the Professor*. He even branched out into speech writing for the likes of Nancy Reagan and Patrick Stewart. As it turned out, The Secret of My Success would be the final script he produced for the screen, and while it was never explicitly stated by Carothers, it would owe a huge debt to the stage musical *How to Succeed in Business Without Really Trying*.

Universal took on the script but executive Frank Price felt the characters needed fleshing out, so turned to Jack Epps and Jim Cash. The duo was about to have huge success in the summer of 1986 with the movie *Top Gun*, for which they'd produced the script. They were given only eight weeks to knock the Success script into shape and quickly set about the job. The original screenplay featured the nephew and uncle scenario, but the character of Christy was a high class call girl, favoured by the uncle, and someone who the nephew falls for. Epps and Cash altered this, turning Christy into a high powered fellow executive, who also happens to be the CEOs mistress. They also introduced the character of Aunt Vera, a further complication for the nephew. The studio signed off on the script and gave the picture a spring 1987 slot. All they needed now was a cast, and they had one very particular actor in mind for the lead.

Michael J. Fox was born in 1961 in Edmonton, but moved around a lot during his early years due to his father's military (and later, police) career. The family finally settled in Vancouver once his father had retired and Fox attended a local school where he was encouraged by his drama teacher Ross Jones to try out for a new sitcom entitled *Leo & Me*. He landed the role of 'me', giving him his first acting break – though the show would not be screened until 1981. But Fox had got the acting bug, and his work on *Leo & Me* led to a part in the TV movie, *Letters From Frank*. When a casting agent suggested Fox move to Los Angeles to pursue an acting career, he jumped at the chance. Upon arriving and attempting to secure work, the young actor found out he'd need to join the Screen Actors' Guild, but as there was already a Michael Fox, he had to either change his name or use an initial. Forgoing the use of his actual middle name (Andrew), Fox took the J from character actor Michael J. Pollard, someone he admired.

Minor roles in *Class of 1984* and *Midnight Madness* (his first US feature) followed, but Fox struggled to find well paid-long term work. He appeared in all eleven episodes of the drama *Palmertown, USA* before landing an audition for a new sitcom created by Gary Goldberg entitled *Family Ties*. The only problem was that Goldberg wanted Matthew Broderick for the role of Alex P. Keaton, but Broderick refused to be tied to a long term commitment. This rejection led Goldberg to instantly despise any other casting choice put forward for the role – the first one being Fox. Casting director

Judith Weiner pushed for the young actor, feeling he was right for the part, and Goldberg eventually relented and gave Fox another audition. This time around he played the character a little less of a smart Alec and managed to win Goldberg over. Fox, almost destitute by this point, negotiated his contract via payphone, telling Goldberg's people that he'd only be in 'his office' between 3 and 4pm.

Family Ties was a sitcom which saw two ex-hippie parents clash with their conservative children, Fox's Alex P. Keaton in particular. In fact, the show was sold on the tagline "Hip Parents, Square Kids". The initial idea was to focus on the parental figures played by Michael Gross and Meredith Baxter-Birney, but so positive was the audience's reaction to Alex, that by the fourth episode the focus had shifted to him. While not a huge success straight off the bat, *Family Ties* hit its stride (and then some) when slotted after *The Cosby Show*. According to figures released at the time, more than a third of America tuned in. In comparison, at its height, *Seinfeld* commanded 20% of America's audience.

When Meredith Baxter-Birney fell pregnant, shooting on *Family Ties* was delayed, allowing Fox to take on the role of Scott Howard in the movie *Teen Wolf*. It was whilst shooting that picture at the tail end of 1984, that the cast and crew came across another production team, scouting locations for a project called *Back to the Future*. There's some conjecture regarding when Fox got offered the role of

Marty McFly. One story goes that during *Family Ties'* second season, Robert Zemeckis sought Fox for the part, but Gary Goldberg refused to allow the director to approach him. Meredith Birney-Baxter was working reduced hours and in her absence Fox's role in the show was elevated further – and Goldberg couldn't risk allowing the actor to take time off to work on the film. The shooting of *Back to the Future* was delayed a number of times because of casting issues, and Eric Stoltz eventually won the lead role. But after only four to six weeks of filming, he was released from the production, Zemeckis claiming that the actor didn't give the right type of performance for the humour involved. Due to the delays, Birney had now returned to *Family Ties* full-time and Goldberg was willing to give Fox the chance to work on *Back to the Future* – as long as he also kept his commitment to the show.

However, during an interview Fox gave to James Lipton in 2005, he stated that five weeks after bumping into the scouting crew, Goldberg called him into his office and gave him the script. He explained that since Stoltz had been let go, Spielberg and Zemeckis wanted him for the lead and that they'd need him to start work within the week. As stated previously, he gave the actor his blessing, on the proviso that he continued to work on *Family Ties*. There's a possibility that at the time, Fox wasn't aware of the earlier (failed) approach by Zemeckis. Either way, the actor accepted the part and began to work out how he would juggle his commitment to the show and work on the movie. As he would soon find out, it was a difficult and exhausting task. Fox rehearsed *Family Ties* from 10am to 6pm, and then rushed to the set of *Back to the Future* and shot until 4am. He kept this schedule up for two solid months, and while many an actor wouldn't have made it, Fox revelled in it. Having gone from selling his couch for food money to working on not one but two projects, he wasn't about to complain. By the end of that summer, he would see it was more than worth the effort.

Back to the Future was a phenomenon. A huge hit at the box office in North America and around the world, it introduced Fox to a global audience who by-and-large weren't aware of his *Family Ties* work. It would go on to make over $380M worldwide, from a budget of only $19M, and became the quintessential 80s movie. Thanks to the film's success, *Teen Wolf*, released in August 1985 also got a huge boost, with Fox's involvement being milked by the studio for all it was worth. The $1M picture made $33M in North America and at one point, the actor held the top two positions at the US box office. Next up would be the drama, *Light of Day*, in which Fox attempted to prove he could play the dramatic role as well as he did the comedic one. The picture reviewed well, but struggled to find a substantial audience. The public wanted Fox goofing around, and in The Secret of My Success, they were about to get it.

It was the perfect vehicle – allowing him to play a romantic lead, while throwing in more than a dash of slapstick and 1980s style big business. Thanks to his success in 1985, Fox was able to command

$5M for the role of Brantley Foster (aka Carlton Whitfield). While budgetary figures for the film aren't available, it is safe to assume that that salary made up a good portion of its costs. Playing opposite Fox in the role of Christy Wills was to be Kristy McNichol, a young actress who had already made her mark in the TV show *Family*, for which she earned two Emmy awards. Her career had gone from strength-to-strength and she won much acclaim for her performance in the coming-of-age flick, *Little Darlings*, opposite Tatum O'Neal. Aged only 19, she earned an unprecedented six figure sum for her role in *The Night the Lights Went Out in Georgia* and won a Golden Globe for her turn in *Only When I Laugh*.

But having been acting for so long, and in such demanding roles, McNichol had a huge emotional breakdown while shooting *Just the Way You Are* in 1982. When the film broke up for Christmas, she refused to return and it would be a further year before shooting would resume. Rumours of drink and drug problems made studios fearful of offering her parts. It would take some time before her career recovered, and she lobbied hard for the role of Christy. Ross was more than happy with her audition and gave her the part, but two weeks before shooting, executives overruled the director for fear the production would be thrown into disarray if McNichol had another episode. [In a 1989 interview, the actress stated that it wasn't the first, or last time, she was passed over for a part because of her early 80s breakdown]. Ross was now left with no female lead and a shoot that was set to commence in less than a fortnight.

In the end, the role went to Helen Slater, who was still recovering from the failure of *Supergirl* some two years previous. She'd been an odd choice for the role, having just one other credit on her resume (an after-school special entitled *Amy & The Angel*) but Alexander Salkind and his son, Ilya, chose her over more established actors such as Demi Moore and Brooke Shields. Despite success with the *Superman* series, the Salkinds couldn't transform *Supergirl* into box office gold and it flopped with only $14M in takings. Slater then won the lead in *The Legend of Billie Jean*, opposite Christian Slater (no relation). Early hype had the picture pegged to become a hit, but it was largely ignored by the public, making only $3M. When she was called in for The Secret of My Success, Slater was a month or so away from scoring a hit with the comedy *Ruthless People,* in which she played an inept kidnapper opposite Judge Reinhold.

The other two major roles, that of Howard and Vera Prescott, went to Richard Jordan and Margaret Whitton. Jordan was a notable theatre actor and director of some standing, who managed to mix stage work with movie roles for the duration of his career. Similarly, Margaret Whitton had a successful off-Broadway career before winning acclaim for her work on the 1982 picture, *Love Child.* Filling out the remainder of the relatively small cast would be John Pankow, Gerry Bamman and Carol Ann Susi as Carlton's secretary, Jean.

Shooting would take place in and around New York during the summer of 1986. At least three different locations would make up the Pemrose building, with the lobby of 599 Lexington Avenue being used for the water fountain fantasy sequence. Filming appeared to have gone off without too many issues, though David Watkin found himself replaced by Woody Allen's cinematographer, Carlo Di Palma, for reasons unknown (years later, writing in his autobiography, Watkin would confess he still had no idea why he'd been replaced). The only other somewhat minor issue was the height difference between Fox and Slater, resulting in some adjustments being made during sequences in which they kissed or walked side by side. With the shoot completed in August 1986, Ross and Editor Paul Hirsch had eight months to assemble the picture to ensure it met its April 10th release date.

Movie soundtracks enjoyed huge success in the late 1970s, a trend that escalated in the 1980s. Studios used popular artists and bands of the time to provide the music which added not only an extra (and long lasting) revenue stream but was used increasingly as a promotional tool for both the artist and the movie in question. Music videos would often feature clips from the accompanying picture or were specially commissioned with stars featuring either as themselves or their characters. Ross had already seen *Footloose*'s soundtrack become a smash hit, and with the music from *Top Gun* and *Beverly Hills Cop* (to name just two of many) also selling incredibly well, Universal weren't about to miss out.

They commissioned David Foster to write and produce the soundtrack album, having already performed similar duties on *St. Elmo's Fire*. Foster was already a hugely successful songwriter, providing tracks for all manner of artists including Earth, Wind and Fire, Boz Scaggs and Chicago, whose massive resurgence in the early 80s was thanks primarily to Foster's work. For The Secret of My Success, Foster would write or co-write seven of the ten tracks, along with providing its score. The Who's Roger Daltrey supplied vocals for *The Price of Love*, Restless Heart sang *Don't Ask the Reason Why* (which was bizarrely given a different title on the track listing) and Night Ranger performed the title track. The film would go on to feature other tracks that didn't appear on the official soundtrack including Yello's *Oh Yeah* and *Walking on Sunshine* by Katrina and The Waves (which was a missed opportunity given that it featured extensively in the trailer and also played during a major scene in the movie itself).

Reviews for the film were mixed – while no one doubted the charm of Michael J. Fox, they felt the big business story was at odds with the slapstick sequences, particularly the bedroom farce it became in its final quarter. Roger Ebert commented that the picture felt like a 1950s script that hadn't been updated, and more than a few reviews echoed that it was too similar to *How to Succeed in Business Without Really Trying* – though how much that would have influenced the public's decision as to whether to see the film, is debatable.

The Secret of My Success was set to open on April 10th 1987. It would face the second weekend of *Police Academy 4: Citizens on Patrol*, and the third of the Bruce Willis/Kim Basinger comedy, *Blind Date*. It would also be Fox's first major release since *Teen Wolf*, though he was still riding high with *Family Ties*. The film easily took the top spot during its opening frame, making a decent enough $7.7M from its 1,336 screen roll out. A week later and it lost just 5% of business, adding another $7.4M – the Matthew Broderick thriller *Project X* offering no real competition. Weekend three saw the film still safely in the top spot, as its overall total approached $28M – easily covering any estimated costs associated with it. Seven days later, and with only *Creepshow 2* as competition, The Secret of My Success fell just 17.5% on its previous weekend's total. In only a month, it had already out grossed *Teen Wolf*, and showed little sign of stopping there.

The film would stay in the top spot for a further week, before being unseated by the Warren Beatty – Dustin Hoffman bomb, *Ishtar*. Even with the release of *Beverly Hills Cop 2* at the end May, The Secret of My Success held steady in third place, behind the other new release of the week, *Ernest Goes to Camp*. By weekend number nine, it was still in the top five and had amassed almost $55M. In total, the picture stayed in the top ten for an incredible twelve weeks, and ended its domestic theatrical run with $66.9M. Overseas, thanks to the success of *Back to the Future*, it made a further $44M, for a total global finish of $110M ($233.7M in 2015 dollars). In terms of movies released in 1987, The Secret of My Success was the 7th most successful, beating out *Predator, Robocop, The Living Daylights* and *Planes, Trains and Automobiles*. It was also incredible successful on video, ringing up almost $30M in rentals.

A year later Michael J. Fox was back in New York for what could be described as the anti-Secret of My Success. *Bright Lights, Big City* saw the actor play a more mature role than what the public were used to, as a fact checker whose life is falling apart – heavy partying, drug taking and the departure of his model wife all taking their toll. The actor received a number of positive notices, but the film failed to recoup its $25M production budget. Fox then returned to the *Back to the Future* series, shooting back-to-back sequels released in 1989 and 1990. Both were smash hits, but another foray into adult fare with *Casualties of War* struggled to find an audience, though again, Fox's work alongside Sean Penn won praise. In 1991, he made the romantic comedy *Doc Hollywood*, and it was whilst shooting the picture that he noticed a twitch in one of his fingers. Over the course of the shoot it got worse, and a visit to a specialist revealed he had the early onset of Parkinson's disease. He battled with the condition but kept it to himself and his family, and continued to work.

But he struggled to find the right roles after *Doc Hollywood. Life with Mickey, For Love or Money* and *Greedy* all failed to light up the box office, though turns in *The American President, The Frighteners* and a cameo in *Mars Attacks* kept him in the public eye. In the meantime, he'd returned to TV, in the popular sitcom *Spin City*. He stayed with the show for four years, before Charlie Sheen took up the mantle. In 1998, he went public about having Parkinson's disease and has since become a spokesperson for fellow sufferers. He has lobbied for an increase in stem cell research and, through his own charity, has raised over $100M. He continues to act and do voiceover work and also made a number of TV show appearances to celebrate the 30th anniversary of *Back to the Future*.

Helen Slater starred in *Sticky Fingers* after The Secret of My Success, and appeared opposite Billy Crystal in *City Slickers*. Since then, she has mixed TV movie work with guest appearances in various shows including *Smallville, Grey's Anatomy* and *CSI: NY*. She has also ventured into music, releasing a number of albums. Continuing his stage and screen career, Richard Jordan appeared in *The Hunt for Red October* in 1991, along with numerous theatrical acting and directing jobs. In 1993, while shooting *The Fugitive*, he was diagnosed with brain cancer and had to withdraw from the production. He died in August that same year. Margaret Whitton continued to dabble with film, appearing in *Major League* and its sequel and in Mel Gibson's *The Man Without a Face*. She returned to the stage in 1995 and has since become an independent film producer. After her role as Jean, Carol Ann Susi appeared in numerous film and TV shows, including reuniting with Herbert Ross on *My Blue Heaven*. In recent times, she had lent her voice to the unseen mother of Howard Wolowitz on *The Big Bang Theory*. Susi succumbed to cancer in November 2014.

Director Herbert Ross had a misfire with *Dancers*, but scored big with the popular weepy, *Steel Magnolias*. He re-teamed with Steve Martin for *My Blue Heaven*, which he followed up with *Undercover Blues* and *True Colors*. *Boys on the Side*, a drama starring Whoopi Goldberg and Drew Barrymore would be his final directorial effort. He died in 2001 aged 74. Screenwriters Jack Epps and Jim Cash produced the scripts for the Tom Hanks hit, *Turner & Hooch*, the Warren Beatty project, *Dick Tracy* and *Anaconda*. Cash passed away in 2000, and Epps retired from the industry in 2004, after writing the *Anaconda* sequel, *The Hunt for the Blood Orchid*. Finally, David Foster continued to work in the music industry, providing Whitney Houston with the smash hit, *I Have Nothing*, for *The Bodyguard*. He would produce debut albums for Josh Groban and Michael Buble, amongst others, as well as providing music for the 2002 Winter Olympics. He is currently the chairman of Verve Records.

Because it focused so heavily on the culture and fashions of the 1980s, The Secret of My Success has not aged well. Its theme of big business-corporate takeover seems very much of the times too but there is still much to enjoy. Michael J. Fox anchors the film, providing many of its best moments – whether that's evading his boss in a mid-film chase sequence, attempting to charm a co-worker or fighting off the advances of his aunt. Largely forgotten by all involved (the film doesn't even warrant a mention in Fox's memoirs), The Secret of My Success is a slice of pure 1980s entertainment worthy of re-discovery.

Similar to The Secret of My Success...

Back to the Future

A stone cold 80s classic that is arguably the most well-known movie of the decade.

Using Doc Brown's DeLorean time machine, Marty McFly travels back to 1955 and inadvertently disrupts the meeting of his parents. This threatens Marty's own existence and he's left scrambling to get them back together while also preparing for a lighting strike that he and the 1955 Doc Brown hopes will send him back to the future.

A fantastic movie that doesn't put a foot wrong and contains some of the most iconic moments in cinematic history. A pitch perfect cast is supported by a cracking script, great special effects and a superb soundtrack. While the well-received sequels expanded the story, the first film remains the best and continues to entice fans, both old and new.

Trivia: *The Power of Love* was the second song Huey Lewis submitted for the soundtrack after Robert Zemeckis and Bob Gale rejected his first effort. After seeing a rough cut of the movie he also went on to contribute the track, *Back in Time*.

Wall Street

Charlie Sheen plays Bud Fox, a junior stockbroker hoping to make a name for himself and gain the attention of Wall Street legend, Gordon Gecko. Using insider information about an airline, he's able to convince Gecko to take a chance on him. As their profits mount, so do the stakes, and Bud soon begins to wonder where his and Gecko's loyalties really lie.

Oliver Stone's drama about stockbrokers, insider trading and corporate America summed up the excesses of the 1980s better than almost any other film of the time. Michael Douglas gives an Academy Award-winning turn in a picture full of great performances and helped create a memorable new type of villain in the guise of Gordon Gecko. For a lesson in 80s fashion, culture and trends, one need look no further than Wall Street.

Trivia: The studio wanted Warren Beatty to play Gecko, Stone wanted Richard Gere, who eventually passed. Michael Douglas was cast despite everyone warning Stone that he was more a producer than actor.

Working Girl

Trying to make her way in the world, Tess McGill pitches an idea to her new boss, Katherine. Initially supportive, she dismisses the idea, but secretly plans to pass it off as her own. When Katherine breaks her leg on a skiing trip, Tess decides to make her move and teams up with executive Jack Trainer to pitch her idea. But just as things appear to being go well for Tess – both professionally and personally, Katherine makes her return.

Like *Wall Street*, Working Girl is great example of the time. Melanie Griffiths gives a career-best performance in a cast which includes the likes of Sigourney Weaver, Joan Cusack and Harrison Ford. A critical success – the film, director, leads and soundtrack were all Oscar-nominated – Working Girl proved to be a winner at the box office too, making an impressive $102M worldwide. The fashions may have aged, but the picture retains much of its charm and laughs.

Trivia: Kevin Spacey was a very late replacement for another actor and learned his lines in the car on the way to the set.

Young Sherlock Holmes

Before a lifetime of adventure, they lived the adventure of a lifetime

Studio: Paramount Pictures

Release Date: December 6th 1985

Director: Barry Levinson

Starring: Nicholas Rowe, Alan Cox

Budget: $18M – 2015 Equivalent: $40.1M

U.S Box Office: $19.7M – 2015 Equivalent: $43.9M

Meeting for the first time at college, Sherlock Holmes and John Watson soon find themselves investigating a series of mysterious deaths. Discovering a link between the victims, the would-be detective uncovers an even greater danger and will need to rely on all his powers of observation and deduction if he and Watson are to survive the Pyramid of Fear.

Easily one of the most popular literary characters of all time, Sherlock Holmes has appeared in countless movies, TV shows and almost every other form of media since his first appearance in 1887. If anything, in recent years, his popularity has reached even greater heights with new films, TV shows and a novel courtesy of Anthony Horowitz. Created by Sir Arthur Conan Doyle, the stories focused on consulting detective Sherlock Holmes and partner John Watson and the many cases they would be called upon to investigate. Yet through all the tales, very little is given to the circumstances of their first encounter – or their lives before that time. Doyle himself had the pair meet when Watson was looking for a room to rent, and a mutual friend put him onto Sherlock Holmes. In 1985, Chris Columbus, Barry Levinson and Steven Spielberg offered their own turn of events, starting many years before *A Study in Scarlet*, with Holmes and Watson meeting at college.

By the time Young Sherlock Holmes came to him, Chris Columbus already had one major success under his belt and another on the horizon. *Gremlins* had been a smash hit in the summer of 1984, and he'd soon repeat that with *The Goonies*. Both movies had been executively produced by Steven Spielberg through his company, Amblin. He tasked Columbus with writing what was essentially a Sherlock Holmes origin story – an idea that both excited and terrified the young screenwriter. With little-to-no back story for the famous detective (or his partner) in Conan Doyle's tales, Columbus sunk himself into the entire back catalogue in an attempt to discover what made Holmes tick. He would take many leads from the stories (along with the novels of Dickens) and devised the origins behind some of the methods Holmes would use later in life.

He was particularly interested in the great detective's cold and emotionless state when dealing with his clients and their cases and envisioned a singular incident that would set him on that path. At the same time, Columbus was cautious not to offend fans of the original material, along with the Conan Doyle estate, whose support for the project they wanted to keep [The finished film would carry a closing epilogue stating that the story was affectionate speculation of what might have happened, and had been made with 'respectful admiration and in tribute to the author and his endearing works']. As with many Amblin productions, Spielberg made contributions to the script, specifically the nightmarish hallucination sequences. With work progressing nicely, a search for a director began. Ruling himself out of the role due to his commitment to *The Color Purple*, Spielberg's pick to helm the mystery thriller was an unusual one.

Like many directors of the time, Barry Levinson got his first break in TV, writing scripts for the likes of Marty Feldman, Tim Conway and Carol Burnett, before graduating to movies. Teaming up with Mel Brooks, he worked on the scripts for both *Silent Movie* and *High Anxiety* and was Oscar-nominated (along with his wife) for the Al Pacino movie, *And Justice for All*. In 1982, he made his feature debut with *Diner*, a critically-acclaimed comedy drama about a group of friends who reunite for the wedding of one of the group. The picture made $14M off a $5M budget and helped launch the careers of Steve Guttenberg, Daniel Stern, Mickey Rourke and Kevin Bacon. Levinson was once again nominated for an Academy Award for the screenplay. His next movie, the Robert Redford drama, *The Natural*, would be his first job as director for hire, the script having been written by Roger Towne and Phil Dusenberry. While not as well received as his previous work, *The Natural* made $48M in North America and is still seen by some as the best baseball movie ever produced.

Yet little in his previous work suggested he could make a mystery thriller with action elements – let alone one that would also involve a number of special effects sequences. Spielberg saw something in the 42-year-old director, revealing in a New York Times article prior to the film's release that he felt he (Levinson) was a frustrated action-adventure director. For his part, Levinson jumped at the opportunity to direct Young Sherlock Holmes, feeling it would offer him a wealth of new experiences which he could take on to future projects. The two directors spent much time talking about the movie, agreeing that it should move at a breakneck pace, not giving the viewer a chance to look for plot holes. The key was in the casting; they needed to find actors with a ready chemistry – if Young Sherlock Holmes was a success, there was no reason why it couldn't become a franchise, especially given how much material there was to mine.

Of the two leads, it was John Watson who was cast first. Alan Cox, son of veteran actor Brian, had been performing since he was six years old. His first onscreen role was as Jason in the TV movie, *A Divorce*. He then appeared in the Eric Sykes's curio, *If You Go Down to the Woods Today*, a film about a scoutmaster who takes his troupe into the woods even though he's aware that killings have recently taken place there. Cox continued to appear in numerous TV shows before taking on a role in the Laurence Olivier film, *A Voyage around My Father*. The picture, based on the early life of John Mortimer (creator of *Rumpole of the Bailey*) won much acclaim. Aged only 14, Alan Cox won the role of Watson, but finding Sherlock would prove to be much harder. By the time the casting crew came to Eton, they'd already been searching for three months with little luck. It was Nicholas Rowe's drama master who urged him to try out for the role, having spotted the crew scouring the college for a 'proper young gentleman" as he put it.

The young actor was in his final winter term, and already had a university place in Bristol secured when he tried out for the role of Sherlock Holmes. Impressed with his initial audition, Rowe was called back a further four times, and then given a full costume screen test opposite Alan Cox. There were two other actors up for the part, including a certain Hugh Grant. Unbeknownst to Rowe, it was Alan Cox who may have been partly responsible for him being cast. After the screen test, the new Watson expressed that he liked the 'tall guy with the big nose best'. The casting director couldn't deny the duo had a ready chemistry that had been somewhat absent with others they had seen (including Grant, one assumes). A video of the screen test was sent to Steven Spielberg, who along with Henry Winkler (TV's The Fonz, taking his first full producer credit) agreed. Things moved very quickly after that, with Rowe receiving the news that he had won the role during the Christmas of 1984 and that shooting would commence January 1985.

While the search for Holmes and Watson had been going on, Sophie Ward won the role of Elizabeth. Like Alan Cox, Ward started her acting career at a relatively young age, appearing in *The Other Window, The Copter Kids* and *Full Circle* before her 13th birthday. Forgoing drama school, she trained under veteran ballerina Merle Park before being deemed too tall to continue. She appeared in numerous theatrical productions before winning the part of Elizabeth Hardy in Young Sherlock Holmes.

In the role of Professor Rathe, a teacher who takes a shine to Holmes was noted stage and screen actor Anthony Higgins. Favouring theatre, Higgins won acclaim for his work in *Romeo and Juliet*, and went on to tour with the Royal Shakespeare Company and the National Theatre, winning the Time Out Actor of the year award in 1979. Young Sherlock Holmes wouldn't be his first time working with Steven Spielberg, having had a small part as Major Gobler in *Raiders of the Lost Ark*.

The remainder of the cast was rounded out by Freddie Jones, Susan Fleetwood and Roger Ashton-Griffiths as Lestrade. Michael Hordern would supply the voice of the older Watson, narrating the tale.

With an $18M budget supplied by Paramount Pictures, filming on Young Sherlock Holmes commenced in January 1985 to meet a December 1985 release window. The picture would shoot for around four months, across a number of British locations including Penshurst Place, Belvoir Castle and Eton College. For set-based sequences, Elstree Studios were utilised. There were no major issues during filming except for Alan Cox having a growth spurt, resulting in some of the later shots of him being taken from more of a distance. Spielberg also had to pay for grass to be replaced at Radley College in Oxford when fake snow destroyed it during filming. The real headaches, however, appeared with the film's extensive (and ground-breaking) visual and special effects work, of which Young Sherlock Holmes would employ many different types. Central to the film's plot is a number of terrifying hallucinatory sequences, along with Holmes taking to flight in a bizarre bike-glider device. In charge of making much of this appear on screen was Dennis Muren and his team at Industrial Light and Magic. By 1985, Muren was already an industry legend, having pioneered so many techniques that continue to be used today, but even he was wary of what lay ahead on Young Sherlock.

For the flying contraption set-piece, the crew had no real option other than to build a life-sized replica and suspend it from wires above Belvoir Castle. Despite the cost and practicality of building the machine, shooting it was relatively painless and required minimal work in post-production. The same couldn't be said for the harpies' attack on the character of Waxflatter, which utilised a technique called go-motion in which a computer controlled both the movement of the harpies and the camera itself. This method gave the creatures' wings a natural motion-blur. But the task of refining the movements and masking the camera rig took a group of animators many months to achieve. While Spielberg was largely absent during filming, another set piece would be one of the few instances in which the producer disagreed with his director – the hallucination that sees Watson attacked by a larder of food.

Spielberg loved the idea, and was impressed with Dave Carson's concept sketches. To shoot the sequence Muren and Co. opted to go with rod puppets as opposed to animation. He reasoned that using puppets they could shoot a number of different takes with ease, but with animation, they only really had one shot to get it right. Levinson felt the scene was a little silly and got worse the longer it went on, whereas Spielberg's view was the opposite and he urged Muren to go even further. In the end, Levinson won out and the scene and its excesses were cut back. Had it gone ahead, it would have felt at odds with Holmes' hallucination, an emotionally-charged incident involving his parents. There were issues with some of the matte painting work too, with Chris Evans vocalising his unhappiness during an interview with Cinefex. He stated that the job was made much harder due to being called in after plates had already been shot. Had he been on set sooner he could have easily solved many of the issues he subsequently had to overcome. Evans' would also create the first ever digital matte shot on Young Sherlock Holmes, which was used during the hugely ambitious stained-glass knight sequence.

If one scene stands out in the movie, it is that of the stained-glass knight. Another hallucination set piece, it would be the first time that a completely computer-generated character was used in a movie [Some argue that technically *Tron* holds this title with the polyhedron character of Bit]. Dennis Muren wasn't sold on the idea of creating the knight digitally because he felt computer-generated imagery hadn't advanced enough to be convincing. However, he was willing to give Lucasfilm's computer graphics division a chance at creating something potentially ground-breaking. To be on the safe side, he also factored in time at the end of the post-production period in case the sequence needed to be created using more conventional methods. Adding to the complexity of the job ahead was the fact that the character was essentially 2D, but needed to look 3D – and menacing. The team was in unknown territory; if they needed a tool to do a job, they had to create it themselves. Work progressed slowly, yet the team continued to make breakthroughs in both the scene and the software they were using. A new rendering tool meant they got to see a test run in around five minutes as opposed to two hours.

John Lasseter, a name that would become synonymous with computer-generated imagery in the near future, spent many hours using a 3D space digitiser, scanning in co-ordinates of a clay model of the knight they'd created. Muren continued to support the venture, while pushing the staff hard to raise the level of believability in the character. The team even ended up using tape measures and blueprints on the actual set to ensure everything was where it should be, in terms of where the knight would be walking in 'their' version of the scene. Though the methods seem antiquated by today's standards, much of what they achieved sowed the seeds for almost everything that would follow in terms of computer-generated imagery. It would take a full six months of work to finish the scene, which lasts less than 2 minutes in the film, with the knight himself appearing for only 30 or so seconds of that time. Yet it would go on to become one of the key promotional aspects of the film, often appearing as a supplementary clip to footage of Holmes and Watson. The work behind many of the film's effects (both digital and practical) was also covered by an extensive article in Cinefex magazine.

Young Sherlock Holmes was due for release in December 1985. The main trailer used to announce and promote the film pushed the action angle for all it was worth, selling it as an *Indiana Jones*-style romp rather than a murder mystery. Indeed, to reinforce the idea further, the picture received the full title of Young Sherlock Holmes and the Pyramid of Fear in the U.K and Australia. Initial signs that the film wouldn't perform well began to creep in with the reviews. While they were generally between average and positive, more than one pointed out that the film became undone when it veered too far into Indiana Jones territory. Rowe and Cox did receive good notices, both for their performance and on-screen chemistry. Furthermore, it appears Columbus' handling of the material was deemed respectful of its origins while existing as its own thing. As with *Krull* and *The Last Starfighter*, one of the issues in promoting Young Sherlock Holmes was the lack of star power on which to hang the picture. While the principal actors worked tirelessly, giving TV and magazine interviews, they were by and large unknown to the general public, meaning the film itself had even more work to do if it was to become a success.

Winter isn't generally as busy as the summer in terms of film releases, but there were still a number of major showings that Sherlock would need to face off against. *Rocky IV* had opened the week before to huge business, and was giving no sign of being ready to give up the top spot. Perhaps a bigger concern was the release of *Spies like Us* on the same December 6-8th weekend. One of its stars, Chevy Chase, was having the best year of his entire career, seeing not one but two hits in the summer (*Fletch* and *National Lampoon's European Vacation*). A week later would bring *The Jewel of the*

Nile, the much anticipated sequel to the 1984 hit, *Romancing the Stone*. There were older releases to contend with too, including *King Solomon's Mines* and a still-going strong *Back to the Future* (entering its 23rd weekend on general release) that could all be a thorn in Holmes' side. However, with the Christmas break coming up, most pictures would receive something of a boost – every day of the holiday week generally playing like a Friday or Saturday.

In the end, none of it really mattered. Young Sherlock Holmes opened in fifth place, making a poor $2.5M. As expected both *Rocky IV* and *Spies like Us* won the weekend, with $11.1M and $8.6M respectively. Holmes was further beaten by *Santa Claus the Movie* and *White Nights*, which had expanded out of limited release. Weekend two wasn't much better either, with the film suffering a 37% drop on its already low opening frame. A huge expansion in its third weekend, readying for a Christmas boost, did nothing to help and it slipped quietly out of the top ten. While it managed to re-enter the chart on the following weekend (scoring the best total of its release), it was short lived. A month on from its release it had barely clawed back more than half of its budget. By mid-January, it was gone altogether, having made a disappointing $16.9M. When all was said and done, Young Sherlock Holmes had earned $19.7M.

Nicholas Rowe would spend almost a year promoting the film around the world, but its lacklustre performance in the U.S was repeated elsewhere. It would go on to gain traction on the home video market, and has become a regular feature on network TV in the intervening years, but was never the money spinning franchise starter Spielberg and Columbus had hoped for. In a baffling turn, two years after the film's debut, a video game adaptation was released exclusively for the MSX. *Young Sherlock: The Legacy of Doyle* was an official license (the back cover even featured photos of Nicholas Rowe and Alan Cox) yet followed a completely different story.

At least the efforts of Muren and Co. were rewarded with an Academy Award nomination for Best Visual Effects in 1986, though the film ultimately lost out to *Cocoon*, whose effects were also produced by ILM. The work pioneered by the computer graphics division on Young Sherlock would serve countless others over the years, influencing such pictures as *Terminator 2: Judgment Day* and *Jurassic Park*. Dennis Muren remains the most decorated person in Oscar history, having won nine Academy Awards to date.

In what seems like an inexplicable move to the modern audience, Lucasfilm decided to offload the computer graphics division the following year, selling it to Steve Jobs. John Lasseter and others went with it, and formed Pixar, which would become the most successful computer animation company in the world. It was purchased by Disney in 2006 for 7.4 billion dollars. As part of the deal, Lasseter became chief creative officer for Disney's animation division, while still retaining control at Pixar. Completing the circle, so to speak, Disney purchased Lucasfilm in 2012, with ownership of Industrial Light and Magic coming as part of that deal.

Sadly, for the three main leads, Young Sherlock Holmes would be the biggest movie of their careers. After struggling to get a foothold in Hollywood (including failed auditions for *The Secret of My Success* and *The Name of the Rose*), Nicholas Rowe returned to England and went to Bristol University, as he had originally planned. While he did some TV work in the following years, he would not appear in a feature until 1996's *True Blue*. More TV roles would come, along with a cameo in the Guy Ritchie film, *Lock, Stock and Two Smoking Barrels*. He has continued to mix stage, TV and film work. In an interesting curio, he once again played Sherlock Holmes in the Bill Condon movie, *Mr. Holmes*. The picture, about the retired detective (now played by Ian McKellen) looking back over his life, featured a TV show based on some of his adventures. It is in these adventures that Rowe once again reprised the role that made him famous more than twenty years ago.

After Sherlock, Alan Cox was absent from screens until an appearance in the UK hospital drama, *Casualty* in 1990. He'd go on to other TV work but similar to Nicholas Rowe, wouldn't appear in a feature for many years. He too would mix stage and screen roles, and recently had a cameo in the Sacha Baron Cohen film, *The Dictator*. In contrast, Sophie Ward worked consistently post-Sherlock, with turns in *Wuthering Heights*, amongst much other TV and movie work. She had recurring roles in *Dinotopia, Heartbeat* and *Land Girls*, and made headlines in 1996 when it was revealed she had left her husband for Rena Brannan, a female writer. The pair were wed in a civil partnership ceremony in 2000. Anthony Higgins, in an interesting twist, would play the famous detective in the 1993 TV movie, *Sherlock Holmes Returns*, in which he found himself awakened in modern times. He would continue to act on stage and screen, his most recent role being in the Tim Roth drama, *United Passions*.

While the people in front of the camera may not have fared quite so well, Barry Levinson went from strength-to-strength. He followed up Young Sherlock Holmes with *Tin Men, Good Morning, Vietnam* and *Rain Man*, for which he won a best director Oscar. Personal project *Avalon* (part of his Baltimore series of pictures with *Diner* and *Tin Men*) was followed up by *Bugsy*, but dream project *Toys* in 1992, was a costly misfire. Since then he has mixed blockbusters (*Disclosure, Sleepers*) with satire (*Wag the Dog, Man of the Year*). In recent times, he has even turned his hand to the horror genre with *The Bay*. His latest feature, the comedy *Rock the Kasbah*, which stars Bruce Willis and Billy Murray, was released in 2015. Steven Spielberg directed *The Color Purple* while Levinson was working on Young Sherlock. It would be the first of a number of adult-orientated projects he would undertake, which would include *Empire of the Sun, Always* and *Schindler's List*, which he shot while completing post-production work on the blockbuster, *Jurassic Park*. He remains one of the busiest and most successful producer/directors in cinematic history.

Sherlock Holmes has seen a huge resurgence in popularity in the last few years. The Guy Ritchie films, starring Robert Downey Jr and Jude Law, kicked things off in 2009. Six months later, under the guidance of Steven Moffat and Mark Gatiss, the BBC introduced *Sherlock*, a modern day take on the characters, which featured elements of Conan Doyle's original stories. The show proved incredibly popular and made superstars out of Benedict Cumberbatch and Martin Freeman. It also helped spawn a US equivalent entitled *Elementary*, with Jonny Lee Miller and Lucy Liu. As mentioned above, Bill Condon directed *Mr. Holmes*, a film starring Ian McKellan as the titular detective, looking back on his life. Some of this success may explain why in 2012, word began to surface of a Young Sherlock Holmes remake. Paramount Pictures hired the writer of *The Lion King 3* to pen the script, and secured Chris Columbus to produce (as Warner Bros. had done on their stalled *Gremlins* remake). At the time of writing, no further news has been forthcoming.

Star power aside, it is hard to see why Young Sherlock Holmes didn't perform better at the box office. The film is well-remembered by those who have seen it and even Holmes purists consider it a solid attempt at the character's origins. The chemistry of the leads is there for all to see and it is a shame we didn't get to see them embark on further adventures together, especially given the groundwork laid down by the first film. It remains an enjoyable thriller with some truly terrifying sequences and while the fabled stain-glass knight doesn't hold up quite so well, it is still a fantastic creation, without which *Terminator 2* may not have had its T-1000, nor *Jurassic Park* such convincing dinosaurs. Given the enduring popularity of the characters, Young Sherlock Holmes is more than worthy of a second chance.

Here are three more if you liked Young Sherlock Holmes...

Indiana Jones and the Last Crusade

The third Indiana Jones movie sees the adventurer team up with his father on a quest for the fabled Cup of Christ. Pursued once again by the Nazis, the Jones family manage to stay one step ahead despite the double-crossing and diversions. The film also sees the welcome return of John Rhys-Davies and Denholm Elliot, though sadly the latter appears to have been dumbed down for laughs.

Harrison Ford and Sean Connery make a fantastic partnership and the movie even finds time to give Indiana a backstory of sorts. A hugely enjoyable action romp, with nefarious villains, effects and action sequences, including the memorable 'three trials'. After the darkness of *Temple of Doom*, The Last Crusade was a fitting return for the finest action hero of them all.

Trivia: The Grail Knight was meant to be played by Sir Laurence Olivier, but the legendary actor was too ill to take on the role.

F/X Murder by Illusion

Rollie Tyler is a special effects artist hired by the justice department to fake the death of a Mafia informant so he can quietly go into witness protection. The plan appears to go flawlessly until attempts are then made on Tyler's own life by Justice Agents. At the same time, Manhattan cop Leo McCarthy begins to take an interest in the case, sure there is something off about it all.

Bryan Brown is great as Rollie Tyler, a man who has to call upon the skills of his day job to keep himself alive. Brian Dennehy is equally good in a role that was expanded for the sequel – *F/X 2 The Deadly Art of Illusion*. An impressive little thriller with an interesting premise at its heart.

Trivia: As well as the sequel, F/X also spawned a short lived TV show that ran for 40 episodes in the late 1990s.

Basil the Great Mouse Detective

An animated take on the Sherlock Holmes story that also serves as an origin story of sorts. Basil of Baker Street is already a renowned mouse detective when his services are sought by Olivia, a young mouse whose father has been kidnapped by the devious Professor Ratigan. Dawson, a mouse just returned from war, helps Olivia locate Basil, who agrees to take on the case when he realises Ratigan is involved.

Based on the Eve Titus' Basil of Baker Street book series, The Great Mouse Detective was Disney's 26th animated feature, and was notable for its use of computer-generated imagery. It's an interesting take and serves as a wonderful introduction to its human counterparts. Animation felt like it lost its way in the 80s, at least in the mainstream, but Basil the Great Mouse Detective showed it was alive and well. According to some, it served as the start of the Disney animation renaissance.

Trivia: In terms of animated features, the clock tower sequence marks the first time that traditional animation techniques were put into a computer-generated scene.

Dragnet

'Just the facts'

Studio: Universal
Release Date: 26th June 1987
Director: Tom Mankiewicz
Starring: Dan Aykroyd, Tom Hanks
Budget: $20M – 2015 Equivalent: $42.5M
U.S Box Office: $57.3M – 2015 Equivalent: $121.7M

Summer. 1987. Joe Friday is an old school, by-the-book cop and something is rotten in the City of Angels. Working with new laid back partner, Pep Streebeck, he has to investigate a series of bizarre crimes orchestrated by P.A.G.A.N – People Against Goodness And Normalcy. It doesn't take Joe long to realise that if wants to deal out justice, he's going to have to take a leaf out Streebeck's book, even if it means putting his precious job on the line.

The idea of taking a TV show and creating a spin-off movie isn't a new one. TV companies soon caught on that they had a built-in audience who would pay money to see their favourite characters on the big screen. In the 1970s and 80s, audiences were treated to all manner of shows that had their plots stretched to movie length – with middling results. Dragnet, released in 1987 was a different sort of beast. Based on the hugely successful TV show, it attempted to pay homage to its source, while also parodying it, taking the straight-laced police officer Joe Friday and throwing him into 1980s Los Angeles.

While it may be somewhat forgotten today, the original Dragnet was ground-breaking and incredibly influential. The show was created by Jack Webb, an actor who had begun his career in comedy with limited success. By the late 1940s, he'd switched to drama, appearing in the private detective show, *Pat Novak for Hire*. But it was a role in the film *He Walked by Night* that would play the biggest influence on Dragnet. The picture was based around the exploits of Erwin Walker, an ex-soldier who embarked on a violent crime spree in the mid-1940s, culminating in the murder of a highway patrolman. In the film, shot semi-documentary style, Webb played a crime lab technician. The background to the story gave him the idea for a police procedural series based on real life cases. With technical assistance from police chief William H. Parker and Sergeant Marty Wynn, Dragnet debuted on radio in 1949.

The show took a little time to find its feet and the lead character of Joe Friday (portrayed by Webb) went through some changes in those first episodes. What instantly set Dragnet apart was its realism and attention-to-detail. It never glamorised the job, rather showing how mundane the day-to-day of it could be – though it was not without its action or heroics. Webb made sure the show was accurate and covered all aspects of police work, from the initial investigation and forensics, through to arrest and interview procedures. The radio programme also introduced the famous Dragnet 'Four note' theme, entitled 'Danger Ahead'. Curiously, the piece wasn't actually written for the show, but rather lifted from the 1946 film, *The Killers*. Each episode would open with a short announcement, informing the audience that the story they were about to hear was true and that only the names had been changed to protect the innocent. Webb's Joe Friday would then detail his circumstances via a tightly clipped, almost rhythmic narration.

Dragnet went on to become an incredible success, running for over 8 years and spanning 314 episodes in total. At the same time, it transferred to TV screens, beginning in 1951. Again, Webb was front-and-centre as Joe Friday, investigating crime in and around Los Angeles. The small screen version was even more popular than the radio show and spawned the first theatrical Dragnet movie in 1954. The episode, *The Big Little Jesus* also holds the title of being the first colour TV programme shown on Network television in North America. The TV series ran for 276 episodes, coming to an end in

1959 – a decision made by Webb, though it must be noted that the show's popularity was starting to wane in its final years. The actor-director then took over detective show *77 Sunset Strip*, but the changes he orchestrated (including removing all but one central cast member) alienated even the most hardened fans. After five quite successful seasons, it was cancelled mid-way through its Webb-controlled sixth. Another failure followed in the guise of *Temple Houston*, described by critics at the time as "Perry Mason goes west".

With a move away from Warner Bros. in 1967, Webb decided to bring back Dragnet. With his partner from the original version now locked into another TV show, he hired Harry Morgan, who had played a number of parts in the Dragnet radio show, as well as making an appearance in its TV counterpart. In an effort to drum up interest, Webb shot a TV movie, on the strength of which NBC commissioned a full series (the movie would not be screened until 1969). To differentiate itself from the original show, the Dragnet revival had its debut year added to the title (Dragnet 1967, Dragnet 1968 etc.). When the series ended four years later, Webb went on to create *Adam-12*, another police procedural show that focused on patrolmen and women. This too proved successful and spawned the spin off, *Emergency!* which followed the lives of the first paramedics working for the LA County Fire department. It ran for six seasons, with Webb producing through his Mark VII company (as had happened with his previous shows).

By 1982, Webb was once again looking to bring Dragnet back. He had five scripts written and because Harry Morgan was now contracted to *After MASH*, Webb had tapped *Adam-12* star Kent McCord to be his new partner. But years of smoking and drinking, not to mention the stress of writing, directing and producing, all finally caught up and Jack Webb died on December 23, 1982 from a heart attack. In tribute, the LAPD retired Joe Friday's badge, number 714, and provided an honour guard at Webb's funeral. The revival was scrapped and with shows like *Hill St. Blues* proving popular, there was little reason for anyone else to champion it. Yet while there was no new show, old episodes of Dragnet (both the original and the 1960s series) were still in heavy rotation on network television. It was while flicking through TV channels one night, that producer David Permut caught an episode. He passed it by and switched over to see Dan Aykroyd spitting out dialogue at a lightning pace on Saturday Night Live. He switched back to Dragnet, and again, back to Aykroyd and the pieces fell into place.

David Permut had made his name with the *Richard Pryor: Live in Concert* movie in 1979, the first ever theatrically released stand-up movie. When the idea of a Dragnet film featuring Dan Aykroyd came to him, he wasted no time. The very next day he spoke to the actor's agent, Bernie Brillstein, explaining that he wanted Aykroyd for what he envisioned as a Dragnet spoof. Brillstein committed the actor in principle immediately. Permut then called in to see Frank

Price at Universal Pictures, who currently held the rights to the show. The producer recalled during an interview for The Ultimate Writer's Guide to Hollywood, that he had no screenplay or even an outline at the time of meeting with Price and simply entered his office and hummed the famous four-bar Dragnet theme. Price knew it instantly. Permut explained that Dan Aykroyd was already on-board and it didn't take much to convince Price of the project's potential – especially when he considered that he (Aykroyd) had had five major hits in the space of a few years. Even though he had no script, by hiring Dan Aykroyd, Permut also gained a successful screenplay writer – not to mention a huge Dragnet fan.

A Canadian native, Dan Aykroyd had made a name for himself as a writer and performer on *Saturday Night Live*, as a member of the "Not Ready for Prime Time Players" troupe. The youngest of the cast, he'd actually worked with producer Lorne Michaels back in Canada, on the short lived comedy show, *The Hart and Lorne Terrific Hour*. The actor soon gained a reputation for his impressions, along with the many characters he created. Indeed, such was his talent and intensity that Eric Idle stated that Aykroyd was the only cast member he could see as a 'Python'. Even at this early stage in his career, he had a knack for reeling off paragraphs of information in a fast, clipped tone – something that was no accident. From an early age, he'd been obsessed with Dragnet and Jack Webb, copying his speech patterns and mannerisms, and bringing them into his own impressions and characters.

It was while working on *SNL* that Aykroyd first met John Belushi. The location for their meeting, a blues club in which Aykroyd was playing, set the spark that helped create The Blues Brothers. What began as a novelty segment on *Saturday Night Live* soon gained a life of its own and the duo performed shows as Jake and Elwood Blues, as well as releasing an album. All of this culminated in the hit movie, *The Blues Brothers*, in 1980. This actually marked the second time the duo had appeared together on the silver screen, the first being the Steven Spielberg disappointment, *1941*. They would star together once more, in the 1981 comedy hit, *Neighbours*, before Belushi died from a drug overdose in March the following year. Aykroyd continued to write and perform, with a notable turn in the 1983 hit comedy, *Trading Places*, opposite *SNL* alumni, Eddie Murphy.

Ghostbusters in 1984 cemented Dan Aykroyd's reputation, and along with Elwood Blues, the character of Ray Stantz is what he is best known for to this day. After the global success of *Ghostbusters*, Aykroyd appeared in two smaller films. He re-teamed with Bill Murray on *Nothing Lasts Forever*, a still-as-yet unreleased science fiction curio which also featured *Gremlins* star Zach Galligan. This was followed by the John Landis comedy-thriller *Into the Night*. He would work with Landis again on *Spies like Us* in 1985, before settling down to script Dragnet with fellow SNL writer, Alan Zweibel. Despite their experience, the writing duo struggled to get a script that both they and the studio were happy with. Universal's Frank Price, knowing the clock was ticking, turned to Tom Mankiewicz in an attempt to knock the script into a workable shape.

By the time he was brought onto the project as its third writer, Tom Mankiewicz was already a legendary script doctor, having worked officially (and unofficially) on some of Hollywood's biggest pictures. The writer was born into movies – his father was Joseph L. Mankiewicz, the formidable screenwriter, producer and director. Tom made his first official Hollywood debut as third director on the John Wayne picture, *The Comancheros*. He received his first on-screen credit (that of Production Associate) for *The Best Man*, a film on which he worked numerous behind-the-scenes roles. Following in his father's footsteps, the young Mankiewicz turned to script writing, producing *Please*, the tale of a suicidal girl in the last ninety minutes of her life. Despite much interest, no studio would buy the script, but it did go some way to acting as a calling card and helped secure him work on Nancy Sinatra's *Movin' with Nancy*. This, in turn, led to him writing the book for the musical version *of Georgy Girl*. Unbeknownst to Mankiewicz, one of the performances was attended by David Picker, who along with Cubby Broccoli, was looking for someone to re-write *Diamonds are Forever* in attempt to lure back Sean Connery.

Signing on for two weeks, Mankiewicz ended up staying on *Diamonds are Forever* for six months, sharing a screenplay credit.

He went on to script *Live and Let Die* and co-wrote *The Man With the Golden Gun*, as well as performing an uncredited rewrite on *The Spy Who Loved Me* and contributing to *Moonraker*. During this period, he also turned in the screenplay for *Mother, Jugs & Speed*, which led to director Peter Yates hiring him to rewrite *The Deep*. Mankiewicz was now gaining a reputation as the go-to/fix-it guy for problem scripts. Richard Donner brought him aboard *Superman I & II* in attempt to streamline the 400-page screenplay. He'd stay with the project for more than a year, controversially receiving a creative consultant credit, which was objected to by the Screen Writers Guild. [Mankiewicz won out in the end, though did agree to have his name appear after the original screenplay writers on *Superman II*]. He turned his hand to TV next and was offered a deal by Aaron Spelling and Leonard Goldberg – if he would re-write their TV movie, *Double Twist*, they'd let him direct it. Mankiewicz agreed and created the extended pilot for what became *Hart to Hart*. The feature spawned a long-running TV series, along with eight further TV movies – the last of which Mankiewicz directed (along with several episodes).

Noticing his talent, Warner Bros. locked him into an exclusive deal fixing movies for them. He worked on *Gremlins, The Goonies* and *WarGames*, as well as turning in the first draft on *Batman*. He re-teamed with Richard Donner on *Ladyhawke*, receiving both a screenwriting and creative consultant credit. Leaving Warner Bros, Mankiewicz found himself contacted by Frank Price, who requested he work with Aykroyd and Zweibel on Dragnet's script. The studio weren't keen on the first draft, and to a degree, Mankiewicz agreed. He met with Aykroyd and they discussed what worked and what didn't. A bizarre subplot involving the theft of people's kidneys (which Aykroyd claims he threw in to mess with Universal) was amongst the first things to go. All up, Dragnet went through three drafts – the original, one that Mankiewicz and Aykroyd wrote and the final one, on which Mankiewicz worked with Zweibel.

At that point, Ted Kotcheff of *First Blood* fame was on-board to direct, but he and the writers clashed. The things Kotcheff wanted fixing were exactly what the three writers felt worked – and vice-versa. Frustrated, Mankiewicz was about to leave the project when Price offered him the chance to direct it instead. He agreed and Dragnet entered pre-production with a price tag of $20M attached.

The key to the film was the chemistry between Joe Friday and his partner. Given that the script contained what was essentially a fish-out-of-water scenario (Friday and his 1950's ideals in the Los Angeles of the 1980s), his partner had to represent everything he wasn't. Aykroyd, having envisioned John Belushi for the role of Pep Streebeck, pushed for his brother, James to be cast, but he wasn't available; neither was second choice, Albert Brooks. Instead they met with a young actor who'd just begun to make a name for himself. Tom Hanks had seen some success with the short-lived sitcom *Bosom Buddies*. When the show was cancelled after its second season, a guest appearance on *Happy Days* brought him into contact with Ron Howard, who at the time was prepping the mermaid rom-com, *Splash*. Howard saw him for the part of the wisecracking brother (eventually played by John Candy) but Hanks proved he could play the lead. The film was a sleeper hit in 1984, and Hanks' career was further boosted by the success of bawdy comedy, *Bachelor Party*. While misfiring with *Volunteers* (again opposite John Candy), Hanks scored big with *The Money Pit*, and to a lesser degree with *Nothing in Common*, opposite Jackie Gleason. Mankiewicz loved that Hanks was unpretentious – he wanted the role in Dragnet because he thought it was a funny script and he'd 'love the company he'd be keeping'.

The role of the Reverend Whirley went to Christopher Plummer, while the Hugh Hefner-like Jerry Caesar was to be played by Dabney Coleman, someone who Tom Hanks had worked with on *The Man with One Red Shoe*, a few years earlier. Coleman met with Mankiewicz at his house and came up with the idea that his character should be from the south and have a lisp. During the course of their meeting, Coleman revealed he'd devised a complete backstory for Caesar – with which the director was happy to go along. Casting the 'virgin' Connie Swail proved a little tougher. At one point, Dan Aykroyd suggested his wife, Donna, but the director vetoed the choice. It was after a viewing of *American Flyers* that he discovered Alexandra Paul. At the time, she'd appeared in a few films but had never heard of Dan Aykroyd (or Dragnet). And that was something that played to her advantage when she auditioned – her lack of 'knowledge' gave her performance a sense of innocence, exactly what the casting team were looking for in the character.

Two familiar faces rounded out the cast. Jack O'Halloran, who had worked with Mankiewicz on *Superman* and its sequel (playing the mute character of Non) came on-board as the larger-than-life villain, Emil Muzz. And in a throwback to the original show, Harry Morgan signed on to reprise the role of Bill Gannon (now a captain). To further the link with the original, Dan Aykroyd would play Joe Friday, the nephew and namesake of the legendary detective. There'd be further cues and asides to the old show in the movie, such as the brand of cigarettes Friday smokes – Chesterfields, who were sponsors of the original radio show. Two further ex-Dragnet actors appeared in cameo roles – Peter Leeds would play Roy Grest while Kathleen Freeman gave a memorable turn as Enid Borden. In one final throwback to the second generation of the show, the movie's working title was Dragnet 1987. This title stuck well into the film's production, and was only altered in the final months (when promotional work began) to avoid confusing uninformed members of the public.

Shooting took place in and around Los Angeles at the tail end of 1986 and into 1987. Dragnet was set for release in the summer and while it was Mankiewicz's first major feature, he'd had enough experience on other sets to handle filming with little issue. But one thing he did notice almost immediately was the differing acting styles of the two leads. With Dan Aykroyd, he'd get the shot on the first or second take – because after that the actor would lose his intensity. Tom Hanks on the other hand, needed three to four takes before he was up to speed. Noticing this early on in the shoot paid dividends and allowed the first takes to concentrate on Aykroyd, before switching focus to Hanks. Both actors were equally aware of their styles and thanked Mankiewicz for coming up with the solution. In terms of characters, Aykroyd was Jack Webb/Joe Friday. He spent much time working on Webb's clipped style and rat-a-tat delivery. He'd walk around the set listening to tapes of Webb's voice and perfected it to such a tee that Harry Morgan swore blind that if he closed his eyes and listened, Jack Webb was who he heard.

With filming finished, Mankiewicz began to assemble his first edit. He didn't cut much out to begin with and asked Frank Price if he could screen the movie without feedback to get a feel for the flow. He already knew it ran much too long and not everything worked. However, unbeknownst to the assembled crew, Sid Sheinberg's son had snuck into the screening and reported back that it was a disaster – it was too long and wasn't funny. When he was confronted by Lew Wasserman (the head of Universal) over the state of the movie, Mankiewicz decided to reassemble the cast for re-shoots before continuing with his edit. The director would later state in his autobiography that those extra scenes were what pulled the film together and made it work. Ever cautious of their own portrayal, the

LAPD sent off-duty officers to every screening to get their own feedback – they wanted to ensure they were being laughed with, not laughed at. Fortunately for all concerned, their opinions were positive.

Critics weren't as impressed, and the film scored only average reviews. While most found it funny, they took exception to how it differed from its source. More than a few also expressed their dislike of the re-imagined Dragnet theme, supplied by The Art of Noise. The picture was set to open at the end of June 1987. It would be up against direct competition in the guise of Mel Brooks' *Spaceballs*, as well as the second frame of *The Witches of Eastwick. Beverly Hills Cop 2* was also a very real threat despite being over a month old. The news didn't any get better in the following weeks either, with *Innerspace, Adventures in Babysitting, Revenge of the Nerds 2* and *Summer School*, all set to debut before the end of July.

Dragnet came out shooting and bested *Spaceballs* by almost $4M in that first weekend, taking the top spot with $10.5M. The popularity of Dan Aykroyd, plus the built-in audience awareness (and the reshoots) appeared to have paid off for Mankiewicz and Universal. A week later, it was still at number one, dropping around 33% of business from that opening weekend. A decent showing in the week meant that after only ten days, Dragnet had recouped it production costs. It slipped down two places in weekend three, up against *Revenge of the Nerds 2* and the expansion of Stanley Kubrick's *Full*

Metal Jacket, but still managed to add another $6M to its total. After a month on general release, the film had doubled its costs and was still out to over 1,200 locations. *Nerds 2* had come and gone, and Dragnet was still clearing an average of $2M each weekend. It survived in the top ten for a total of six weeks and ended up making $57M in North America, with a further $6M overseas. In terms of the year 1987, it was the fourteenth biggest film, out-grossing the likes of *Outrageous Fortune, Spaceballs* and *Planes, Trains and Automobiles*. Like most movies of the time, it performed well on the home video market too.

With such a solid return on its budget, talk of a sequel soon began to circulate. However, while Dragnet was finishing its run, Tom Hanks had gone on to shoot *Big*, which propelled him to global stardom. After that, according to Mankiewicz, it was difficult to get him to play second fiddle to Dan Aykroyd. A number of other ideas were put forward, including having John Candy replace Hanks. A new team was brought in to write the script – the original writers having projects of their own to work on. While they were a few years from success, the Farrelly Brothers turned in a draft that had its moments, but never really gelled as a whole. In terms of feature films, that was the end of Dragnet. The show did return to TV screens in 1989 as *The New Dragnet*. At around the same time, another Jack Webb originated project, *Adam-12* also got a new lease of life. *The New Dragnet* ran for 52 episodes (and crossed over with the new *Adam-12*). The show was resurrected once more in 2003, with Ed O'Neill as Joe Friday. It stuck to the original blueprint for the first season, before turning into more of an ensemble drama (Friday ended up being promoted, reducing his screen time). It was cancelled five episodes into its ten episode second season, with the final five shows appearing on a different network.

After Dragnet, Tom Hanks went on to become one of the biggest stars in Hollywood, and indeed the world. *Big* was a critical and financial success in 1988, which led to *The Burbs* and *Turner & Hooch*. There were a couple of misfires (*Punchline, Bonfire of the Vanities*) before he emerged with an incredible string of successes, beginning with *A League of Their Own* in 1992. By 1995, he'd won two Academy Awards (For *Forrest Gump* and *Philadelphia*) and re-teamed with Meg Ryan on *Sleepless in Seattle*. By the end of the 90s, he'd had nine movies earn over $100M each. The 00s saw him diversify further, and he remains one of the most successful and popular actors of the modern age.

Dan Aykroyd followed Dragnet with *The Great Outdoors* (opposite John Candy) and *Ghostbusters 2*, which while a financial success, was not as well-liked as the original. He received an Academy Award nomination for his turn in *Driving Miss Daisy*, but then watched his career almost completely derail with the directorial effort, *Nothing but Trouble*. In the 90s, some *Saturday Night Live* cast members got movies made based on their characters. Dan Aykroyd gave *Coneheads* a shot, but the film failed to repeat the success of similar *SNL* spin-offs such as *Wayne's World*. From that point forward, the actor seemed happy to take on supporting roles, and gave a fantastic performance in the 1997 picture, *Grosse Pointe Blank*. A year later, he brought back another *SNL* creation – *The Blues Brothers*. However, *Blues Brothers 2000* was a failure, making only $14M from a budget of $28M. Aykroyd continues to take on film roles and is also part of a company selling vodka in skull shaped bottles.

Alexandra Paul went on to become a global star thanks to her work on the hit TV show, *Baywatch*. After the show ended, she teamed up with Pierce Brosnan for the action dramas, *Death Train* and *Nightwatch*, before moving on to a number of TV movie roles. She has also co-written and co-produced the documentaries *Jampacked* and *The Cost of Cool: Finding Happiness in a Materialistic World*. Christopher Plummer and Dabney Coleman continued their careers through the 90s and beyond. Coleman joined Tom Hanks in the 1998 picture, *You've Got Mail*, while Plummer appeared in the English language remake of *The Girl with the Dragon Tattoo*.

Tom Mankiewicz looked to be heading for the big time after Dragnet and was set to work on *Sleeping with the Enemy*, before a change of guard at the studio left him out in the cold. Taking a meeting with his former agent and discussing his dissatisfaction at how things had turned out with *Enemy*, he managed to annoy his current agency, Mike Ovitz's uber-powerful CAA. No one would take his calls after that and he quickly found himself unemployable – a situation not helped when rumours were circulated that he was a heavy drinker and therefore unreliable. Only Richard Donner stood up for him and helped put together the John Candy movie, *Delirious*. While Mankiewicz states this was the happiest filming experience he'd had, financial troubles at MGM saw it barely receive a release. He would make no further theatrical features and only directed three more times – an episode of *Tales From the Crypt*, TV movie *Taking the Heat*, and the final *Hart to Hart* film, *Till Death do us Hart*. He all but retired from Hollywood after that, but did once again join Richard Donner to assemble *Superman II: The Richard Donner Cut* in 2006. Tom Mankiewicz died in 2010 from pancreatic cancer.

There's no denying that the partnership of Aykroyd and Hanks works well in Dragnet and means that even today, the picture can be enjoyed despite some of the references falling flat. It moves at a brisk pace and has some solid laughs, including a brilliant final pay-off. Dragnet may not be as fondly remembered as *Beverly Hills Cop* or *The Naked Gun*, but that doesn't make it any less worthy of your time.

Liked Dragnet? Try one of these…

Midnight Run

Another stunning action comedy from *Beverly Hills Cop* director, Martin Brest. Robert De Niro plays bounty hunter Jack Walsh, tasked with bringing Jonathan Mardukas back to Los Angeles. What seems like a simple job is complicated by the Mafia, who want Mardukas dead, the FBI, who want Mardukas to testify and Mardukas himself, who is terrified of flying, resulting in the pair having to cross the country by train, car and even hitchhiking.

The chemistry between the leads is spot on as we witness a genuine bond began to form throughout the picture's runtime. The supporting cast, including Yaphet Kotto and John Ashton are equally good and help make Midnight Run almost as a strong a movie as *Beverly Hills Cop*, though with less financial success. A great 80s feature more than worthy of re-discovery.

Trivia: Three TV movie sequels were screened in 1994, with Christopher McDonald taking on the Jack Walsh role.

Remo Williams: The Adventure Begins (aka: Remo: Unarmed and Dangerous)

Based on *The Destroyer* paperback series, Remo is an action adventure comedy that sees Fred Ward recruited into a secret organisation after his death is faked. With a new identity and a new face, he's trained by the mysterious Chiun in the deadly art of Sinanju. These new skills allow him to dodge bullets and run across water, amongst other things. Before too long, he's sent to investigate a corrupt weapons programme at a US military base and has to call upon his recently-gained talents to stay alive.

Big things were hoped of the picture and with a series of books to adapt, a franchise was certainly in the offing. Despite the great interplay between Ward's Remo and Joel Grey's Chiun, audiences didn't warm to the movie. A shame, as there's much to enjoy, in particular a fight sequence on and round the Statue of Liberty. Not a classic by any stretch, but an enjoyable curio all the same.

Trivia: Director Guy Hamilton rewrote the script when he signed on-board, and the Statue of Liberty sequence was one of his contributions.

Spies Like Us

John Landis directs Dan Aykroyd and Chevy Chase in what is essentially an update of the old Crosby and Hope *'Road To'* movies. The pair stars as recently-qualified field agents, a task they achieved despite making a complete mess of the entrance exam. What they don't know is that they're actually being sent into Russia as decoys, while the real agents complete their mission.

The great chemistry between the leads is what makes the picture work so well, whether they're bluffing the exam, performing fake surgery or escaping from the KGB. The cold war and threat of a nuclear strike is very much of the time, but really serves only to get Chase and Aykroyd into more increasingly dangerous situations. A solid comedy from all concerned, that also includes a memorable debut for Vanessa Angel.

Trivia: Co-star Donna Dixon is actually the wife of Dan Aykroyd. The film is also noted for the number of directors who cameo, which include Sam Raimi, Martin Brest, Joel Coen and Frank Oz.

-----

48 Hrs.

The Boys are Back in Town

Studio: Paramount Pictures
Release Date: 10th December 1982
Director: Walter Hill
Starring: Nick Nolte, Eddie Murphy
Budget: $12M – 2015 Equivalent: $29.9M
U.S Box Office: $78.8M – 2015 Equivalent: $196.8M

Jack Cates is on the trail of escaped convict and cop killer Albert Ganz and his partner Billy Bear. After a hotel shootout leaves two more officers dead, Cates seeks the help of Ganz' former partner, Reggie Hammond, currently serving time for armed robbery. Released into Cates' custody for 48 hours, the duo might just be able to catch Ganz – if they don't kill each other first.

The history of the buddy movie can be traced back many years, starting off with the likes of Laurel and Hardy in the 1930s and Abbott and Costello in the 1940s. Over time, its make-up has changed but essentially it consists of two often mismatched people put into a situation where they must work past their differences toward a common goal. While the 60s and 70s added further to the genre, splicing it with the road movie in the case of *Easy Rider* or the western as in *Butch Cassidy and the Sundance Kid,* it was the 1980s where it truly shone. Gene Wilder and Richard Pryor may have scored big with *Silver Streak* and *Stir Crazy*, but it was Walter Hill's 48 Hrs. that ushered in a whole new age of buddy movie, that continues to this day.

Walter Hill was born in Long Beach, in 1942, and due to early childhood illnesses and an on-going battle with asthma, spent many of his formative years bedridden or housebound. Embracing this time alone, the young Hill learned to read early on in his life, and devoured countless books and comics, as well as becoming an avid fan of radio serials, and later on, TV shows. In periods of wellness, he would venture to the local cinema, but generally avoided kids' films, favouring the Western instead. By the age of fifteen, and having seemingly outgrown the asthma that had blotted his childhood, Hill thought about becoming an athlete, but the call of writing was always in his mind. He knew even then that regardless of what he did, he would at some point return to writing. After some time spent in Mexico, he wound up attending school in Michigan, studying literature and history. Upon finishing, Hill was drafted into the army, and returned back home to Long Beach to wait to be assessed. It was during this time he met up with friend Gene Waters, who introduced him to a group of people who made educational films for Encyclopaedia Britannica. When the army rejected him because of his childhood illness, Hill was offered a research job on the Britannica educational films. Within a short space of time, he'd move from research to actually writing the scripts and found directing them to be a natural progression.

When the contract came to end, he took on a job in the Universal Pictures mailroom in an effort to meet people who worked in the industry. He was writing in every free moment he had and was fortunate enough to get on the Directors Guild training programme, which in turn allowed him to work as an apprentice on various TV shows of the time. He'd spend over a year in TV, going between the likes of *Bonanza* and *The Wild Wild West* on a fortnightly basis. He secured the role of second assistant director on *The Thomas Crown Affair* and *Bullitt* (for which he would be uncredited), before taking on a similar job on the Woody Allen feature, *Take the Money and Run*. By his own admission, he did little beyond administrative work on the picture – though did get to direct some of the re-shoots. A dabble with directing commercials for TV left him cold and made him realise that that wasn't a path he wished to pursue. During this time, he continued to write, but struggled to get scripts finished, estimating that at one point, he had twenty-six 'first acts' written.

However, when he did finally complete his first screenplay, *Lloyd Williams and His Brother*, it sold quickly. Despite the studio renewing the option on it, the script remained unproduced, but it was enough to catch the eye of Warner Bros, who asked Hill to pitch something to them.

Hickey & Boggs, an old-school detective story was his idea. Warner Bros. liked it enough to fund a draft, but did little when the script was completed. In the meantime, Polly Platt, ex-wife of Peter Bogdanovich, read *Hickey & Boggs* and recommended Peter hire Hill to work on the script for *The Getaway*. At the time, Bogdanovich was directing *What's Up, Doc*, and in the downtime the duo worked on *The Getaway*. Having completed around 25 pages, they returned to San Francisco, where Bogdanovich was promptly fired by Steve McQueen. Rather than continue, Hill rewrote the script from scratch and worked alongside newly-hired director, Sam Peckinpah. *The Getaway* was a smash hit and led to more script work for Hill. He wrote *The Mackintosh Man* for Paul Newman, by way of settling a lawsuit with Warner Bros. that related to an unwritten screenplay contract and the sale of *Hickey & Boggs*. He was then hired to rewrite *The Drowning Pool*, again for Paul Newman, but was let go when the producers objected to the direction his script took. All this set Hill up for *Hard Times*, a movie that would be his feature directorial debut.

Producer Larry Gordon had a script about a bare-knuckle fighter, set in San Pedro. When he moved to Columbia Pictures, he offered Walter Hill the chance to direct – if he would re-write the script. He agreed, and working for scale (essentially a fixed industry rate), re-worked the script and directed the picture. *Hard Times* went on to become a hit, and in his own words, 'turned out to be the best deal I ever made' – Hill was still making money from it in 2009. He re-teamed with Gordon on *The Driver*, but their previous success was not repeated. When financing on a western they planned to make fell through, Gordon and Hill moved forward with *The Warriors*. The producer had secured the rights to Sol Yurick's novel when they lapsed from the previous rights holder. They pitched the film to Paramount, who gave them the budget and greenlight for production. Hill would clash numerous times with Paramount CEO Michael Eisner over the content of the picture, leading Larry Gordon to act as peacemaker on more than one occasion.

The Warriors, a violent action feature about a street gang attempting to get back to their own turf, was released with little fanfare in February 1979. When violence broke out before and after screenings, Paramount allowed cinemas to break their contract and pull the film. They went as far as removing trailers from TV and theatres, promoting the picture by way of small print ads. The notoriety helped *The Warriors* break out into the mainstream, and it went on to make $22M from a budget of only $4M. It was successful on the burgeoning home video market too, and spawned a short-lived TV show entitled *The Renegades*. In the meantime, Hill finally got the go ahead for a western, which would become *The Longriders*. He followed this up with the thriller *Southern Comfort*, about a troop of National Guardsmen who find themselves fighting for survival against a group of Cajuns. Hill would also famously have a hand in the creation of *Alien*, the history behind which would fill many, many pages and is *still* contested by some of those involved.

It was Larry Gordon who had the original idea for 48 Hrs. back in the mid-70s. The story would see a violent criminal kidnap the daughter of the Louisiana governor and strap dynamite to her head. If the ransom wasn't paid within the designated time, he would kill her. Gordon envisaged the meanest cop partnering up with toughest prisoner (who happened to be the kidnapper's ex-cellmate) to bring the guy down. They'd initially despise each other, but a grudging respect would grow during the course of the story – each knowing they will benefit if the situation comes to a satisfying conclusion. Roger Spottiswoode wrote one of the earliest drafts, with the hope of directing it. Hill and Gordon encouraged him to 'Write himself into the job' but little came of it. Another draft was crafted by Bill Kerby, and a third by Tracy Keenan Wynn when the project moved to Paramount. By the time filming began, at least six people had had a hand in the screenplay, including Steven E. de Souza (making his feature writing debut after working on a TV pilot for producer Larry Gordon) and Hill himself.

48 Hrs was initially seen as a vehicle for Clint Eastwood, but in something of a reversal, Eastwood wanted to play the criminal. Playing the cop, he argued, would spill over into the work he did as *Dirty Harry*. Even when the idea of Richard Pryor as the prisoner was put forward, Eastwood was still against playing the cop, and opted for a role in *Escape from Alcatraz* instead. The project slipped into limbo and Hill went off to shoot *The Longriders* and *Southern Comfort*. Larry Gordon wouldn't let the project die and called Hill out-of-the-blue one day and asked if he'd be interested in directing Nick Nolte in 48 Hrs.

By the time Nolte was offered the role of Jack Cates, it was said that Burt Reynolds, Mickey Rourke and Sylvester Stallone had all passed on it, as had Kris Kristofferson. Nick Nolte had been acting for just over a decade when he won the role in 48 Hrs. He'd started his career off as a model, before moving into acting, though his first few roles were largely uncredited or one-off appearances in such fare as *The Streets of San Francisco* and *Emergency!* It was his turn in the TV mini-series *Rich Man, Poor Man* that bought him attention and critical recognition and paved the way for his first major starring role in *The Deep*. He won further good notices for his work on *Who'll Stop the Rain* (1978) and *North Dallas Forty* (1979). When he took on the 48 Hrs. job he was coming off the back of romantic drama, *Cannery Row*, in which he'd starred opposite Debra Winger. A big, imposing figure, Nolte was perfect for the grizzled Jack Cates.

Having agreed to direct, Hill set about re-writing the script with the aid of Larry Gross. By the time they came to start shooting the picture, seven years had passed since Roger Spottiswoode had turned in his initial draft. A May 1982 start date was in place, with a view to release the film in December of that same year, but there was still the issue of casting the other lead, that of Willie Biggs (later renamed as Reggie Hammond). According to at least one source, Gregory Hines was initially cast in the role, but had to drop out due to scheduling conflicts with *The Cotton Club*. Richard Pryor was the studio's number one choice, but he passed in favour of starring in *The Toy*. Both Howard E. Rollins Jr. and Denzel Washington were said to have also tried out for the part, but in the end, Hill found his Willie Biggs thanks to his then-girlfriend, a theatrical agent who represented a popular *Saturday Night Live* player by the name of Eddie Murphy.

Eddie Murphy was born in 1961 and discovered his talent for comedy when he and his brother spent a year in a foster home due to their mother being too ill to care for them. Devouring the work of Richard Pryor, Bill Cosby and Jerry Lewis (to name but a few), the young Murphy began crafting his own short stand-up routines and made his stage debut at the age of 15. He went on to play all manner of clubs and expanded his routine when a manager of one such place offered him a dollar for every minute he was on stage. By 1980, he found himself playing Manhattan's Comic Strip club, further building his act and popularity. According to Neil Levy, a talent co-ordinator on *Saturday Night Live*, Murphy began calling him daily from September onwards in an attempt to get an audition for the show. Even after getting constant knock-backs and the fact that "the black cast member had already been chosen", Murphy refused to give up and eventually got the chance to try out as an extra. Levy was blown away and fought hard for him to be taken on as a full-time cast member – going so far as threatening to quit if it didn't happen. At the time, *SNL* was faltering in the ratings, due in large part to the departure of its creator, Lorne Michaels, who had been unable to broker a deal with NBC. This, in turn, led to many of the regular writers and players quitting the show also, leaving the producers scrambling for talent.

Murphy, along with Joe Piscopo, saved *SNL* from the axe with a variety of sketches and characters that proved an instant hit with the public. His creations made him a household name and he would go on to be the second most popular actor on the show, after John Belushi. Yet even with such success, Murphy wanted more. He quickly grew tired of being referred to as his characters when meeting the general public, going so far as to kill off one of his creations as part of a *SNL* sketch. When his agent suggested him for 48 Hrs., the director, and especially the studio, were more than happy to entertain the idea. For his part, Murphy was interested because he wouldn't have to carry the picture alone. He also liked the fact that it was action thriller with comedy elements, rather than being an out-and-out comedy role. In a 1982 interview given to *Entertainment Tonight*, the young comedian half-joked that he couldn't really lose. If the film was a hit, it showed he could be serious as well as funny. On the flip side, if it flopped, he could blame the fact that he was a comedian put into a film where he called upon to be serious, something he wasn't known for. The actor was also responsible for the character's name change, from Willie Biggs to Reggie Hammond.

The first complication was that Murphy was committed to *Saturday Night Live*, which would run over into when shooting on 48 Hrs. was set to commence. Rather than lose the actor, Walter Hill shuffled around the schedule, shooting some of Nolte's scenes first, along with those featuring co-stars Annette O'Toole, Sonny Badham, James Remar and David Patrick Kelly (the latter two having worked with Hill previously on *The Warriors*). After two weeks, Murphy was free from *SNL* (until the next season) and joined the production. Something that Hill *hadn't* figured on was finding himself no longer the right man for the job – at least in the eyes of the Paramount and Michael Eisner. When he signed up, 48 Hrs. was a violent action thriller with some comedy elements. Now Eddie Murphy was involved, the studio wanted to tone down the violence and up the comedy – and in Hill they saw a writer/director who could shoot great action sequences, but had never done comedy. They figured they'd rather lose the director than risk squandering Murphy.

Hill stood his ground, and got to work shooting the main sequences of the film now that all the cast was present. Having come from stand-up and *SNL*, Murphy had little acting experience, and a coach was hired to help him cover the basics. His energy and enthusiasm also went a long way, and he was easily able to hold his own against his far more experienced co-star. However, Eisner wasn't impressed and pushed Hill to make the film funnier. According to the director, Eisner couldn't comprehend or visualise how funny a scene would be when it was actually shot, with the addition of actions, gestures and sight gags. The chemistry between Nolte and Murphy was there for all to see in the dailies; Hill and Larry Gross continued to refine the script on a day-to-day basis to play to the actor's strengths and increasing confidence with each other. [Nolte claimed in the 2008 documentary *No Exit* that much of his and Murphy's dialogue was improvised, but Hill states they were writing and rewriting dialogue up to the very last day of the shoot]. Still, Eisner passed down pages of notes via his executive, Don Simpson, who was simply biding his time before he could secure a production deal. Even then, Simpson's lifestyle was making people nervous.

Initially Hill read the notes, but as time went by he became more and more insulted by them, eventually passing them straight on to the man that Larry Gordon had put in charge of the day-to-day running of the production – Joel Silver. Even he grew weary after a while and passed them on to his secretary to read over. 48 Hrs. would mark the first time that Silver received a full producer credit – the first of many. The issues weren't only with the amount of comedy either. When shooting got back to Los Angeles, the set was visited by a group of Paramount executives who sat through dailies from the hotel shootout sequence and deemed it far too violent. They felt that no matter how funny the film was after that, it would not recover, and told Hill he'd never make another picture for the studio again [When Hill did again work for Paramount, the executives had long since gone]. Despite his reservation, Michael Eisner did at least find edited footage of Murphy to be funny (though not funny enough for his liking). Some years later, Hill would reveal that Paramount wanted to fire Murphy – not because he wasn't funny, but rather that he wasn't 'Richard Pryor funny'. As the shoot came to a close, any doubts about Murphy were extinguished when they shot the 'Redneck bar' sequence. Even though he'd never appeared in a movie before, after that scene was completed, Murphy was a bona fide film star – something that didn't go unnoticed by Don Simpson.

Work began on editing the picture in time for its December release date. James Horner would provide the film's instrumental soundtrack, while The Bus Boys, who would open for Eddie Murphy's stand-up shows, contributed two songs. As has been noted before, the cinematic landscape in the early 1980s was much different to how it is today. A wide theatrical release would top around 1,200 screens, and VHS was already being branded as the killer of cinema. In a move that would seem inexplicable to a studio executive today (or even ten years ago), 48 Hrs. opened up against two other major comedy releases – one of which (*The Toy*) starred Richard Pryor. There was other competition too (though not all direct) in the guise *of First Blood, An Officer and a Gentleman* and *E.T the Extra Terrestrial*, which was in its 27th weekend on general release and still making money. 48 Hrs. cost $12M to produce, so a good few weekends would see it home and dry. Reviews were incredibly strong, with many singling out Murphy's star-making performance and the chemistry between the leads as being the highlights. The picture currently holds a 95% approval rating on Rotten Tomatoes and was one of the best reviewed films of that year.

48 Hrs. opened on December 10th 1982, and made an OK $4.3M during its first weekend. *The Toy* won the top spot with $6.3M, while *Airplane 2: The Sequel* slipped into second place, earning $5.3M. It's worth noting that *The Toy* was on over 530 screens more than 48 Hrs (and 200 more than the *Airplane* sequel) giving it a ready advantage. A week later, another comedy joined the fray; Dustin Hoffman picture, *Tootsie*, knocked *The Toy* off the top spot and contributed to 48 Hrs. dropping down to fifth place. The studio weren't too concerned as it had already made back most of its budget in the first ten days, and word-of-mouth was white hot. The same couldn't be said for *Airplane 2*, which tumbled from second to sixth. A week later and *Tootsie* was still at number one, but 48 Hrs. had crept back up the chart, and actually increased on the previous weekend's takings (without the aid of any extra screens). Over the

New Year period, the film dropped down the chart again, yet saw another increase in takings. At this point, it had been on general release for a month and comfortably earned back its costs. What not one realised at the time was that 48 Hrs. was just getting started.

An increase of seventy screens during the January 7-9 weekend helped push the film to its highest chart position yet, sitting behind *Tootsie*, which was doing incredible business. The two films would occupy those same positions for the next three weeks. Only in its ninth weekend, did 48 Hrs. drop down a place, when *The Entity* was released. By now, the picture had crossed the $50M mark and *The Toy* was all but a distant memory. By the end of February, 48 Hrs. was still in the top ten and actually moved back up the chart just as it began its exit from screens. *Tootsie* finally gave up the top spot in its 14th week to the Tom Selleck actioner, *High Road to China*. The following weekend was almost an entirely new top ten, as studios released (or re-released in the case of *Raiders of the Lost Ark* and *The Sword in the Stone*) eight films. Only *High Road, Tootsie* and *Ghandi* survived, and 48 Hrs. fell to eleventh place. All told, it stayed on general release for twenty weeks, finishing its North America run with $78M – almost eight times what it cost to produce. It was the seventh biggest film of 1982, and enjoyed a very long and successful run on video too. Eddie Murphy was nominated for a Best Newcomer Golden Globe, Hill won the Grand Prix award at the Cognac Festival du Film Policier and James Horner's score earned him a Los Angeles Film Critics gong.

48 Hrs. thrust Murphy from TV comedian to global superstar almost overnight. Paramount, now knowing what they had, moved to sign him onto an extended contract. Yet at the same time, they never gave Walter Hill much credit for his contribution. In fact, according to an interview Hill gave to the Directors Guild a few years back, Paramount (or rather, its executives) actually took credit for the film's success, telling Hill it was only funny because they'd pushed him to make it funnier. He made his next two films, *Streets of Fire* and *Brewster's Millions*, for Universal Pictures.

Given how successful 48 Hrs. was, it didn't take long before talk of a sequel surfaced, but it would take eight years before it got to the screen. The two leads returned for the 1990 release, *Another 48 Hrs.*, as did Walter Hill. In the interim, Eddie Murphy had become one of the biggest stars of the decade, while Nolte continued to win solid reviews for his dramatic work. After receiving $450,000 for the first film, Murphy made between $7M and $9M for its sequel and took top billing (and a 'story by' credit). Nolte saw his salary rise from $1M to $3M. This time around, Jack Cates, facing a charge of manslaughter, recruits the newly-paroled Reggie Hammond to help clear his name and apprehend villain The Iceman. Hill's initial cut ran for 145 minutes and was edited down to 120 minutes for its release. However, after *Total Recall* stormed the box office a week before *Another 48 Hrs.* was to make its debut, Paramount panicked and hastily hacked another 25 minutes from the picture. Complete characters and sequences were removed and actors such as Brion James saw their roles drastically reduced. In a somewhat baffling move, the studio also cut the scene in which Cates explains to Hammond how he has only 48 hours to clear his name. The film performed well, doubling its production budget in North America, and making a total of $153M globally. Nevertheless, given Murphy's previous box office hits, it was seen as a disappointment and critics savaged it. Talk of a second sequel soon dried up.

For much of the 1980s, Eddie Murphy could do no wrong. He followed up his debut with *Trading Places*, opposite Dan Aykroyd, to even greater success. His stand-up concert movie *Delirious* was also a smash hit on video, though its controversial content earned him protests and threats. Such was his appeal, after the Dudley Moore comedy *Best Defence* tested poorly the studio had Murphy shoot a few scenes that they could insert into the picture. His part didn't feature any other member of the main cast (a scene he did share with Moore was later cut) and amounted to little more than a cameo but that didn't stop Paramount from promoting *Best Defence* as if Murphy was a fully-fledged co-star. If the studio had been impressed with his box office so far, they were blown away by what he did next. *Beverly Hills Cop* was produced by Don Simpson and Jerry Bruckheimer and became one of the most successful pictures in movie history. As of today, it remains the sixth biggest R-rated picture ever released – and that is without inflation being factored in. Only *Titanic* stayed at number one for more consecutive weeks.

1984 had some major releases, including *Ghostbusters* and *Indiana Jones and the Temple of Doom*, and *Beverly Hills Cop* topped them all.

For many, it marked the high point of Murphy's career – both critically and financially. He would have many other successes, such as *The Golden Child, Beverly Hills Cop 2* and *Coming to America*, but by the time he directed vanity project, *Harlem Nights*, audiences had moved on. After *Another 48 Hrs.*, the actor tried various genres, with middling results. Romantic-comedy *Boomerang* did quite good business, but *Vampire in Brooklyn* and *The Distinguished Gentleman* sank quickly. A return to the *Beverly Hills Cop* franchise was a major failure in 1994, earning just $42M. However, *The Nutty Professor* proved a big success, as did his voice work on Disney's *Mulan*. Now with a family of his own, Murphy switched to PG-friendly pictures, much to the disappointment of his older fans. Success from a *Nutty Professor* sequel and *Dr. Dolittle* eclipsed previous disappointments and some future ones (*Metro* and *Holy Man)*, though he did receive positive notices for his work on the comedy drama, *Life*, opposite Martin Lawrence, and *Bowfinger* with Steve Martin.

Shrek in 1999 became a major turning point and a huge success. Murphy provided the voice of Donkey and went on to reprise the role in three further movies and numerous TV specials, but he continued to struggle with live action. While *Daddy Day Care* made over $100M, *Showtime, I Spy* and notorious (and hugely expensive) flop *The Adventures of Pluto Nash* could barely muster $75M between them. Many were surprised when he took on a dramatic role in the 2006 picture *Dreamgirls*, earning a supporting actor nomination in the process. Since then he has seen success again with *Shrek* sequels and failure with *Meet Dave, Imagine That* and *One Thousand Words*, which sat on the shelf for some time before receiving a release. Murphy is still set to return as Axel Foley in a fourth *Beverly Hills Cop* as some point in the future.

Nick Nolte favoured drama moving forward, though wasn't averse to comedy (*Three Fugitives, Down and Out in Beverly Hills*). He re-teamed with Walter Hill on *Extreme Prejudice* and again on *Another 48 Hrs*. He was nominated for an Academy Award for his work on *Prince of Tides* (1991), *Affliction* (1997) and *Warrior* (2012). He remains an in-demand actor, appearing in eight features since 2012.

Walter Hill continued to direct, but his next picture, *Streets of Fire*, failed at the box office, though subsequently gained cult status. His work with Richard Pryor on *Brewster's Millions* saw him return to success briefly, before three disappointments in a row (*Extreme Prejudice, Red Heat* and *Johnny Handsome*) helped convince him to make the 48 Hrs. sequel. His 1992 picture *Trespass*, featuring Ice-T and Ice Cube remains an underrated gem, but his return to the western genre with *Geronimo* in 1993 and *Wild Bill* in 1995 failed to find an audience, likewise the Bruce Willis film, *Last Man Standing*. After the disastrous *Supernova* and boxing drama *Undisputed*, Hill switched to TV, winning awards for his work on *Deadwood* and *Broken Trail*. His latest theatrical release was the 2013 Sylvester Stallone picture, *Bullet to the Head*.

Don Simpson and his partner Jerry Bruckheimer would go on to make some of the biggest pictures of the 1980s and 90s, including the aforementioned *Beverly Hills Cop* (and its first sequel), *Top Gun, Days of Thunder* and *The Rock*. Similarly, Joel Silver became *the* action producer of the next two decades, having a hand in the likes of *Commando, Predator, Die Hard 1 & 2,* the *Lethal Weapon* series and *The Matrix trilogy*. He also produced *Streets of Fire, Brewster's Millions* and *Bullet to the Head* for Walter Hill.

Viewed today, 48 Hrs. still packs a violent punch that's offset perfectly by Murphy and Nolte's interplay. Many would argue that the original *Beverly Hills Cop* aside, Murphy has never been better, and it remains one of the strongest examples of the genre. Its influence ran throughout the 1980s and 90s and even today's action comedies owe it a debt. Despite changes in fashion and attitude, 48 Hrs. has aged incredibly well and remains not only a great comedy thriller, but also serves as witness to the making of a superstar.

More like 48 Hrs…

Lethal Weapon

Danny Glover as a cop nearing retirement and Mel Gibson as his new suicidal partner make the perfect pairing. Aided by Shane Black's fantastic script and Richard Donner's direction, Lethal Weapon may well be the best buddy movie ever made. This first film in what would become a four movie series is a much darker affair than the later entries and all the better for it.

Gary Busey adds menace as Mr. Joshua, but this is Gibson and Glover's movie, and as the stake gets higher, Donner continues to ratchet up the set pieces, culminating in an action packed and breathless third act. Despite being an actor of some experience, it's arguable that it was Lethal Weapon, and not *Mad Max*, that made Mel Gibson a star in America. A great example of what a movie should be – violent, outlandish but never less than absolutely entertaining.

Trivia: A veritable who's who of Hollywood turned down the role of Riggs before Mel Gibson got the job, including Kurt Russell, Kevin Costner, Rutger Hauer and Jeff Goldblum.

Running Scared

Something of a hidden gem, featuring Billy Crystal and Gregory Hines as two wisecracking Chicago cops who decide to put in for early retirement when a bust goes awry. Returning from vacation, the duo discovers that the dealer (Gonzales, played by Jimmy Smits) has been released on bail and vow to bring him to justice before they retire to Florida.

The chemistry between Crystal and Hines is spot on and they both play their roles with ease. Even when the plot takes a more serious tone, they've got a line to lighten up the moment. Running Scared isn't nearly as well-known as it deserves to be, and often finds itself overshadowed (or ignored completely) in favour of the bigger, showier cop movies of the 80s. A superb action comedy that should be on everyone must-watch list.

Trivia: The original script was written with Gene Hackman and Paul Newman in mind, and it was director Peter Hyams who suggested they rework it with younger actors as the leads.

Stakeout

Another great buddy movie, starring Richard Dreyfuss and Emilio Estevez as two cops tasked with staking out the apartment of an escaped criminal's ex-girlfriend. Trouble ensues when Dreyfuss accidentally befriends (and falls for) the girl they're meant to me watching, played by Madeline Stowe. If that wasn't enough to contend with, they also have to deal with the practical jokes from the stakeout day-shift and the possibility that Aidan Quinn's violent criminal might just be heading to see his old flame.

A cracker of a movie, with Dreyfuss and Estevez making a great team. The pair bounces off each other with ease, and the romantic subplot adds further hilarity and tension. The comedy also helps to balance out the violence perpetrated by Quinn's Montgomery as he travels towards the inevitable showdown. Knowing what he is capable of adds further tension to proceedings. A sequel followed in 1993 but lost much of the charm despite the leads reprising their roles.

Trivia: During the movie trivia scene, Estevez quotes a line spoken by Richard Dreyfuss' character in the movie Jaws.

Fright Night

There are some very good reasons to be afraid of the dark

Studio: Columbia Pictures

Release Date: 2nd August 1985

Director: Tom Holland

Starring: William Ragsdale, Chris Sarandon

Budget: $9M – 2015 Equivalent: $20M

U.S Box Office: $24.9M – 2015 Equivalent: $55.5M

When Jerry Dandrige moves into the house next door, horror fan Charley Brewster suspects he could be a vampire. Maybe it's the coffin he saw being taken into the house or the blood-curdling screams he hears in the dead of night. But when his girlfriend doesn't believe him and his best friend thinks he's crazy, Charley turns to the one man he knows can help – Fright Night host Peter Vincent. But even he isn't all he appears to be.......

Horror was one of the main staples of 1980s cinema as it emerged from the campy Hammer movies of the 70s into something of a much darker, more violent nature. The genre moved into the mainstream with the likes of the *Friday the 13th* and *Nightmare on Elm Street* series, as well as becoming a major catalyst in the uptake of the video recorder, helped no end by the infamous video nasty period. Hollywood studios were quick to realise that while horror movies were successful, their very nature shut off a large percentage of the potential audience. John Landis, with *An American Werewolf in London* and Sam Raimi's *The Evil Dead* showed that comedy, however dark, could work in a horror movie. But it would be a fine line to tread – too much comedy would water down the horror, too graphic the horror and no matter how funny the film, you would not get your audience back. There are few better examples of a movie getting that balance just right than Tom Holland's Fright Night.

Tom Holland was born in Poughkeepsie, New York and caught the acting bug in high school, appearing in numerous plays. A summer-long stint at a local playhouse all but convinced him to quit school and act full-time. However, his parents had other ideas and managed to sway the young Holland into finishing school and attending college. He graduated in 1962 and moved on to study drama at a New York university, as well as receiving tutelage at the Herbert Berghof Studio and the world famous Actors Studio, under the guidance of Lee Strasberg. Working with some of the players and directors, he came to realise that if he could write a script, it could lead to directing. He struck up a friendship with Stewart Stern, scripter *of Rebel without a Cause*, who taught Holland how to write for film. Outside of the classroom, Holland struggled to find work as an actor and ended up, initially at least, making more money from modelling. He supplemented this by taking on all manner of behind-the-scene jobs on TV shows and films – something that would aid him later on in his career.

He was fortunate enough to get noticed by Jack Warner, who signed him to a Warner Brothers contract. Tom Holland, or rather Tom Fielding as he became known (there was already an actor by the name of Holland) made his voice acting debut on the Eli Kazan movie, *America America*, dubbing dialogue. He moved on to appear in a number of TV shows of the time, including *Temple Houston* and *77 Sunset Strip*, before realising he could make more money working back in New York. He took on soap opera work, landing a recurring role on *A Time for Us*, but when the show was cancelled, he once again found himself in Los Angeles. He did however manage to land the lead role in *Josie's Castle*, opposite George Takei; sadly, the film suffered numerous production problems and was ultimately re-edited and sold as a sexploitation movie. As the acting work dried up, Holland took to appearing in various TV commercials (as many as 200, he would later state), before deciding to give up acting altogether and return to school to study law. After getting through the first difficult year, he considered quitting, but instead stuck with law, while writing film treatments and screenplays in his spare time. It was while waiting for the results of the bar exam that he sold his first script, *The View from 30*, to Dick Berg, for $1500.

Despite passing the bar and graduating, he opted to pursue a career in screenwriting. While *The View from 30* wasn't produced, another treatment of Holland's was used as the basis of *The Initiation of Sarah*, a movie-of-the-week that was essentially a *Carrie* knock-off. The picture garnered huge ratings and notoriety thanks to a sequence involving a young Morgan Fairchild in a fountain. The writer later stated that it was 'the first [programme on American television] to have a wet T-shirt scene in it'. Holland received his first proper writing credit on the 1981 film, *The Beast Within*. While the picture failed to do much business, it did convince him that he had chosen the right career path, and he went on to write cult hit, *Class of 1984*. Next, he teamed up with Richard Franklin to work on the made-for-TV sequel, *Psycho II*. According to Holland, Franklin was the leading scholar on Hitchcock to emerge from USC and gave him an in-depth education on the fabled director as the pair began to construct the script. Even in those pre-internet days, there were plenty of people ready to rally against a sequel to Hitchcock's seminal classic and critics readied their knives.

Made for TV sequels were quite a popular thing back in the late 70s and early 80s. Much like the straight-to-DVD sequels of the 90s, these TV movies had built-in audience awareness, but rarely featured any of the stars of the original and were made on shoestring budgets. Holland poured his heart into *Psycho II*, and with Franklin's knowledge, turned in a very workable script with plenty of nods to Hitchcock's original. An offer went out to Anthony Perkins, with a view to him reprising his most famous role, but he turned it down. The studio began to look for a new Norman Bates, and when Perkins heard that Christopher Walken was up for the part, he quickly changed his mind and signed on-board. Holland tells a different version of events, one in which Perkins still wasn't interested – but changed his mind upon reading the script. Whatever the truth, with Perkins back on-board, Universal elevated the picture to theatrical status. It became a surprise hit with both critics and the public, earning generally positive reviews and $34.7M at the box office in 1983.

Around the same time, Holland wrote (and sold) the scripts for *Cloak and Dagger*, a spy adventure thriller that would be released on a double bill with *The Last Starfighter* and horror movie *Scream for Help*. It would be Michael Winner's treatment of the latter that convinced Holland that he must direct whatever he wrote next to avoid it suffering a similar fate. Having had success with *Class of 1984* and *Psycho II* and proving himself a reliable talent, he now had some clout within Hollywood. While writing *Cloak and Dagger*, he'd had the idea for a story in which a teenager obsessed with late night horror shows is convinced his neighbour is a vampire, but obviously, no one believes him. Holland was happy with the initial idea but couldn't figure out how to expand it further, and so it sat in his head for a year while he continued with other projects. But the story never went away, and it was while talking to John Byers at Columbia Pictures that he finally cracked it – he'd have the teenager seek the help of one of the late night horror show hosts.

Once the central device was in place, the script came together very quickly, and went from treatment to finished screenplay in only three weeks. Columbia Pictures offered to finance the film, providing Holland could bring it in for $9M. As the newly made director would find out, the studio weren't all that interested in his horror-comedy, their sights were set on what they were sure would be the blockbuster of the year, the John Travolta-Jamie Lee Curtis movie, *Perfect*. But Holland was off, and set about casting for what would become known as Fright Night. Key to the picture were the roles of the vampire Jerry Dandrige, the neighbour Charley Brewster, and the horror show host, Peter Vincent (Holland's tribute to Hammer Horror stars Peter Cushing and Vincent Price). The supporting cast would consist of Charley's girlfriend, Amy, his best friend Evil Ed and Dandrige's 'assistant', Billy.

Given that Peter Vincent was written with horror icon Vincent Price in mind, it seemed natural to Holland to approach him for the role, but the actor turned him down, having become tired of the horror genre and being typecast. It was Guy McElwaine, head of Columbia Pictures at the time, who suggested Roddy McDowall for the part.

Having worked together on *Class of 1984*, Holland was more than open to the idea of a reunion. The actor jumped at the chance and had some of his own ideas on how to portray the character. By the time of Fright Night, McDowall was a veteran of some standing. He began acting at an early age, and won his first major role in the film *Scruffy*, when aged nine. Due to the outbreak of World War 2, McDowall's family moved to the United States, where his career took off thanks to appearances in *How Green was my Valley* and *Lassie Come Home* (on which he met lifelong friend, Elizabeth Taylor). Aged only sixteen, he was voted one of the Stars of Tomorrow by exhibitors.

He was fortunate enough to make the transition from child to adult star, and began to take on more theatre work – notably in Orson Welles' adaptation of *Macbeth*. By 1952, he'd again switched back to cinema, making seven pictures for Monogram, before leaving Hollywood to take on Broadway and television – a move which would see him win an Emmy and a Tony award in the same year (1961). Throughout the sixties, the actor would mix film with TV work on a regular basis. He appeared in the legendary *Cleopatra*, winning acclaim for his role, but missing out on an Academy Award nomination when the studio accidently submitted his name in the wrong category (Best Actor instead of Supporting Actor). However, it would be his work on the *Planet of the Apes* series for which he would be remembered. His portrayal of the sympathetic ape Cornelius in the original film won much acclaim, and saw him reprise the role in the second sequel (scheduling conflicts prevented him from appearing in the first sequel, *Beneath the Planet of the Apes*). He would return again in *Conquest of the Planet of the Apes*, playing the son of his original character, and again in its sequel, *Battle for the Planet of the Apes*. For the short-lived TV spin off series, McDowall would play the ape Galen, a character unrelated to the original films.

By the time Fright Night came around, the actor was still much in demand. He'd appeared in various TV shows, including recurring roles in *Fantasy Island* and *Tales of the Golden Monkey* as well as more than ten movies since 1980. As mentioned, he worked with Tom Holland on the surprise hit, *Class of 1984*, and was eager to take on the role of Peter Vincent simply because he'd 'never played a character that old before'. Like the rest of the cast, McDowall was tasked with coming up with his character's backstory and also had some ideas for the old horror movies that had made Peter Vincent famous. His primary inspiration came from the Cowardly Lion in *The Wizard of Oz*, along with bad actors he recalled from his childhood.

The key role of vampire Jerry Dandrige was a little harder to cast. Chris Sarandon had been a jobbing theatre and TV actor for a number of years before getting his big break opposite Al Pacino in *Dog Day Afternoon*, a role for which he was Oscar nominated. He continued to take on theatrical roles (favouring Shakespeare) as well as appearing in such pictures as *Lipstick* and *The Sentinel*, a Michael Winner horror film that all but killed Sarandon's interest in the genre. His previous picture before Fright Night was the Goldie Hawn comedy, *Protocol*. When his agent showed him Tom Holland's script, Sarandon refused to even entertain the idea of appearing in another horror film, but his agent continued to push him to read it. When he finally relented, Sarandon found himself impressed, coming to the conclusion that it was real labour of love that 'had fun with the genre, without making fun of it'. However, he was still cautious, especially given that Holland hadn't directed a feature before. He agreed to meet the first-time director and was quickly taken with him, especially when he [Holland] acted out or described every single shot or scene during their first meeting. Sarandon was sold and signed on to play Dandrige. Like Roddy McDowall, he too had some ideas of his own, many of which would make it into the picture.

The two established names were joined by the newcomer William Ragsdale. The young actor had just one minor credit to his name when he won the lead role of Charley Brewster. Fresh out of acting school, a casting director friend suggested he try out for the part of Rusty in the Peter Bogdanovich film, *Mask*. While that didn't work out (the role went to Eric Stoltz), casting director Jackie Burch, who had also worked on *Cloak and Dagger*, remembered Ragsdale and convinced him to try out for Fright Night. A young Charlie Sheen had been up for the part, but Holland felt that he was too much of a hero, were as Ragsdale was the perfect everyman. It still took four or five auditions before he secured the role, by which point the vast majority of the cast were already in place. Getting the call on Halloween, Ragsdale found himself on the Fright Night stage less than two weeks later.

In contrast, Jonathan Stark, who would play Billy Cole, Dandrige's modern day butler (and possible lover) was cast so early on that he was convinced he'd lost the role after hearing nothing more about it in over six months. Stark had impressed Holland during the audition by playing the role funny instead of evil, leading to the script being refined. The part called for Cole to be well-built, something Stark got round at the initial audition by wearing multiple layers of clothing. In the time between winning the part and shooting actually commencing, he'd had time to bulk up properly.

Stephen Geoffreys managed to get a part in the movie thanks to not being Anthony Michael Hall. Geoffreys and Hall were managed by the same agent at the time, and when Jackie Burch was casting *Weird Science*, she contacted their agent with a view to seeing Anthony Michael Hall for the part of Gary Wallace. Due to a mix up, the agent sent Geoffreys by mistake, which led to an embarrassing meeting. While he wasn't right (or even considered) for *Weird Science*, he did make an impression on Burch. When his agent sent him the Fright Night script, he was shooting comedy *Fraternity Vacation*. He pushed to audition for the role of Charley

Brewster, only to be told they had him in mind for the part of Evil Ed. A little taken back, but still happy to be involved, Geoffreys readily accepted.

There's a little confusion as to when the role of Charley's girlfriend, Amy, was cast. According to some sources, it was the final part to filled, yet during a reunion discussion in 2008, actor William Ragsdale stated that his final audition was with Stephen Geoffreys and Amanda Bearse, who was cast as Amy Peterson. Tom Holland mentioned they'd seen a number of actresses but none had the girl next door quality that Bearse possessed. In an interesting twist, Amanda Bearse had already worked with two of the Fright Night cast before – she'd appeared with Stephen Geoffreys in *Fraternity Vacation* and with Chris Sarandon in 1984's *Protocol*. The remainder of the cast were rounded out by Dorothy Fielding as Judy Brewster and Art Evans as Detective Lennox.

In something of a rarity, Holland and his cast had the luxury of two weeks' rehearsal time prior to the shoot commencing. This gave them time to refine the script and figure out how certain sequences would need to be shot. It also provided the cast with the time to work on their character biographies. Roddy McDowall had plenty of ideas, and saw Peter Vincent as a terrible actor who'd made some awful movies – and was now reliving them via a cable TV show. McDowall was also instrumental in changes made to the end of the movie and Vincent's fate. Chris Sarandon strived to make Jerry more human and sympathetic, despite his vampire nature. It was the actor's idea to have Amy appear to be the reincarnation of one of his lost loves revealed via an old portrait in Jerry's house. It was while doing some research that Sarandon discovered that the vast majority of bats were actually frugivores. He decided his character would probably have a fair bit of fruit bat DNA in his make-up, so had him munching on apples in a number of scenes. The actor explained it as a 'palette cleanser after draining blood from his victims'.

Shooting commenced in the December of 1984 and ran through to late February. Because all studio eyes were on the Travolta/Curtis movie, *Perfect*, the cast and crew of Fright Night were left to their own devices. At $9M, it was the lowest budgeted movie that Columbia had funded in recent times and little was expected from it. The rehearsals had served as a stage play version of the movie and worked out so well that it was rare for Holland to use more than three takes when it came to shooting. Roddy McDowall kept everyone amused during the downtime with stories of old Hollywood, and was rarely without his video camera when not part of a scene. [A keen movie archivist, McDowall was one of the first people ever investigated for copyright infringement, in 1974, when it was discovered he was transferring film prints to tape in an effort to preserve them]. However, the shoot was not without its issues – the most serious of which would be William Ragsdale breaking his ankle during a scene shot on Christmas Eve. The schedule was hastily reworked, with action sequences pushed back to when the actor was able to perform them safely. To get around scenes in which Ragsdale's feet would be visible, the crew made slits in his shoe and covered any exposed parts of the cast with black cloth.

In a sense, the visual effects crew also had a rehearsal period, except theirs was on the big budget 1984 release, *Ghostbusters*. Fright Night would claim to be the first vampire movie to spend over $1M on its effects. Heading up the team was the award winning Richard Edlund, who had begun his career working for fledgling effects company Industrial Light and Magic, on *Star Wars*. He would share an Academy Award for his efforts, and went on to work on both *The Empire Strikes Back* and *Return of the Jedi,* along with *Raiders of the Lost Ark* and *Poltergeist*. Any problems Edlund and his crew might encounter on Fright Night were things they'd already solved while shooting *Ghostbusters*, saving much time and expense.

Much of the hardship the cast had to endure came from the make-up they had to wear to realise their characters. The two who suffered most for their art were Chris Sarandon and Stephen Geoffreys. The final transformation of Dandrige would see Sarandon endure over eight hours of make-up each time it was required for a shot. Given his theatrical background, and to stop himself going stir crazy, the actor assisted the crew in the process by applying the finger nail extensions and hand make-up himself. Geoffreys had it even worse; it took an incredible eighteen hours to create Evil Ed's final form. At one point, while attempting to fill the costumes mouthpiece with a solution to create a drool-saliva effect, the actor complained about the taste – the crew realised to their horror that they were in fact pouring dental glue into the mask (and therefore Geoffrey's mouth).

While other cast members didn't have to endure full make-up, they did need to wear contact lenses for some sequences. At the time, the technology wasn't very advanced, meaning the lenses were made of a tough plastic that was hand painted, lacquered and then polished smooth. Their use rendered most actors practically blind and they could only endure short periods of work with them in. Amanda Bearse found filming incredibly difficult one day and after a scene was stopped because of the pain, it was found the set of lenses she was wearing hadn't been polished. Jonathan Stark could only wear one at time – wearing both made a chase scene impossible for him to shoot without constantly stumbling. Wanting to get a sequence finished, Stephen Geoffrey's kept his lenses in for forty minutes, resulting in scratches to his eyeballs that took many months to heal.

A quick piece of visual effects work also helped the film in another way. Towards the end of the shoot, Holland asked creature designer Randall William Cook if he could come up with a shark mouth for one of the vampires. With neither time or money on his side, Cook spent the weekend creating a crude device and told the director if he focused on the effect for more than a few seconds, the audience would realise just how poorly crafted it was. However, the rig ended up working much better than anticipated and featured in the movie for much longer than expected. More importantly, it provided the basis for Fright Night's iconic poster.

Whatever the cast and crew had to endure for the movie, they did it together, each buoying up the spirits of the other. Indeed, more than one actor involved in Fright Night has since gone on to state it was the happiest filming experience of their career. With shooting completed in the February of 1985, Holland began to assemble his edit in time for the film's August 2nd release date. Having been impressed with Brad Fiedel's work on *The Terminator* score, he was hired to provide the instrumental soundtrack on Fright Night. A novelisation, written by Craig Spector and John Skipp was released to coincide with the film's debut and sought to add more backstory, particularly to Jerry Dandrige.

Columbia were too busy promoting *Perfect* for its June release to give much time or money to Fright Night, though a fairly wide 1,500+ screen/location roll-out was planned. Reviews for the picture were very strong, with Chris Sarandon and Roddy McDowell coming in for much of the praise. Roger Ebert scored it three out of five stars noting that 'Fright Night is not a distinguished movie, but it has a lot of fun being undistinguished. It currently holds a 91% rating at Rotten Tomatoes. The reviews would go some way to helping the picture get noticed as it had little in the way of star power. The make-up and special effects work would also feature heavily in its publicity. In another case of films aimed at a similar demographic opening on the same weekend, Fright Night would go up against the John Hughes comedy, *Weird Science*. There was still strong competition in the guise of *Back to the Future* (now in its fifth weekend) and *National Lampoon's European Vacation*, while *Summer Rental* and *Real Genius* were only a week away. Fright Night's screen count of 1,584 gave it an advantage over *Weird Science*, whose PG-13 rating could potentially attract a wider audience.

Fright Night got off to a great start, making an impressive $6.1M during its opening weekend, slotting in behind *Back to the Future* and *European Vacation* (*Weird Science* dropped in at number four). Given that the studio had largely ignored the picture during its production, they suddenly sat up and took notice – especially now that *Perfect* had crashed and burned to terrible reviews and worse box office. A week later, with two new releases thrown into the mix, Fright Night dropped down to sixth place, but lost only 30% of business compared to its previous weekend. Even before that second frame had begun, the film had recouped its $9M production budget and scored some great word-of-mouth. A big drop occurred in weekend three, caused primarily by the studio's bizarre decision to reduce its screen count by a third. Nevertheless, it was faring better than *Weird Science*, which had already tumbled out of the top ten.

The loss of another 282 screens in the following week, plus increased competition from *Teen Wolf* and the *Ghostbusters* re-issue pushed Fright Night down to eleventh place. Despite the fall, the film had now more than doubled its production budget. It remained in the top twenty for a further month, and while its release was a relatively short one, Fright Night had managed to become something of a sleeper hit for Columbia. Had they not removed it from theatres quite so quickly, it would have easily cleared $30M in takings; as it was the picture had to settle for a total theatrical gross of $24.9M. In terms of horror in 1985, only *A Nightmare on Elm St: Freddy's Revenge*, made more money.

Fright Night went on to perform well on the home video market, which by the mid-eighties, was in full swing. Even if people hadn't heard of the film, the movie's poster which adorned many a video shop window, got them interested enough to take a chance on it. A few years after its release, a comic book series was launched and ran for 27 issues, beginning in 1988. The first two issues followed the events of the movie. Later stories covered the adventures of Charley Brewster and Peter Vincent, as they battled all manner of monsters, including Evil Ed and a resurrected Jerry Dandrige. 1988 also saw the release of a videogame adaptation for the Commodore Amiga which put the player in the role of the vampire, tasked with turning as many people before sunrise.

Talk of a movie sequel soon began to circulate, but it would take four years before *Fright Night 2* saw a very limited release. Producer Herb Jaffe retained the rights to the characters and attempted to get a follow-up off-the-ground, and while Tom Holland was interested in returning to direct, a reduced budget and his commitment to *Child's Play* saw him bow out. Instead, Tommy Lee Wallace, of *Halloween III* fame, stepped in to helm the picture (with Holland's blessing). Both William Ragsdale and Roddy McDowall would return, but like Tom Holland, Chris Sarandon was committed to *Child's Play*, if indeed he had been approached to return in one capacity or another. An early draft of the script was said to contain a return for Amanda Bearse's Amy, but by that point she was involved in *Married....With Children*. According to Wallace, by the time he joined the sequel, the character of Amy was nowhere to be seen, instead replaced by Charley's new girlfriend, Alex. Stephen Geoffreys was approached to reprise his Evil Ed character, but didn't like the script. Instead, he opted to take the lead in *976-Evil*.

The sequel would see Charley in denial that the events of the first movie took place, passing Jerry Dandrige's actions off as those of a bizarre serial killer. When he goes to see Peter Vincent, who has lapsed back into his old TV show ways, he spies four coffins being taken into the house next door and meets a girl called Regine, who is revealed to be Jerry Dandrige's sister, out for revenge. Things are further complicated when Charley is bitten and Peter Vincent institutionalised for attacking Regine live on-air. With so much time having passed since the first film, much of its good will had been lost. Reviews for *Fright Night 2* were poor to average at best, and the studio dumped the film into just 145 theatres in May 1989. It made $2.9M in total.

Despite the film's failure, Roddy McDowall loved playing the character of Peter Vincent and planned to get together with Tom Holland and pitch a third film to Carolco Pictures chairman, Jose Menendez. Sadly, before the meeting could take place, Menendez and his wife, Kitty, were murdered by their sons, Lyle and Erik. It's worth noting that Julie Carmen (who played Regine) claimed during a 2008 cast reunion, that *Fright Night 2* was barely released because the studio was in free-fall after the murders, and pulled all their pictures from theatres. This, however, cannot be the case as the sequel was released in May 1989 and the Menendez murders occurred in August of that same year.

More than 25 years after the original release, a Fright Night remake went into production. Directed by Craig Gillespie of Lars and the Real Girl fame, and written by Marti Noxon, it would follow the template of the original closely. Colin Farrell appeared as Jerry, Anton Yelchin as Charley Brewster and David Tennant as Peter Vincent, who this time around is a Las Vegas magician. They'd be joined by Christopher Mintz-Plasse as Evil Ed and Imogen Poots as Amy. Chris Sarandon would also make a cameo, as a victim of Farrell's vampire. He would be credited as Jay Dee, in a tribute to his original character. The film reviewed very well but struggled to find much of an audience. It made $18.3M in North America, with a further $22.7M overseas. A second film was released two years later, but oddly *Fright Night 2: New Blood* was more or less another retread of the original (and the reboot). None of the cast returned and it debuted to little fanfare on VOD in October 2013.

After the original Fright Night and its sequel, William Ragsdale went on to appear in the sitcom *Herman's Head*, which ran for three seasons. He also starred in the poorly received *Mannequin on the Move* and famously played Ellen's 'final' boyfriend in her TV series. Since then he has had roles in *Gross Pointe, Judging Amy* and *Justified*, while also appearing in numerous TV movies. It's arguable that Fright Night remains his biggest movie success, but unlike a number of 80s stars, he has worked consistently in the intervening years. Amanda Bearse appeared in the hit sitcom *Married....With Children*, where she also turned her hand to directing a number of episodes. Since that time, she has appeared on screen only occasionally, opting to direct instead of act. Stephen Geoffreys appeared in horror *976-Evil* and had a supporting role in *At Close Range*, but struggled to find further work. More than one observer has commented that his refusal to return for *Fright Night 2* may have done his career more damage, though given the film's lack of success, this is questionable. During the 1990s, he appeared in a number of gay pornographic movies (under the alias Sam Ritter) before returning to mainstream movie work with 2007's *Sick Girl.*

Chris Sarandon would appear in the film he's most notably famous for, *The Princess Bride*, in 1987. The romantic comedy saw him portray villain, Prince Humperdinck. He went on to work again with Tom Holland on the demonic doll flick, *Child's Play* and lent his voice to Jack Skellington in the beloved *Nightmare Before Christmas*. Since then he's mixed smaller movies with TV and theatre. Even with a huge body of work behind him, Roddy McDowall continued to act at an almost frightening pace. Along with TV, movie and voiceover work, came appearances in such documentaries as The *Magical World of Chuck Jones* and *The Fantasy Worlds of Irwin Allen*. He died of complications from lung cancer on October 3rd 1998. Tom Holland followed up Fright Night by directing Whoopi Goldberg in the cop comedy, *Fatal Beauty*, after which he co-created the cult horror hit, *Child's Play*. In the 1990s, he directed the Stephen King adaptations *Thinner* and *The Langoliers*, along with a number of TV movies. In 2013, he created the web-based horror series, *Twisted Tales*, and at the time of writing is working on another King story, *The Ten O'Clock People*.

Like much horror released in the 1980s, Fright Night's effects don't stand up quite so well but are still very effective. Its light relief complements the more tense and horrific moments. Even now, it is easy to see the passion and fun the cast and crew had making it and all concerned remain proud of their achievement. Indeed, when the studio refused to fund a commentary track for a DVD release, the cast and crew assembled and recorded not one but two of their own (available via the Icons of Horror website). The soundtrack is a perfect slice of 80s synth too, and while McDowall came in for much praise during the film's initial release, it really is Sarandon's show. He adds many layers to the character, showing him as seductive, frightening and even vulnerable. Fright Night remains an enjoyable horror comedy that treads the line between them both perfectly.

Oh, you're so cool, Brewster

If you're looking for fun and scares, why not try one of these…

An American Werewolf in London

John Landis' jet-black horror comedy remains a lesson in special effects and genre splicing. When two Americans take a shortcut across the moors, they end up encountering something that leaves one of them dead and the other much worse. Aided by Rick Baker's revolutionary (and award-winning) make-up work, the film is still rightly seen by many as the yardstick for all werewolf movies – and its transformation scene is still unrivalled.

Despite the comedy of some of the situations, the film has more than its fair share of horrific and terrifying moments, none more so than the nightmare-within-a-nightmare sequence and the pursuit in the Underground station. An American Werewolf is one of the best horror movies of the decade and indeed, of all time. It also achieves that rare trick at making an audience laugh while simultaneously horrifying them.

Trivia: The film was actually written in 1969 and inspired by a bizarre burial ritual Landis witnessed in Yugoslavia when working on *Kelly's Heroes*.

Poltergeist

A typical everyday family move into a new home, little suspecting the horror that awaits them, and in particular, their young daughter Carol Anne. After she begins communicating with something inside the TV, strange things begin to occur that soon escalate in their ferocity. The family decide to enlist the help of a group of parapsychologists who discover there is more than one spirit invading the house and that they're being controlled by the 'beast'

A frightening piece of entertainment, made all the more real by the perfectly average surroundings. The story behind the film is equally as interesting, being that there is to this day, much conjecture as to who truly directed it – the named director Tobe Hooper or its producer (and story creator), Steven Spielberg. Whoever was responsible, Poltergeist is a great horror movie that often gets forgotten thanks to the period being heavy on the gore and nasties.

Trivia: For the swimming pool sequence, real human skeletons were used as they were cheaper to buy than the manufactured plastic ones.

House

Written by Fred Dekker, who directed *The Monster Squad*, House is the tale of an author who moves into his recently deceased aunt's old house. Still coming to terms with his tour of Vietnam, divorce and his missing son, Roger Cobb begins having nightmares he finds seeping into reality. As things escalate, Cobb discovers a portal into another dimension were even more horrors, and perhaps redemption awaits.

House was a minor hit upon release in 1987 and was followed by three sequels, though only the final (*House IV*) had any real connection with the original. The film blends horror and comedy, favouring the former over the latter, unlike *House 2: The Second Story*, which is a more lightweight affair. An enjoyable but slight movie, House is often forgotten amongst the bigger horror hits of the decade.

Trivia: House was originally written to be part of a *Twilight Zone*-style horror anthology. When the project failed to get off the ground, Dekker expanded the idea into a feature-length movie.

The Sure Thing

A sure thing comes once in a lifetime… but the real thing lasts forever

Studio: Embassy Pictures
Release Date: March 1st 1985
Director: Rob Reiner
Starring: John Cusack, Daphne Zuniga
Budget: $4.5M – 2015 Equivalent: $10M
U.S Box Office: $18.1M – 2015 Equivalent: $40.3M

Walter 'Gib' Gibson is having no luck with the girls at his college. Sympathetic, his friend Lance offers him a 'Sure Thing' – a no-strings attached liaison with a beautiful girl. All he has to do is get across the country in time for Spring Break. But the path of true lust is never a smooth one, especially when Gib finds himself car sharing with Alison Bradbury, a girl with whom he had a disastrous study date...

In the early 1980s, the teenage movie genre was split into two factions. On the one side was raunchy comedy, spurred on by the massive success of *Porky's* and its many imitators. On the other, was the more thoughtful comedy-drama, buoyed by the likes of John Hughes' *Sixteen Candles* and Amy Heckerling's *Fast Times at Ridgemont High*. These pictures attempted to give cinema-goers a more realistic portrayal of the struggles (and dreams) the modern teenager lived with – while also attempting to make money from the demographic that made up most of the audience. While Hughes was likely the most influential, and certainly the one recalled when talking about teen movies of the 1980s, that's not to say there weren't others of equal, if not better, standing. The same went for the stars of these pictures; Molly Ringwald and Anthony Michael Hall may have been synonymous with the time and the genre, but for many, no one played the awkward or lovelorn college student better than John Cusack. The actor would appear in a number of teen comedies throughout the decade, but it would be his work on The Sure Thing, that brought him to the public's attention.

The idea for The Sure Thing was based on the real-life experience of writer Steve L. Bloom. Opting to go to Brown College in New England, Bloom was regaled with tales of 'Wonderful Wednesday' by his friend Wayne, who attended college in Atlanta. Wayne explained that on the day groups of students would come together at a local hotel and get up to all sorts of no-good. Having listened to

Bloom's tales of failure with the opposite sex, Wayne set him up with a 'sure thing' – a no-strings attached sexual encounter. All he had to do was get himself there for Spring Break and the rest would be taken care of. Sharing a car with a group of students, Bloom did indeed get himself there, though never eluded as to whether he met Wayne's sure thing. What it did do was inspire the young student to write a short story/treatment about someone placed in the same situation and the moral decisions he faced (The character at this point was named Richard Gowens). After graduating, Bloom went on to attend film school at USC, where he was joined by his old college roommate, Jonathan Roberts. While at Brown, Roberts (and others) had been responsible for writing the satirical guide, *The Preppy Handbook*.

The duo decided to write something together based around Bloom's Sure Thing story. They aligned themselves with Roger Birnbaum, an executive who was looking to make the jump to producing and began to pitch the idea to anyone who would listen. Studio after studio turned it down – in part because the only thing the trio could present was an idea; they had no script or even examples of their writing, and nothing to prove they could turn in a useable screenplay. They had begun to resign themselves to the fact that the story would not get produced. Their last shot was Embassy Pictures, pitching to Jeff Young. According to Roberts, the pitch they gave turned out to be longer than the actual movie. Young was impressed by the enthusiasm and asked for the weekend to think about it, but

Birnbaum knew that if they waited, the answer would be no. [In a documentary produced to celebrate the film's 20th anniversary, Embassy executive Lindsay Doran, who was in the room for the pitch, states that Young was indeed planning on turning the film down because while he liked the story, he felt it was too familiar and the writers too much of a risk. It also appeared very similar *to It Happened One Night*].

The fledgling producer asked the writers to step outside while he talked with Jeff Young on a one-to-one basis. In Birnbaum's own words, he all but got on his knees and begged Young to take a chance with The Sure Thing. He explained that the writers would work for scale and produce as many drafts as Young felt were required – also at scale. The budget would be kept low ($4.5-6M) so even if things didn't work out, the risk for Embassy would be minimal. Birnbaum himself was taking a chance, he knew if The Sure Thing failed his career as a producer would be a short one. The second pitch worked, and Young agreed to take a chance on the writers and greenlight the picture. The duo set to work in the latter half of 1982 on an outline script, with a second draft dated April 20th 1983. The script would get at least one more pass prior to shooting commencing, at the hands of the man Embassy Pictures had chosen to direct – Rob Reiner.

Rob Reiner was born in 1947 to legendary comedian/writer/director Carl Reiner and his wife Estelle. His first break into showbiz came via bit parts in such 1960s fare as *Batman, The Beverly Hillbillies* and *The Andy Griffith Show*, before he switched to writing for *The Smothers Brothers Comedy Hour*. His big break would come in 1971, playing the role of Michael Stivic in the hit sitcom *All in the Family*. Reiner would appear in eight seasons of the show – 174 episodes in all, and win two Emmy awards, as well as being nominated five times for a Golden Globe. He also contributed three scripts to the show and continued to create and write other projects, famously co-scripting the first episode of *Happy Days* and directing the short TV film, *Sonny Boy*. After leaving the show in 1978 (*All in the Family* would run for another season and receive a four-season spin off in the guise of *Archie Bunker's Place*), Reiner began developing the rock mockumentary *This is Spinal Tap*, on which he would go on to make his feature directorial debut for Embassy Pictures.

It was while working on *Spinal Tap* that he received the script for The Sure Thing. Again, according to Embassy exec Lindsay Doran, Reiner was the only director they sent the script to, partly because they'd had a positive experience working with him on *Spinal Tap*. They also knew he'd be able to punch up the latest draft of the script with his own thoughts and ideas. The director got to work while still assembling the edit of his first movie (a monumental task given the huge amount of footage that was shot). Reiner took the script apart and began with the two main characters of Walter 'Gib' Gibson and Alison Bradbury. Instead of creating situations and dropping them in, he worked on expanding their depth, allowing the situations to become almost secondary to the emotional obstacles they faced. Both Bloom and Roberts credit Reiner for improving all aspects of the script, from the dialogue and pace to the overall structure.

With all parties happy, work could begin on casting. The producers, which now included Henry Winkler, turned to Roger Birnbaum's friend Fred Roos for a recommendation. At the time, Roos was working with Francis Ford Coppola's Zoetrope Productions, but had previously been a casting director of some standing. He'd been responsible for casting *The Godfather, Five Easy Pieces* and *American Graffiti*, amongst many other movies and TV shows and recommended fellow Zoetrope employees Jane Jenkins and Janet Hirshenson. With Reiner and Birnbaum, the duo discussed the budget, the script and the type of people they had in mind for each role. One of the biggest restrictions was budget – an established or in-demand player would cost a lot more to cast and may also come with baggage. A relative unknown would obviously be cheaper, but with limited experience, the casting team (and by extension the production itself) would not be sure what they would be getting. For the role of Gib, Anthony Edwards' name was put forward; at that point the young actor had already appeared in a number of roles, including a small part in *Fast Times at Ridgemont High* and a recurring role in the TV series, *It Takes Two*. He was also set to make a name for himself as Gilbert in *Revenge of the Nerds*, a picture set to debut in the summer of 1984.

At the same time, another actor came in to try out for the role and impressed the casting team enough for them to inform Rob Reiner that he should consider him for the part over Edwards. John Cusack was born into an acting family – his father was an actor and documentary film-maker and siblings Susie, Ann, Bill and in particular, Joan, have all acted. At a young age, John became part of the Piven Theatre Workshop, set up and run by the parents of one of his oldest friends, Jeremy. It wasn't long before he made his on-screen acting debut in the Rob Lowe/Andrew McCarthy comedy *Class* (it also marked the first of many collaborations with his sister Joan). He worked with John Hughes next, on *Sixteen Candles*, playing a geek friend of Anthony Michael Hall's Farmer Ted and followed that up with a part in *Grandview U.S.A.* The Sure Thing looked set to be his fourth film based on the recommendation of Jenkins and Hirshenson, but Rob Reiner wasn't interested and opted not to see Cusack audition.

The issue Reiner had with Cusack was his age – at 17 he was still classed as a minor, and that would restrict the amount of hours he could legally work on set each day. It might also extend the length of the shoot and that would raise costs. Anthony Edwards remained the frontrunner but while the director was in Los Angeles the casting team informed him that Cusack was also in town, and that while he may not be right for The Sure Thing, Reiner should meet with him with an eye to using him on a future project. The actor was still struggling to find work and had taken to sleeping on friend's couches between attending as many auditions as possible. When Cusack came in, the director was blown away and knew that he had to cast him over anyone else he'd seen – including Edwards. But the age issue still remained, and the shoot was set to commence a full three months before Cusack would turn eighteen. Delaying was out of the question, and the budget didn't allow for the kind of schedule that would be required to accommodate the restricted shooting hours.

The only solution, if they wanted Cusack as the lead, was for him to seek emancipation from his parents. That would mean they were not responsible for their son's well being, his choices or his earnings – he would be, for all intents and purposes (and, more importantly, in the eyes of the law), an adult. It also allowed him to pick the hours he wished to work, enabling the production to proceed as if Cusack was 18. Roger Birnbaum agreed to become the actor's legal guardian during the shoot, and a teacher was on set most days to help Cusack continue his education. Even though Anthony Edwards was now out of the running, Reiner kept him on-board and set him to play Lance, Gib's best friend and the one who sets him up with The Sure Thing. Noted Swedish actress Viveca Lindfors was cast as Gib's lecturer Professor Taub. Lindfors was already a major player in her native land before making the jump to Hollywood in the mid-1940s, and by the time she won the part in The Sure Thing, had already appeared in over sixty film and TV shows.

The small, but essential, role of Gary Cooper proved a difficult one to cast. Despite the character (and his partner) appearing on-screen for only a short amount of time, they couldn't find anyone who could make the role work. At one stage, there was something of a crisis of confidence, and Reiner and Co. discussed completely re-writing the part. It was only when a young Tim Robbins tried out for the role, and played it funny instead of straight, did they realise what had been missing from the other auditions they'd seen. In the original draft, Robbins and his partner, played by Lisa Jane Persky, were written to be constantly bickering. The part was rewritten to have them singing show tunes for much of their screen time, something that worked much better (and funnier) when in contrast to Gib and Alison's behaviour. Other minor roles went to Boyd Gaines and Joshua Cadman, along with a cameo for Steve Pink, who would go on to write *Grosse Pointe Blank* with Cusack some years later.

The hunt was now on for the two female leads, Alison Bradbury and the 'sure thing' herself. Reiner and the casting team saw a number of girls for both parts, but none quite had the qualities they were looking for. Daphne Zuniga, a young actress who'd had a couple of minor roles at that point, auditioned very well as Alison, and had a ready chemistry when screen tested with Cusack. By her own admission, Alison was very similar to Zuniga – both very serious about their work, very strict and methodical. In the documentary, *The Road to The Sure Thing*, Rob Reiner states that one of the reasons he cast Daphne Zuniga was because she was the kind of smart girl next door he could have seen himself dating back in college. The role of the nameless 'sure thing' was another difficult one to cast, and along with the role of Alison, one of the last ones to fall into place. Again, they saw many young girls, both actresses and models, before Nicolette Sheridan walked into the room. At the time, she had no actual acting credit to her name, though she would appear in the TV show *Paper Dolls* prior to the release of The Sure Thing. However, despite the lack of experience, she auditioned very well and both Reiner and Birnbaum knew they'd found the one, informing Sheridan that she'd got the part as she was on the way to her next audition.

With casting complete, and the shooting script ready, principal photography began on March 5th 1984 (two days before *This is Spinal Tap* made its theatrical debut). The shoot was set to run for 48 days, with the majority of filming taking place in Los Angeles and Stockton, California. Reiner was very keen to let the actors ad lib and come up with their own ideas and takes for each scene. Cusack flourished in this and had much input throughout the shoot. He would later state that for every ten ideas he threw out there, Reiner would take on at least three or four. This gave the young actor more confidence, and while Zuniga was more comfortable sticking to the script, she soon warmed to the improvisation – in some ways mirroring the way her character comes out of her shell. Sheridan's first scene to be shot was the one featured in the opening titles, with her character on the beach. The costume department went through at least twenty different bikinis before settling on a plain and simple white one – the idea being that the outfit should not be the centre of attention, rather the Sure Thing's body should be. A large house just behind that opening beach shot would be utilised for the picture's dream sequences.

It was John Cusack who came up with the beer shotgunning idea too, which Reiner used in a number of scenes. The script called for a different kind of trick, but when Cusack showed the director what he could do, it was written in. The first actual scene to be shot was the one in which Gib goes to meet Alison to study, but their first rooftop scene, which takes place moments later in the film, was shot some time later. This wouldn't be the only time when two seemingly follow-on scenes where shot many weeks apart. The pool sequence for example – the first part when Cusack's tirade ends with him diving into the water was shot near the start of filming, but the following scene, in which he stands drenched and waiting for Alison to appear, was shot a month later. This meant the continuity people had to match the character's wet clothes between the two scenes. The pool sequence itself was shot three times – each one ending with Cusack falling into the water a different way. Daphne Zuniga didn't get off scot-free either. In the scene where she flashes another car, the actress removed her bra with such force that it also pulled off the tape that was meant to be covering her breasts.

A story from Rob Reiner's father, Carl, helped create one of the most memorable sequences in the film. When Alison gets picked up after hitchhiking, she narrowly avoids being assaulted thanks to a seemingly crazed Gib. Reiner senior recounted a story to his son, about seeing a girl being beat up by a guy in the street. Knowing he couldn't win a straight fight, he ran over to the fighting couple and began to act even crazier than the guy hitting the girl, forcing him to eventually flee. A variation of this idea was written into the script and played not only as a great scene in itself, but helped to show Alison's resistance to Gib softening. The sequence also reinforced Reiner and Birnbaum's idea that only things that could realistically happen would make it into the picture. Another such example was the bar scene – this time based around a Christmas Eve writer Steve L. Bloom spent stuck in a strip joint. The part also led to a rights issue; originally Gib and the barflies were meant to sing *White Christmas* but they couldn't get permission to use the song, *The Christmas Song* standing in for it instead.

By-and-large, the shoot continued to go smoothly, but ran into a minor issue with the party scene that takes place toward the end of the picture. The budget (rumoured to be between $4.5-6M) was fairly stretched as it was, and there was little in the way of money to clothe a bunch of partygoers (or dress the scene). To get around the issue, costume designer Durinda Wood came up with the novel idea of having a competition – $100 to the best dressed partygoer. It meant that, major players aside, the cast of extras clothed themselves. Further money was saved on at least one set too. Instead of creating the huge beer bottle collection that adorns the wall in Lance's bedroom, the crew simply hired one wholesale that they'd found in a local college dorm room while scouting locations. As filming drew to close, Viveca Lindfors arrived on set to shoot her scenes. While the actress only appeared in three quite short sequences, she made a memorable impression, particularly in the picture's final moments. Filming wrapped on May 3rd, with the final piece shot being the last scene of the movie.

Everyone went their separate ways as Reiner began to assemble his first cut. In the meantime, *This is Spinal Tap* had come-and-gone, and while it didn't set the box office alight, it would go on to become one of the biggest cult classics of all time. Even if The Sure Thing didn't make much of a splash, Reiner was already talking up a future project tentatively titled *When Harry Met Sally...* The soundtrack was pulled together and would feature such artists as Huey Lewis and the News, The Eagles, Wang Chung and Rod Stewart, who provided the opening track, Infatuation. The initial edit opened with Alison looking for a ride back west but this was removed so as to establish the characters before anything else. The finale was also refined, and instead of cutting back-and-forth between the two couples, Reiner chose to focus more on Alison and her boyfriend, removing the scene in which the Sure Thing asks Gib if he loves her ('her' being the Sure Thing). With the release set for March 1st 1985, the studio tested the near-completed picture in St. Louis and Paramus, New

Jersey. Audiences loved it and warmed to characters; Cusack in particular came in for much praise and the film was rated highly for keeping its footing firmly in reality.

When critics got to see the finished picture, their praise was much the same. Roger Ebert called it a 'small miracle' for the way it handled teenage romance, especially in an era where sex comedies such as *Porky's* had become the norm. Similarly, Janet Maslin, writing in the New York Times stated that The Sure Thing proved that 'Traditional romantic comedy can be adapted to suit the teenage trade'. The picture currently holds an impressive 87% approval rating on Rotten Tomatoes. Unlike today, March of 1985 was a relatively quiet one. Back in those days, potential summer blockbusters stuck strictly to the May-July release window. At the time *Beverly Hills Cop,* which had been released back in December 1984, was still in the top spot, a place it had occupied for twelve straight weeks.

The Sure Thing didn't need a big start – a solid opening and a decent follow-up frame would enable it to recoup its modest production budget. It was set to open on the same weekend as *Missing in Action II: The Beginning* (a follow-up that came just four months after the release of the original picture). It wouldn't offer much in the way of direct competition, but *The Breakfast Club*, which was still going strong, certainly would. The following week would see no major releases opening but the week after bought *Porky's Revenge* and *The*

Last Dragon, with *Police Academy 2: Their First Assignment*, waiting in the wings. On its debut weekend at 1,115 locations, The Sure Thing slotted into fifth place, making a not-bad $3.1M. Given the film's lack of star power or hype, chances are the studio was quite pleased with that figure. It was also more than two thirds of what *This is Spinal Tap* made in its entire theatrical run. *The Breakfast Club* was one step ahead, making around $500K more while *Beverly Hills Cop* continued defy belief, making $5.1M on its thirteenth weekend.

A week later, The Sure Thing moved up into fourth place and saw a drop of only 7.4% on the previous weekend's taking. By the end of its tenth day on release, it had recouped its budget and got ready for the onslaught of *Porky's Revenge*. *Witness*, the Harrison Ford drama, had also ended *Beverly Hills Cop's* run at the top. Weekend three saw no change in position for The Sure Thing as it crossed the $10M mark and dipped another 7% on the last frame. Sadly, a week later with four major releases entering the fray, it was all change. *Friday the 13th – Part V* took the top spot, *Porky's Revenge* dropped in behind while *The Last Dragon, Baby: Secret of the Lost Legend* and *Mask* (which expanded out of limited release) ensured it was an all-new top five. The Sure Thing dropped down to eighth place and lost a hundred or so locations in the process. More new releases (and a re-issued *Return of the Jedi*) saw the picture tumble outside the top ten but it continued to play well right up until its exit from theatres and ended up with a solid $18.1M – more than tripling its production budget. The bikini-clad Nicolette Sheridan adorning the poster may well have been a factor in the film become a success on the home video market too.

The Sure Thing showed John Cusack was adept at being both a comedic lead and somewhat serious actor. Despite being successful at roughly the same time, he was rarely lumped in with The Brat Pack. His next picture, the criminally-neglected (and brilliant) *Better Off Dead* was another romantic comedy, though a lot less grounded in reality. While not a success, it too proved popular on video. He moved on to more serious fare with *The Journey of Natty Gann*, before re-teaming with Rob Reiner for a minor role in *Stand by Me*. Two further teen-comedies followed – *One Crazy Summer* (with Demi Moore) and *Hot Pursuit*, and then a reunion with Tim Robbins on the music industry satire, *Tapeheads*. But Cusack was eager to be taken seriously and made the switch to more adult-oriented fare with *Eight Men Out*, TV movie *Fat Man and Little Boy* and as Roy Dillon in the well-received picture *The Grifters*, opposite Annette Benning and Angelica Houston. He also created a memorable character in Lloyd Dobler, star of Cameron Crowe's romantic drama, *Say Anything....*

In the early 1990s, he worked twice with Woody Allen. First on *Shadows and Fog* and again on *Bullets Over Broadway*. Even though he gave a spirited performance in the latter, he was the only one of the four leads who was not nominated for an Academy

Award. He went on to appear opposite Anthony Hopkins in *The Road to Wellville* and Al Pacino in *City Hall*. In the later third of the decade, he stepped up his output, appearing in summer blockbuster *Con Air*, lending his voice to the animated *Anastasia* and playing a hitman attending his high school reunion in arguably his best film, *Grosse Pointe Blank*. He rounded out the year by appearing in Clint Eastwood's *Midnight in the Garden of Good and Evil*.

As the millennium approached, he continued to work at quite a pace, winning strong notices for *Being John Malkovich*. That was followed up by a trilogy of romantic comedies – *High Fidelity* (featuring a cameo by Tim Robbins), *American Sweethearts* and *Serendipity*. He switched again later in the new decade, adding horror (*Identity*, *1408*) and thriller (*The Ice Harvest, Runaway Jury*) to his repertoire. He'd have one more major hit, the disaster flick *2012*, and one more throwback to his teen years in *Hot Tub Time Machine* before his career took something of an odd path. While he has continued to work consistently, it has been on much smaller movies in most cases, or taking a cameo part in an ensemble picture. He has continued to diversify, going so far as to appear as a villain in a number of features – though sadly few saw the inside of a movie theatre. He remains a popular actor and has found a whole new audience thanks to the success of *Dragon Blade*, an action adventure released in 2015 that saw him team up with Jackie Chan.

Post-The Sure Thing, Daphne Zuniga appeared in a number of smaller movies and one-off TV roles, before scoring the female lead in the Mel Brooks' Star Wars spoof, *Spaceballs*. She, then, appeared opposite Tom Berenger in *Last Rites* and Eric Stoltz in *The Fly II*. However, her most enduring role came in 1992 when she landed the part of Jo Reynolds in the Aaron Spelling show, *Melrose Place* – a spin-off of the hugely successful *Beverly Hills 90210*. She would stay with the show for four seasons and also had a cameo as the same character in the pilot episode of a further spin-off entitled *Models Inc.* When she left *Melrose Place* in 1996, she struggled to find the same level of success and appeared in a string of low budget films and TV movies. She returned to episodic drama in *American Dreams* (2004), *Beautiful People* (2005) and *One Tree Hill* (2008). She also had chance to return to two of her earlier roles, as Jo Reynolds for the short-lived return of *Melrose Place* and lending her voice to Princess Vespa for *Spaceballs: The Animated TV Series*.

Tim Robbins went on to have a hugely successful career as an actor, writer and director. He appeared in such notable pictures *as Jacob's Ladder, The Shawshank Redemption* and *The Player*. He also directed *Bob Roberts* (which featured John Cusack), *Cradle Will Rock* and the critically-acclaimed *Dead Man Walking*, which starred Sean Penn and Susan Sarandon. Anthony Edwards appeared opposite Tom Cruise in the smash hit *Top Gun* in 1986, but it was the hugely successful drama, *ER*, for which he remains best known for to this day. As an actress of some standing, Viveca Lindfors continued to appear in film and TV shows throughout the remainder of the 1980s and well into the 90s, including a part in the original *Stargate* movie. She passed away in 1995. As for The Sure Thing herself, Nicolette Sheridan, she followed a similar path to Daphne Zuniga, winning a recurring role in the hit drama *Knots Landing*. Throughout the 1990s, she appeared in a number of TV movies, before landing the part of Edie Britt in the hugely popular *Desperate Housewives*. Sadly, after her exit from the show, she spent more time in court suing the network for wrongful dismissal than in acting roles.

Roger Birnbaum went on to have very successful career as a movie producer, before forming the production company Spyglass Entertainment. Over the last 25 years, he's worked on the *Rush Hour* series, *Bruce Almighty* (and its sequel), *The Legend of Zorro, Wanted* and many, many more. Following his work on The Sure Thing, Rob Reiner went on to direct two of the most popular romantic comedy dramas ever made in the guise of *The Princess Bride* and *When Harry Met Sally....*He won acclaim for his work on the Stephen King adaptations *Stand by Me* and *Misery* and saw success with *A Few Good Men, The American President* and *The Bucket List*. He has also continued to write, produce and act, appearing in the Martin Scorsese picture *The Wolf of Wall Street*.

Even at the time of its release, The Sure Thing was a light romantic comedy, far and away from the nudity-filled sex romps out around the same time. Compared to more modern teen movies such as the *American Pie* Series, it seems tamer still, yet that is part of its timeless charm. Birnbaum, along with Reiner, Bloom and Roberts set out to see if they could take a 1930s love story and modernise it for a contemporary teenage audience – something that many felt they achieved. The film never talks down to the viewer and the chemistry of the two leads is there for all to see. The Sure Thing may not make any top romantic comedy lists but is more than worthy of a place amongst the best of them.

Did you enjoy The Sure Thing? Try one of these…

Better Off Dead

An off-beat comedy that stars John Cusack as the recently dumped Lane Myer and his attempts to kill himself. Living with his bizarre family, that includes his genius younger brother and a mother who is quite literally the worst cook in the world, Myer's life gets worse when he challenges the school jock (and the guy who stole his girlfriend) to a skiing competition.

Making his directorial debut, Savage Steve Holland packs the film with wacky characters and situations, including an animated title sequence, a stop-motion hamburger-led music video and a psychopathic newspaper boy. Cusack is perfectly cast as the lovelorn lead and is ably supported by the likes of Curtis Armstrong's Charles De Mar. Better Off Dead is the ultimate underrated (and barely-seen) jewel of the 1980s.

Trivia: Despite a really great critical reception, Cusack famously hated the movie and told Holland as much when he screened it prior to the pair commencing work on *One Crazy Summer.*

Summer School

Mark Harmon stars as gym teacher Freddy Shoop, a guy more than ready for summer vacation with his girlfriend. When the planned summer school teacher quits after winning the lottery, Shoop finds himself blackmailed into taking on the job by the vice principal. Tasked with getting a bunch of oddballs and dropouts through remedial English is not the summer he had planned.

However, the group form a bond of sorts, especially when Shoop grants each student a favour, providing they study in return. This leads to him helping one of them learn to drive, go to Lamaze classes with another and even allowing a classroom screening of *The Texas Chainsaw Massacre*. Summer School is a slight but hugely enjoyable comedy that was minor hit in North America and popular on the home video market.

Trivia: The original Summer School teacher is played by Carl Reiner, the film's director.

Say Anything…

What could essentially be known as the final part of the John Cusack growing pains trilogy (along with *The Sure Thing* and *Better Off Dead*), Say Anything… was the directorial debut of *Rolling Stone* reporter, Cameron Crowe. After graduating, Lloyd Dobler decides to seize life by both hands and asks the super-smart Diane Court out on a date. Much to their surprise, the couple hit it off, but as they begin to fall love, realise the path isn't always a smooth one.

A funny, poignant movie with a great turn from both Cusack and Ione Skye, along with strong support from the likes of Lily Taylor, John Mahoney and John's sister, Joan. Perhaps best known for the *'In Your Eyes'* scene, Say Anything… is a wonderful picture to which anyone who has ever been in love can relate.

Trivia: In the iconic 'radio above the head' sequence, the original track used was *Bonin in the Graveyard* by the band Fishbone, of which Cusack was a huge fan. Peter Gabriel's *In Your Eyes* was added in post-production.

Cobra

Crime is a disease. Meet the cure.

Studio: Warner Bros.

Release Date: May 23rd 1986

Director: George P. Cosmatos

Starring: Sylvester Stallone

Budget: $25M – 2015 Equivalent: $57.3M

U.S Box Office: $49M – 2015 Equivalent: $105.2M

When Los Angeles finds itself terrorised by the brutal Night Slasher and his New World cult, Marion 'Cobra' Cobretti of the Zombie Squad is called in to hunt them down. An unconventional cop, he represents the police department's last resort. But when a witness to a Night Slasher murder escapes with her life, Cobra must go on the run to protect her, even if means taking on the killer and his entire army.

By the early 1980s, Sylvester Stallone was already a major star. He'd seen dramatic and financial success with *Rocky* and its sequels and given America another everyday hero in the guise of John Rambo and *First Blood*. The actor had proven himself to be something of an all-round talent, capable of not only acting, but writing and directing too. Yet, when a troubled script came his way, one that had already been through numerous re-writes and over a million dollar's' worth of development, even he wasn't sure they'd got the right person for the job. Nonetheless, Stallone signed on the dotted line to re-write and star in *Beverly Hills Cop*.

How *Beverly Hills Cop* came into existence is a tale of some dispute. According to an interview published in the New York Times to mark the film's release, Michael Eisner claims the idea was inspired by an incident that took place in Hollywood in the mid-1970s. Driving a station wagon that had clearly seen better days, he was pulled over for speeding and found himself impressed (and annoyed) by the police officer's efficient manner and condescending attitude. Reflecting on the incident a short time later, he realised the cop was more offended by the car (than his crime) given that it didn't fit the Hollywood image. Returning to the Paramount lot, he talked with his assistant Don Simpson and stated there could be some value in a story about a Beverly Hills police officer and his day-to-day dealings with the rich and famous. Yet despite numerous attempts, no one was able to crack the story.

However, Simpson claimed he came up with the idea for *Beverly Hills Cop* a couple of years after Eisner's run-in had taken place and that it was he who also introduced the 'fish-out-of-water' angle – that being an East-LA cop relocating to a Beverly Hills precinct. He pitched the idea to screenwriter Danilo Bach in 1977, who began working on the concept, only with little progress. Further attempts were made to develop the story, but it was only when Bach returned to the idea in 1981, that he cracked it. *Beverly Drive* as it was then known, featured a Pittsburgh cop named Elly Axel, who comes out to Hollywood to investigate the murder of an old friend and butts heads with the local police force and a successful businessman, whom he is convinced is behind the crime. At this point, the script was more straight action than comedy, and after Bach gave it another pass, Simpson bought in other writers.

After *Flashdance* became a hit in 1983, Simpson along with his producing partner, Jerry Bruckheimer, decided to brush off the *Beverly Drive* script and make it their next project, hiring Daniel Petrie Jr. to rework it. Petrie punched up the fish-out of-water elements, finally creating a good balance between action and comedy. The producers (and Paramount) loved what had now become *Beverly Hills Cop*. Elly became Axel Foley, a Detroit cop out in Beverly Hills investigating the murder of an old school friend. Simpson pushed to cast Mickey Rourke in the lead role and paid $400,000 to keep him under contract while further changes were made to the script. Delays would see Rourke leave the project; he opted to appear in *The Pope of Greenwich Village* instead. Sometime later, and with some surprise, the producers received news that Sylvester Stallone had now signed on to star as the lead, and having read the script, planned on re-writing it to his strengths.

By his own admission, Stallone thought the script had been sent to him by accident. The actor had spent many years struggling to make a career (he made his debut in the soft-porn feature *The Party at Kitty and Stud's*) and ended up taking on numerous bit-parts before landing a starring role in the 1974 drama, *The Lords of Flatbush*. A year later, he appeared in *Capone* and the cult classic, *Death Race 2000*. However, it was what he did next that essentially set up his career for life. The history behind *Rocky*'s creation is the stuff of Hollywood legend. After watching Muhammad Ali fight Chuck Wepner, Stallone came home and wrote for three twenty hour days, at the end of which he had the script for *Rocky*. He began to shop it around various studios and was offered $300,000 by Irwin Winkler and Robert Chartoff for the rights, who planned to hire Robert Redford or Burt Reynolds for the lead. However, Stallone had other ideas and held fast – if the picture was to be made, he was to be the star. After much discussion and a substantial cut in its proposed budget, the actor got his way.

Rocky was a phenomenal success, both critically and financially. It went on to be nominated for ten Academy Awards, winning three of them. The writer/actor quickly moved into directing with *Paradise*

Alley in 1978 along with a starring role in *F.I.S.T.* A year later, he returned to writing, producing the screenplay for *Rocky II*, which he also starred in and directed. Again, the film was a smash hit, grossing over $200M worldwide. He went on to appear with Michael Caine in war drama *Escape to Victory* and in the well-received thriller *Nighthawks*, opposite Billy Dee Williams and Rutger Hauer. 1982 saw another successful *Rocky* sequel, along with the birth of a new hero (and franchise) with *First Blood*, in which Stallone appeared as Vietnam veteran John Rambo, a man who gets on the wrong side of a small-town sheriff and ends up unleashing hell. By the time the script for *Beverly Hills Cop* came to him, the actor was one of the most successful in the Hollywood.

Stallone got straight to work and the first thing he stripped out was the comedic fish-out-of-water elements, replacing them with a lot more bloody action and violence. Axel Foley became Axel Cobretti, the character of Michael Tandino became Cobretti's brother and childhood friend Jenny Summers became the love interest. An ultra-violent opening and lavish end sequence which included Cobretti driving a Lamborghini into a train saw Paramount voice their concerns about the budget. With pre-production well under way and a start date set, the studio called a meeting with Stallone and the producers. Paramount still wanted their fish-out-of-water story, and they wanted it cheaper than the current *Beverly Hills Cop* was set to cost. Stallone wanted to make his version, and after two days of discussion, agreed to leave the project. According to Daniel Petrie, the actor was given the choice to go back and make the film he originally signed on for (based on Petrie's script) or take what he'd added to the story and make his own project – providing it didn't end up involving a cop in Beverly Hills.

Stallone chose the latter, leaving Paramount frantically scrambling to find a replacement lead for *Beverly Hills Cop* just two weeks before shooting had been set to commence. Simpson turned to actor/comedian Eddie Murphy, with whom he'd already discussed the role around the time Paramount was getting cold feet. Murphy agreed and the picture's production was delayed a month while the script was re-worked again. The young actor added his own unique ideas during shooting and the picture went on to become one of the most successful comedies of all time (even without taking inflation into account, it is still amongst the biggest R-rated movies in box office history). Meanwhile, Stallone saw a major misfire with musical *Rhinestone* and the *Saturday Night Fever* follow-up, *Staying Alive* (which he directed). He soon returned to his roots with back-to-back hits *Rocky IV* and *Rambo: First Blood Part 2*, both released in 1985.

In the same year, the actor signed a multi-picture deal with Cannon, the first project being a remake of *Angels with Dirty Faces*, set to co-star Christopher Reeve. Such was the backlash against the idea that the proposed film was soon scrapped. Instead, Stallone began work on what would come to be known as Cobra. While he used some ideas from his aborted *Beverly Hills Cop* script, a bigger influence was Paula Gosling's 1974 novel *A Running Duck* (later re-issued as *Fair Game*). Gosling had sold a movie treatment of the story to Warner Bros. and all but forgotten about it. Indeed, the author didn't even know Cobra was based on her story until a friend spotted her name in the film's credits during a preview screening. Despite serving as the basis for the movie, the finished screenplay bore little resemblance to *A Running Duck*.

With a completed script, Cannon and Warner Bros. (who would act as distributor) signed off on Cobra and the search for a director could begin. For reasons unknown, Stallone declined to helm the project despite having directed five features by that point. Instead, he turned to George P. Cosmatos, an Italian director he'd worked with on *Rambo: First Blood Part 2*. Cosmatos made his directorial debut on the Raquel Welch picture, *The Beloved*, before coming to prominence with *Rappresaglia* (also known as *Massacre in Rome*), a World War 2 drama starring Richard Burton and Marcello Mastroianni. Other pictures followed including *The Cassandra Crossing* and *Escape to Athena*. He teamed up with Stallone to work on the *First Blood* sequel, and the actions of the duo on that feature may well have been the reason why they worked together on Cobra. It has long been rumoured that Cosmatos was just a front man on *Rambo*, with Stallone actually calling the shots on both sides of the camera. Similar stories would circulate on Cobra, strengthened by comments since made by cinematographer Ric Waite.

Given that the movie cost $25M to produce, it had a relatively small central cast, with only three leads and two supporting actors for the most part. Stallone had a hand in casting, with his then wife Brigitte Nielsen winning the role of female lead Ingrid Knudsen. The Danish-born actress had started her career as a model in the early 1980s before landing the role of *Red Sonja* opposite Arnold Schwarzenegger. In the same year, she appeared with Stallone in *Rocky IV* as Ludmilla, the wife of Ivan Drago. As the cast and crew would soon find out, casting the real-life partner of the main star would create its own problems. Taking on what would be the final lead role, that of the Night Slasher, would be newcomer Brian Thompson.

The young actor was a year out of drama school when he auditioned for Cobra. He got into acting by chance when he offered a friend a ride home from school and found out he was trying out for a play. At his friend's suggestion, he auditioned for the role of a Russian ballet instructor in *You Can't Take It With You*. Bitten by the bug, he attended college to study music but ended up doing a Masters in Fine Art instead. It was during his last year of study that he secured an agent, which led to his cinematic debut as one of the three punks who face off against Arnold Schwarzenegger in *The Terminator*. Thompson shot the part in one night, after performing in a three and half hour Shakespeare play.

When it came to Cobra, he ended up auditioning seven times, nearly losing out during the fourth attempt when Stallone came to watch and deemed Thompson too nice. Still, the actor was called back again and again, and eventually given a screen test in full costume and make-up – which left no one in any doubt he could carry the role (interestingly, Thompson found out he'd won the part while performing in a *Conan the Barbarian* stage play).

Rounding out the cast was Reni Santoni as Cobretti's partner, Sergeant Tony Gonzales and Lee Garlington, as a cop with an ulterior motive. There was also a small part for Andrew Robinson, who had famously portrayed Scorpio in *Dirty Harry* (a picture that had also featured Reni Santoni) and Art LaFleur, who played Captain Sears.

With a $25M budget in hand (almost half of which was rumoured to be Stallone's salary) and casting completed, shooting could commence for a May 1986 release date. Within days, the film was running into problems with the script and the schedule, both of which would be altered on-the-fly. According to Brian Thompson, Stallone's ego was also out of control, holding up filming while he fooled around with his new wife or showed off to his bodyguards (who, in the words of cinematographer Ric Waite, were hired to laugh at the actor's jokes and stories). The supporting cast and crew were also forbidden from speaking with the actor when not filming. As he was rumoured to have done on *Rambo*, Cosmatos took a back seat on Cobra, leaving Stallone to call the shots – or rather inform the director of the shots he should be making. Evidence of this came to light when, after viewing dailies the previous night, Cosmatos turned up on set with a list of notes he claimed to have made about the footage – only it was in Stallone's handwriting. Again, according to Waite, this continued throughout the picture.

Being that Cobra was his first major role, Brian Thompson was eager for direction and to discover the motivations of his character (and the cult he led). In a conversation Thompson recalled for the MovieGeeksUnited podcast, Stallone compared The Night Slasher (or Abbadon as he was known in the script) to Hitler. Thompson didn't see the comparison and stated that the cult didn't really do anything for most of the film except chase down one girl. Further discussions about the character weren't forthcoming, leaving the actor to write his own three-page New World manifesto to help fill in the blanks. The actor was further dismayed when he discovered his climactic foundry speech would be shot opposite a script girl as Stallone was off watching a basketball game.

When shooting began to fall further behind, Stallone approached Ric Waite and told him and his crew to work faster. A cinematographer of some experience, Waite was noted for being one of the fastest in the business and put the cause of the delays back onto Stallone and his antics, both on and off-set. Shocked that someone would talk to him like that, he cleaned up his act and began working to schedule, if only for a few weeks. Shooting continued but changes were still happening at a regular rate – notably the proposed night shoot for the motorcycle chase that takes place near the end of the film. Despite all preparations for the sequence having been made, Stallone decided to scrap it in favour of a day shoot, concerned that mosquitoes would make filming at night difficult. For Thompson, there was one final disappointment. As shooting came to a close, Cosmatos informed him that "You could have been good if you had listened to me.".

While the edit was being finalised, work began on assembling the soundtrack. John Cafferty & The Beaver Brown Band supplied the track *Voice of America's Sons*, which played over the end titles, while Sylvester Levey produced a number of instrumental pieces, not all of which made it into the finished film but still ended up on the soundtrack album. Robert Tepper, who had performed *No Easy Way Out* for the *Rocky IV* OST provided the song *Angel of the City*, which became the picture's unofficial theme. Bizarrely, Stan Bush wrote *The Touch* to be used in Cobra – without knowing anything about the film. According to an interview with Geektyrant, Bush agreed to write and perform a track not long after the release of *Rocky IV* and based *The Touch* more on the content of that film than anything in Cobra. Ultimately the track wasn't used, ending up in *Transformers the Movie* instead. In a further odd development, the soundtrack album to Cobra wasn't released until 1988, two years after the film's debut.

The first version of Cobra ran for around 130 minutes and was initially edited down to a two-hour director's cut. The amount of on-screen graphic violence saw the picture run foul of the MPAA who slapped it with an X-rating, all but dooming it from a wide release. Cuts were made to some sequences, with a number of the killings being edited down, shown off-screen or removed altogether. The first murder was heavily modified, removing the shots of the victim having her throat cut and hands severed. Similarly, the murder of Ingrid's photographer friend removed excessive axe blows, while an autopsy scene omitted lingering shots of mutilated female corpses. The violent end of the Night Slasher was also reduced and other graphic moments were sped up to lessen their impact. Conversely, because of the now-choppy editing, some parts were actually slowed down to disguise the fact. Upon being re-submitted, the MPAA granted Cobra an R-rating, and everything was set for the May 23rd release. Then *Top Gun* happened.

The action drama starring Tom Cruise was already gaining a lot of attention prior to its May 16th release date, and even though it received quite average reviews, it opened to a decent enough $8M and some great word-of-mouth. However, Warner Bros. and Sylvester Stallone were wary of the film's potential success; more so given Cobra was to open the following weekend. Perhaps knowing that their film wouldn't score strong word-of-mouth or repeat business, a decision was made to drastically reduce its run time, meaning it would be possible to insert an extra screening session into the day and make more money in the process. It is estimated that between 30-40 minutes were removed from the then finished (and R-rated) cut. Entire plot points and characters were drastically reduced or removed altogether. The knock-on effect of this was that any reference to a removed scene or character also had to be edited out. Any development of the New Order cult was all but deleted, as was most of David Rasche's role. Yet, curiously, most of Stallone's work remained intact. When all was said and done, the film ran just 84 minutes without credits. Warner Bros. pushed the film with a hard-hitting trailer featuring Stallone detailing the amount of violent crimes perpetrated in America on a daily basis.

Critics savaged Cobra upon release, noting its weak plot and graphic violence as being particular sticking points. It currently holds a 13% approval rating on Rotten Tomatoes. However, Sylvester Stallone was still incredibly popular with the public, in fact, it is arguable that the period after *Rocky IV* and *Rambo: First Blood Part 2* saw him at the height of his fame.

The film opened on May 23rd 1986, and while it was a busy summer, the only immediate threat was the aforementioned *Top Gun*, which had knocked *Short Circuit* out of the top spot during its opening weekend. Arnold Schwarzenegger's *Raw Deal* was still a fortnight away, which could give Cobra time to make back its $25M. The film actually got off to a strong start, making around $15M for the Memorial Day weekend and securing the top spot from Cruise &

co (*Poltergeist 2: The Other Side* did give it a good run for its money though). That opening marked the biggest ever debut for a Warner Bros. picture at that point and a week later, the film was still in the top spot, adding a further $7.5M. By that early stage it had recouped its budget but when *Raw Deal* was thrown into the mix the following weekend, Cobra slipped down to third and *Top Gun* moved back up to number one, continuing its journey to becoming the biggest film of 1986.

Back to School and *Ferris Bueller's Day Off* opened in mid-June, pushing everything down a notch or two. By this point, Cobra was approaching $40M and was all but done in North America. In total, it lasted only six weeks in the top ten and ended up making $49M; poor word-of-mouth and a lack of repeat business being partly to blame. Still, the film did a lot better than *Raw Deal*, which ended up making only $16M. However, overseas, Cobra was a smash hit, raking in $110M and pushing the film to an overall global finish of $160M. In the years that followed, the actor came to rely more on the overseas market than the domestic one.

Cobra was a hit all over again on video and cable, where it became one of the most screened films in history. Indeed, Brian Thompson claims that even to this day, almost thirty years later, he is still receiving residual cheques for his work. Elsewhere, Ocean Software, who had secured the rights to produce a videogame based on the movie, scored a critical and financial hit with their tough-as-nails adaptation. This marked the second time they'd collaborated with Stallone, the first being on *Rambo: First Blood Part 2*. The company was gaining a reputation for its licensed games, and produced a string of them in the mid-1980s and 1990s, including *Red Heat, Highlander, The Untouchables* and *Robocop*. They'd go on to work again with Stallone on *Rambo III*. Paula Gosling's novel *A Running Duck*, which had already been re-issued as *Fair Game*, was re-launched as Cobra. Despite the finished movie having little in common with the book, it didn't stop Stallone offering to share a co-writing credit on the re-issue. Gosling politely declined.

In many ways, Cobra marked a turning point for Sylvester Stallone. His next film, arm-wrestling drama *Over the Top* earned only $16M in the February of 1987. A return to *Rambo* a year later didn't fair quite so well either, especially compared to the second movie's box office performance – the situation wasn't helped by *Rambo III* costing (a very expensive at the time) $63M. Thankfully, it played stronger overseas. *Lock-Up* did barely better than *Over the Top*, while the popular buddy movie *Tango & Cash* made $63M off a $55M budget. Even a return to his roots with *Rocky V* didn't work, the film failing to recoup its $42M costs. The actor attempted to reinvent himself in the early 1990s, as a comedy player but both *Oscar* and the disastrous *Stop! Or My Mom Will Shoot!* flopped. *Cliffhanger* in 1993 was a major hit, especially overseas, where it made over $170M. Sadly, this was followed by another string of costly, albeit somewhat enjoyable movies, including *Demolition Man, Assassins* and *The Specialist*.

Copland, in 1997 saw Stallone return to the kind of straight drama he'd done with the first *Rocky* movie, and he won many positive notices for his role as the partially deaf Sheriff Freddy Heflin. The following years were rough for the actor, with only a part in the animated *Antz* gaining any traction with audiences. The triple failure of *Drive, Get Carter* and the barely released *D-Tox* (AKA *Eye See You*) all but finished his career for a time, the only success of the period being multiple roles in *Spy Kids 3D: Game Over*. In order to get back into the game, Stallone returned to the two characters that had made his name in the first place. The success of *Rocky Balboa* and *Rambo* (parts six and four respectively) thrust the actor back into the limelight. He followed this goodwill with the ensemble action feature, *The Expendables* – a solid hit that has so far spawned two further sequels, with another on the cards. Sadly, the long-awaited (proper) team up of Stallone and Schwarzenegger in *Escape Plan* failed to generate much domestic box office despite being a solid enough movie. Most people felt it had come twenty years too late. The actor returned to his roots once more with the *Rocky* spin-off *Creed*, a critical and theatrical hit in 2015.

Brian Thompson took on a number of TV roles after Cobra, working on the likes of *Falcon's Crest, Star Trek: The Next Generation* and *Key West*, a short-lived comedy in which he played a new-age sheriff. In between his TV roles, he appeared in the likes of *Moon 44, Fright Night Part 2* and the Sean Connery picture, *Dragonheart*. In the mid-90s, he won recurring roles in *The X-Files* and *Buffy the Vampire Slayer*. He recently turned his hand to writing and directing on *The Extendables*, a picture about a disgraced action star given the chance to direct a movie in Uzbekistan. Brigitte Nielsen followed up Cobra with a showy part in *Beverly Hills Cop 2*. After a very messy (and public) divorce from Sylvester Stallone in 1987, Nielsen appeared in a string of low budget features including *976-Evil 2, Snowboard Academy* and *Galaxis*, amongst others. Despite never achieving the same level of fame as enjoyed in the mid-80s, the actress has worked consistently, with one of her most recent projects being the all-female Expendables knock-off, *Mercenaries*, in which she appeared opposite Zoe Bell, Kristanna Loken and 80s action star, Cynthia Rothrock.

George P. Cosmatos directed the science fiction film *Leviathan* in 1989, which featured Peter Weller and Rambo co-star Richard Crenna. The story behind his next film is long enough for an article of its own. The Kurt Russell project *Tombstone* had already had its fair share of problems before filming had even gotten underway. Competing with Kevin Costner's Wyatt Earp saw the picture struggle to find funding and distribution. Kevin Jarre, who had written *Tombstone* was fired as its director some way into filming due to a reluctance to cut down his screenplay and for falling behind schedule. Looking for a quick solution (and with a panicked studio on his back), Kurt Russell turned to Sylvester Stallone, who recommended Cosmatos for the job. The new director signed on-board and the film was completed. Later, it was revealed by journalist Henry Cabot Beck, who had visited the set during production, that Russell had actually directed *Tombstone* and that every night the actor had given his director a list of shots he was to make the next day. The duo even developed a secret sign language to be used on set. Cosmatos made Beck swear he would not reveal this fact until after he had died, and the journalist was good to his word, the information appearing in 2005 after the director's passing.

Paula Gosling's novel was filmed again in 1995, under its re-issued title of *Fair Game*. It was seen as a star-making vehicle for model-turned-actress Cindy Crawford, and also featured William Baldwin. While it stuck closer to the plot than Cobra, it too ended up being slashed to pieces during post-production after poor test screening results. Characters were removed or replaced entirely (notably Salma Hayek taking Elizabeth Pena's role) and new scenes were shot to increase the believability of Crawford and Baldwin's relationship. In the end, it was all for nought, and *Fair Game* made only $11.5M against a budget of $55M. It also marked the end of Crawford's very short acting career. As for Cobra's original cut, timecoded VHS copies have surfaced in the intervening years but no official release has ever been forthcoming. This rarity reintroduces much of the violence and character development hacked out by the studio, though how much difference this makes to the film is debatable.

Like many action movies from the 1980s, Cobra doesn't stand the test of time, but that doesn't make it any less watchable. The simplistic plot keeps things moving at a fair pace – it is estimated the longest time between action sequences is six minutes. While much of its dialogue is laughable (as it was upon release), this doesn't detract from the violence of the picture, particularly the killings carried out by Brian Thompson's quite formidable Night Slasher. The film continues to be shown on TV with semi-regularity and even played an influence on Nicolas Winding Refn's *Drive*, with Ryan Gosling claiming the matchstick his character has in his mouth was a trait borrowed from Marion Cobretti. While Cobra isn't remembered as fondly as *Rocky* or even *Rambo*, it remains as endlessly entertaining.

More like Cobra…

Die Hard

A crackerjack action movie, with a never-better Bruce Willis as New York cop, John McClane, the epitome of the wrong man in the wrong place at the right time. Facing off against Alan Rickman's Hans Gruber and his crew, McClane fights tooth and nail in some of the most incredible action sequences of the entire decade. John McTiernan directs with such confidence, building on every set piece with the next and leading to an explosive climax.

Die Hard represents the best of 80s action, and while the latter sequels may have watered things down, the original remains a classic of the genre. Even the supporting characters bring something to the picture, be it Bonnie Bedelia as McClane's almost ex-wife, Reginald VelJohnson's beat cop or Hart Bochner as the slimy executive, Harry Ellis. There's even room for Paul Gleason and 80s A-hole William Atherton. A true classic in every sense of the word.

Trivia: The film was based on the book *Nothing Lasts Forever*, whose predecessor, *The Detective*, had been turned into a movie starring Frank Sinatra. For this reason, Fox was contractually obliged to offer Sinatra the lead role before anyone else.

Commando

Pumping Iron and *Conan the Barbarian* may have bought him to the public's attention, but it was Commando that made Arnold Schwarzenegger an action star. As the one-man army, John Matrix, Schwarzenegger kills the population of a small island in his quest to rescue his kidnapped daughter. The larger-than-life hero quips as well as he shoots, facing off against Bill Duke, Dan Hedaya and the super-camp Bennett, memorably portrayed by Vernon Wells.

Written by Steven E. de Souza, who would work on *The Running Man* and the first two *Die Hard* pictures, the ultra-violent Commando set up a rivalry between Schwarzenegger and *Rambo* star, Sylvester Stallone, as to who was the biggest action hero of the decade. Commando is a guilty pleasure for some, but remains a thoroughly enjoyable film.

Trivia: According to screenwriter Jeph Loeb, the picture was conceived as a vehicle for KISS front-man, Gene Simmons.

Predator

What starts out as a routine rescue missions for Arnold Schwarzenegger and his band of elite commandos takes a far darker and more violent turn when they come up against an alien who's hunting and killing for sport in the jungles of South America. A race to the extraction point soon becomes a fight for survival as one-by-one, the soldiers are picked off by a barely-seen, yet terrifying, killer.

A great ensemble action feature that steadily builds the tension as the situation and the chance of survival becomes more desperate. Schwarzenegger's ragtag team have a real sense of camaraderie, giving their deaths more gravitas that one would expect. A superb final showdown puts the icing on what is another classic 80s action picture.

Trivia: The original inspiration for the script came from a Hollywood joke, that after *Rocky IV*, Stallone had run out of Earth-bound opponents to fight.

Police Academy

The new police recruits. Call them slobs. Call them jerks. Call them gross. Just don't call them when you're in trouble.

Studio: Warner Bros.
Release Date: March 23rd 1984
Director: Hugh Wilson
Starring: Steve Guttenberg
Budget: $4.5M – 2015 Equivalent: $10.4M
U.S Box Office: $81.1M – 2015 Equivalent: $187.9M

Due to a shortage of police officers, the mayor decides that police academies have to take on any willing recruit – no matter how unsuitable they might be. Carey Mahoney doesn't have much of a choice – go to jail or join the academy. With a rag-tag band of recruits, schooled under the watchful eye of the vindictive Lt. Harris, Mahoney might just have what it takes to become one of the future's finest – providing he survives the training!

While much maligned, for a brief period in the 1980s, the Police Academy series was incredibly popular with the public. The rise of the R-rated comedy saw studios falling over themselves to find the next *Animal House* or *Porky's*, which had been a smash hit in the summer of 1981. A whole slew of movies came after, all upping the sex and nudity factor in a hope of attracting the biggest cinema-going demographic. Truth be told, other countries had been making these kinds of movies throughout the previous decade, with the Confessions series in England and the Israeli-made *Lemon Popsicle* proving popular. Police Academy looked set to top them all with its boundary-pushing, 'hard-R' rated script – the only problem was, no one liked it.

The idea for Police Academy came to producer Paul Maslansky while he was on the set of *The Right Stuff*, acting as a representative of The Ladd Company. He had gotten into movie production almost by accident at a relatively young age. Before graduating from college in the mid-1950s, Maslansky set about travelling the world, and wound up in Paris looking to become part of a band (in school he had been a fairly accomplished trumpet player). While in France, he met a Danish film student by the name of Benny Corson, who was intrigued by some of Maslansky's musician friends, many of whom were graduates of Fullbright. Corson suggested the idea of making a short documentary about the college and its students. He told Maslansky that he could get a film crew down from

Copenhagen to shoot it, all they needed was $1500 to make it. They came up with the idea of pitching the documentary to Fullbright College in Paris, and it was left to Maslansky to make the deal.

To his surprise, the college agreed to buy (what was now titled) *Letters From Paris* – but only if they liked it. Maslansky raised the money through friends and family. Rather than make things up as they went, the production 'team' sought a writer to give the documentary some structure. Through friend James Baldwin, Maslansky met Melvin Van Peebles, who would later go on to produce cult classic *Sweet Sweetback's Baadasssss Song*. He provided them with the structure they needed but despite all their efforts, Fullbright opted to pass on the finished product, feeling it was more about music than the education. Still, the documentary was entered in the short film competition at Cannes in 1962, as part of the debutant director series. While Corson didn't win first place, the picture did, and thanks to labour issues in American TV and film production at the time, Maslansky was able to sell the picture for $1500.

A number of other behind-the-scenes jobs followed, and at one point the still relatively young Maslanksy found himself helping manage second unit on *The Long Boats* (1964), a Viking picture being made by legendary director of photography, Jack Cardiff. The managing job saw him dealing with 500 extras, boats, horses and various battle props. He would carry out a similar task on *Jason and the*

Argonauts. Now feeling more confident in his abilities and realising that film was where he wanted to work, Maslansky began discussing producing his first proper picture with director Warren Kiefer. At the time, horror movies were popular and even a half-decent one was assured of interest from a studio. Furthermore, they realised that shooting in Europe would offer an abundance of real life sets and backdrops, adding authenticity and greatly reducing the cost of making such things. Made for $120K, *Castle of the Living Dead* starred Christopher Lee and Donald Sutherland, who made his feature debut in three different roles. The picture marked Maslansky's first feature producing credit and he sold it to American International Pictures, home of Sam Arkoff and Roger Corman.

He stuck with the horror genre for his next producing job, *She Beast*, which was directed by Michael Reeves. There has been talk that Reeves was the actual director on *Castle of the Living Dead*, but in actual fact, he worked second unit (confirmed by Maslansky in 1994). The director would go on to make the legendary *Witchfinder General* before dying from an accidental overdose aged only 25. Maslansky then worked two years at United Artists, but was famously fired for leaving his post to travel to Israel with friend (and CBS Reporter) Ike Pappas, to cover what became known as the Yom Kippur war. Despite making the front page of Variety with his termination, when Maslansky returned from Israel, UA wanted him back on their books, but a disastrous meeting in Paris saw him walk away. Over time, he would work again with Donald Sutherland on

Raw Meat along with acting as executive producer on cult movie, *Race with the Devil*. More production worked followed, including the Martin Luther King mini-series, *King*, in 1978, and the true life drama story, *Lovechild* in 1982. The latter saw studios fighting over the movie rights, only to discover that Maslansky already had them, having secured them via Murray Silver, who he'd met while making *King* (Silver was an attorney acting for the King Family).

Now working for The Ladd Company, the producer found himself without another picture lined up after production on *Lovechild* had finished. Alan Ladd Jr. asked him if he'd go out to San Francisco to represent the Ladd Company on the set of *The Right Stuff*. Arriving early one morning to oversee the shooting of the John Glen tickertape sequence, Maslansky noticed a rag-tag bunch of police officers who were there to act as both crowd control and to feature in the scene. He got talking to the officer who brought down the group and discovered they were actually police cadets from the local academy. When he asked why they were such an unconventional bunch, he discovered that San Francisco had a Fair Employment Policy, meaning the academy had to take on anyone who applied – for at least three weeks, after which they could flunk out those that didn't look to make the grade. This gave Maslansky an idea and that night he went home and wrote a two-page treatment about a group of eager but unsuitable people who all wanted to be police officers.

The next day he pitched the idea to Gareth Wiggin, who was overseeing production on *The Right Stuff*. He liked the idea, and Maslansky asked him to mention it to Alan Ladd upon his return to California. Ladd too was impressed and called Maslansky in to see him after work on *The Right Stuff* was completed. He agreed to finance Police Academy providing it could be made for the right price, which ended up being $4.5M. To turn the treatment into a script, they hired Pat Proft and Neil Israel. Proft was a friend of Maslansky's wife and had written for various comedy shows throughout the 1970s, along with working with Mel Brooks and the Zucker Brothers. Neal Israel had gotten his break working on *Tunnel Vision*, a show which brought Chevy Chase and John Candy to prominence. The duo set to work, using the treatment as their guideline, but the script that came back a few months later was a lot more explicit than anyone expected. Alan Ladd wasn't impressed, and even though they'd begun to shop the script around in hope of finding a director, Paul Maslansky figured the project was done with before it had even got going.

It came as something of a surprise when he received a call one Friday from talent agency APA, who had an agent who wanted to discuss the Police Academy script. The agent informed Maslansky that he had a client by the name of Hugh Wilson, who'd seen the script on the agent's desk and wanted to discuss it with him. The producer had never heard of the guy but agreed to take his call at home that evening. Wilson revealed that he didn't like the script but it had funny moments and the central premise was sound. He then revealed he was the creator of the hit sitcom *WKRP in Cincinnati*. If Maslansky would give him the weekend, he'd rewrite the script. True to his word, by Monday morning, Wilson had completed a major revision which would turn out to be the exact movie they shot. Unbeknownst to all, Wilson was actually looking to get into directing by way of re-working low budget comedy scripts. Thanks to his efforts, he was able to cut a deal to direct Police Academy, as well as being credited for his writing work on it (Israel and Proft would still receive a story credit and shared the screenplay one with Wilson).

With a relatively low budget of $4.5M attached, both producer and director knew they wouldn't be able to afford any of the major comedy stars of the time. They turned to the casting team of Pamela Basker and Fern Champion to help fill out their cast of misfits and authority figures. Despite being an ensemble picture, the character of Carey Mahoney was essentially the lead, a role that ended up going to Steve Guttenberg. The young actor had an uncredited role in the disaster film *Rollercoaster*, followed by parts in *The Chicken Chronicles, Players* and *The Boys from Brazil*. His role in the Village People movie, *Can't Stop the Music* almost ended his career, being an unmitigated critical and financial disaster (though it has since gained a cult following, especially in Australia, where it is shown every New Year's Eve). It was his part in Barry Levinson's comedy drama *Diner* that brought the actor to prominence. He arrived at the Police Academy audition in his father's old police shirt with a bit of an attitude – which the assembled group felt was perfect for Mahoney.

For the role of the bumbling Commandant Lassard, they chose George Gaynes, an actor of some repute who had been in the game since the early 1940s. First gaining recognition on Broadway, the actor switched to movies and TV in the 1960s. Besides acting, he had also studied and performed opera and could speak seven different languages. Gaynes was already known to Hugh Wilson, having directed the final episode of *WKRP in Cincinnati*. Marion Ramsey, who would play the timid cadet Hooks, was performing in a production of *Little Shop of Horrors* when she got the call to audition. Although Ramsey had a powerful singing voice, the night before she had met Michael Jackson, and used his voice as the inspiration for the character. Wilson and Maslansky were instantly taken with it, and she skipped the audition process and went straight to a costumed screen test.

In the role of Mahoney's antagonist, Lt. Harris, G.W Bailey was cast. Another veteran of stage and TV screen, Bailey didn't actually make his film debut until 1979 in the Chuck Norris actioner, *A Force of One*. At around the same time, he was making his name in *M.A.S.H*, playing the recurring role of Luther Rizzo. As the no-nonsense Sergeant Callahan, Leslie Easterbrook was chosen after giving a very frightening audition. She later revealed that her husband was a very intimidating man and that she'd spent the previous two days practicing with him to be as threatening as possible. However, after the audition was over, Easterbrook was fearful she'd come on too strong, but the assembled casting team loved her performance (even if they were a little frightened). Celebrated football star-turned actor, Bubba Smith took on the role of Hightower. A formidable giant of a man, Smith had taken up acting upon his retirement from professional football, with small roles in various TV shows and movies. During the audition, Maslansky explained there was little money in the role but Smith didn't care, he was happy to be involved in the project.

David Graf, who would play the mildly-disturbed, weapon-obsessed Tackleberry attended his audition in full camouflage, while Donovan Scott (Cadet Leslie Barbara) strolled into the room, did a flip and landed straight on his back. Both won their respective roles. Kim Cattrall was another who had been acting for a number of years prior to Police Academy, and had recently gained some notoriety for her part as Miss Honeywell in *Porky's*. She took on the character of rich girl-turned-cadet, Karen Thompson. The remainder of the cast were made up by Bruce Mahler (Fackler) and Andrew Rubin (George Martin), alongside Scott Thomson and Brant Van Hoffman, who played Copeland and Blankes, two cadets who Lt. Harris recruits to intimidate the others into quitting.

One final addition to the cast was Michael Winslow. Paul Maslansky got word of a comic who was opening for Count Basie, and was advised to go and see the show. When Winslow came onto the stage, the sound system malfunctioned and he ended up borrowing a loudhailer from a fire marshal. His act, a combination of stand-up and incredible sound effects, which Winslow himself generated, impressed the producer to such a degree that he and Wilson set about writing Winslow into the script. Before that time, the character of Larvell Jones didn't exist. He would go on to be the most memorable player in the series.

The film shot in Toronto during the summer of 1983, with a disused psychiatric hospital standing in for the Police Academy. Hugh Wilson, coming from TV, had to adjust to shooting for film but didn't let it slow him down, often needing only a couple of takes for each scene – at least when the cast weren't cracking up. Restrictions caused by the budget also meant there wasn't the money for multiple set-ups. He also encouraged the actors to improvise and often asked them prior to shooting a scene 'what they had for him'. There were few issues during the forty-day shoot, but one problem did occur thanks to the way filming had been scheduled. In a memorable scene, cadets Copeland and Blankes, thinking the police academy has the same strict rules as the military, get their heads shaved – something they did for real. It was only after the scene was shot did the production crew realise that the actors were yet to film their arrival at the academy. When it came time for that part to be shot, the actors had to wear ill-fitting wigs to cover their shaven heads.

Even with the budget restrictions, there were at least two moments that needed multiple takes after the cast (and crew) couldn't stop laughing. The 'fight' in the dinner hall, in which Barbara hits Blankes square in the face with a metal tray was repeated so many times that the mild-mannered Hugh Wilson began to lose patience with the actors. Another sequence which saw Tackleberry urge Cadet Barbara to hit him was shot so many times that David Graf's cheek was bright red for some time after. The picture also got an unplanned director cameo after the man they hired to play the bit part 'angry man in car' was found passed out drunk in his trailer. Given they were shooting at night and had no backup, Wilson stepped in, though most of his short scene ended up on the cutting room floor (Maslansky didn't make it into the picture, though he did get his name on the side of a van featured in a chase scene). The sound crew also got a rude awakening thanks to Marion Ramsey. Having had to turn up their recording equipment to catch all of her timid Michael Jackson voice, they were deafened during her single loud outburst in the film's final moments.

Steve Guttenberg's dresser helped out with the hilarious Blue Oyster Club sequences, rounding up over two hundred guys who all had their own leather outfits. To add an air of authenticity, the two men who danced with Blankes and Copeland were qualified ballroom dancers. They also hired a professional for what is arguably the film's most (in)famous moment – Lassard's podium speech. Georgina Spelvin, an adult film star who had gained fame for her role in *Devil in Miss Jones*, took on the part of the hooker hired to get Mahoney thrown out of the academy. Spelvin was originally scheduled to appear in one sequence, but that would change after the film's first test screening.

While the initial edit was being assembled, Robert Folk was hired to compose what would become Police Academy's memorable theme tune. A release date of 23rd March 1984 was put in place, and while Maslansky and Wilson were happy with the movie, they had no real idea how it would play to the public. It contained little in the way of profanity, and its few scant moments of nudity paled when compared to *Porky's* and its ilk. A test screening was scheduled at Preview House, with Alan Ladd, Maslansky and Wilson all present. From the get-go, the crowd loved it, and the dial setup used to measure the film's approval with an audience was off-the-chart, barely dipping through the entire run time.

As the last scene played out and the assembled crew were about to pat each other on the back, they noticed the approval dial had dropped down by a fair amount. It wasn't in the 'don't like' band, but it was significant enough to give them cause for concern. They needed the audience to leave on a high and that wasn't happening. Alan Ladd spoke up first, telling Maslansky and Wilson to go home and think about how they could fix the ending. They met up the following morning, yet before they could even sit down, Ladd announced he'd cracked it. He reasoned that the picture had one huge laugh – the podium scene, and that they should reprise that in the closing moments, but with an added twist. An extra scene was shot for the end which played brilliantly with a new test audience. While the technical aspects were finished off and a trailer put together, Maslansky left for London to oversee production on *Return to Oz*.

The film received middling reviews with critics, though they would prove to be the best of the series. Roger Ebert awarded Police Academy zero stars but noted New York Times critic Vincent Canby gave it a favourable notice. Ebert wasn't the only one who was unimpressed by what he had seen. During a 'Making Of' feature to celebrate its 20th anniversary, Steve Guttenberg revealed that after his agent saw the finished movie, he rushed over and told the actor that he would quickly secure him work on a TV show, as he was unlikely to work in pictures again.

Opening in a quieter part of the year and with little hype, expectations for Police Academy weren't high. However, it would have little in the way of competition save for the Tom Hanks romantic comedy, *Splash*, which would be in its third weekend of release. Maslansky had a lot riding on its success, and even though he'd produced a number of pictures, he'd never had a hit. It would be a tense weekend while he waited to receive word of how the film had done, made tougher by the time difference between California and London (where, as mentioned, he was overseeing *Return to Oz*). Unbeknownst to Maslansky, Alan Ladd had already previewed the film in 300 theatres in the previous week, to great success.

Unable to sit and wait, the producer and Matt Clark, who was acting in *Return to Oz*, went on a pub crawl. When they returned, he asked his wife if they'd had a call about the weekend numbers. She said they had, and it was 'eight something'. Maslansky knew it couldn't be anything as ridiculous as $80M, and began to panic when he realised it must have been $800K. He nervously called Alan Ladd to hear the worst, only to be told the picture was estimated to make $8.2M that weekend, one of the biggest spring openings for a Warner Bros. release. The producer later joked in an interview with Jog Road Productions, that that weekend had essentially built his house.

Police Academy opened in first place with an impressive $8.5M, recouping its $4.5M budget by that first Saturday afternoon. And this was against strong competition from *Splash* which had earned another $6.6M. A week on and the film was still firmly at the top, dipping just 6% on the previous weekend's takings, neither *Greystoke* nor *Romancing the Stone* giving it much trouble. In only ten days it had earned back its budget nearly four times over, and it was just getting started. Another small drop in the following weekend kept the film at number one as it crossed the $30M mark. R-rated competition showed up the next frame in the guise of *Friday the 13th: The Final Chapter* and the comedy slipped down to second. Yet a week later, it was back at the top, and stayed there for the next fortnight. By the time *Breakin'* took the top spot in the first weekend of May, Police Academy had made almost $60M.

In total, the movie remained in the top ten for an incredible thirteen weeks, making $81.1M and becoming the sixth most successful picture of 1984. It is worth noting that that year contained some of the biggest releases of the 1980s, including *Beverly Hills Cop, Ghostbusters* and *Indiana Jones and the Temple of Doom*. Overseas figures were equally impressive, adding a further $65M to its coffers. It was also a smash hit on video, becoming one of the most popular rentals of 1984 and '85. With such success, it wasn't long before Warner Brothers began looking for a sequel – and fast.

A year later, *Police Academy 2: Their First Assignment* was unleashed into theatres. Maslansky returned to produce but Hugh Wilson was replaced by Jerry Paris. The majority of the cast reprised their roles, with the notable exceptions of Kim Cattrall, Leslie Easterbrook and Donovan Scott. New additions would include comedian Bobcat Goldthwait as gang leader Zed, Tim Kazurinsky as timid shopkeeper Carl Sweetchuck, and Art Metrano as Lieutenant Mauser in what was essentially the Lt. Harris role (G.W Bailey has a blink-and-you'll-miss-him cameo in the wedding scene). There were some issues over the amount of screen time given to the new cast members and production was actually shut down for a day or so while a mediator was brought in. This time around the newly qualified recruits are sent to the worst precinct in the city in an effort to help Commandant Lassard's brother clean it up. Lt. Mauser does everything he can to stop them, knowing if they fail he'll become the new captain. Reviews were much worse, and even critics who were fans of the original struggled to find something to like. The public however, were willing to give Mahoney and Co. another chance. The picture opened to $10M, remained in the top ten for eleven weeks and finished up with $55M in takings. It also did a further $27M on video.

Police Academy 3: Back in Training was released less than a year later, and marked the series' switch to the PG rating. Leslie Easterbrook returned to the series, as did Brant Van Hoffman and Scott Thomson. Bobcat Goldthwait and Tim Kazurinsky became series regulars (and new academy recruits) while Art Metrano returned as Mauser (now commandant of a rival academy). The plot would see the gang return to save Lassard's academy when the state announces it can only afford to fund one of them. Mauser does his best to ensure his is the one chosen to remain open- by fair means or foul. A number of jokes were reprised from the first movie, including a sequence at the Blue Oyster Bar and a cameo from Georgina Spelvin's hooker. As before, critics hated the movie but the public were still happy to see the gang back – though not in quite so larger numbers. *Police Academy 3* made $43M throughout its theatrical run, with an opening weekend take of $9M.

Given the low budget costs involved, the studio didn't mind that the sequels weren't as successful as the first movie (or the previous one). April 1987 saw the release of *Police Academy 4: Citizens on Patrol*. The film would mark Steve Guttenberg's final appearance in the series. Along with the cast of regulars, G W Bailey returned as Harris. Newcomers included Sharon Stone and a young David Spade – whose stunt double was played by skateboarding legend Tony Hawk (who ended up getting fired for being too tall and unable to hide his face from the camera). This time around Lassard comes up with the idea of recruiting ordinary members of the public to be part of his Citizens on Patrol program. Now four films in, the series was beginning to struggle even with fans. While it opened to an OK $8M, it ended up making just $28M in total.

With Guttenberg choosing to work on *Three Men and a Baby*, a new lead was required for *Police Academy 5: Assignment Miami Beach*. Newcomer Matt McCoy got the job of Nick Lassard, the commandant's nephew. While much of the cast returned, Bobcat Goldthwait and Tim Kazurinsky were absent (in truth, when Goldthwait couldn't work out a deal with the studio, he opted not to return. The producers figured that without Zed there was little point in having Sweetchuck in the movie, so Kazurinsky was also dropped). Despite debuting at no.1, the film struggled and didn't surpass $20M in North America.

Warner Brothers and Maslansky pressed on with another sequel a year later. The original idea was to relocate the action to London, and the producers approached Ben Elton and Richard Curtis (of *Blackadder* fame) to provide a script. The duo passed on *The London Beat* and the action moved back the United States. *Police Academy 6: City Under Siege* saw Matt McCoy return as Nick Lassard, but it marked the final appearances for Bubba Smith and Marion Ramsey. However, Bruce Mahler, who played Fackler, did return after a two picture absence. Critics had long since given up on the series and with a paltry box office total of $11.5M it seemed the public finally had too. It would be five years before another Police Academy movie was produced.

In 1988, the year the fifth movie was released, an animated TV show was produced. It featured many of the same characters along with some new recruits (and protagonists), as well as a canine division. None of the original cast voiced their characters. It ran for two seasons and spawned a set of action figures and vehicles. Marvel also released a short-lived comic book tie-in. In 1990, came rumours of a video game adaptation for the Nintendo Entertainment System. Screenshots appeared in a number of magazines of the time but the game (or games, there were said to be two different versions) was never released.

The series lay dormant until 1994 and the release *of Police Academy 7: Mission to Moscow*. Only five of the original cast returned for the picture – George Gaynes, Michael Winslow, David Graf, G.W Bailey and Leslie Easterbrook (the former three appearing in all seven movies). Christopher Lee played a Russian commandant who calls in his old friend Lassard when he needs help dealing with mafia boss Ron Perlman. Also appearing in what was only her second feature was Claire Forlani, who would go on to star in Kevin Smith's *Mallrats* and opposite Brad Pitt in *Meet Joe Black.*

In actual fact, G.W Bailey's Harris wasn't in the original script and was hastily added after Bubba Smith dropped out, an incident caused by the producer's reluctance to give Marion Ramsey a part. *Police Academy 7* actually shot some sequences in Russia, and the cast and crew found themselves in the middle of a violent coup. Plans were made to move production to Budapest, but after a few days the incident had been contained and filming could continue. Director Alan Metter disowned the movie after Maslansky insisted on more slapstick comedy (over the cultural difference-based humour Metter preferred). In the end, it was all for naught – Warner Brothers barely released the film and it earned $126K.

That was the end for Police Academy – as far as movies went. In 1997, *Police Academy: The Series* hit the small screen. It ran for one season, comprised of 26 hour long episodes. Only Michael Winslow would return as a regular, though David Graf and Leslie Easterbrook both appeared in single episodes, as did Tim Kazurinsky and Art Metrano – oddly playing different characters to the ones they'd portrayed in the movie series. In terms of the Police Academy franchise, only Michael Winslow has appeared in every film and live action TV show episode.

Of the principal cast, Steve Guttenberg and Kim Cattrall enjoyed the biggest success outside of the series – at least initially. Guttenberg appeared in the 1985 comedy drama *Cocoon, Short Circuit* in 1986 and the smash hit *Three Men and a Baby*, which ended up being the biggest film of 1987. The sequel released three years later was another success, though not on the same scale as the original. Guttenberg was largely absent from screens after that, appearing in just a handful of smaller movies over the next five years. In the 2000s, he turned his hand to directing with *P.S Your Cat is Dead!* and appeared in a recurring role on the TV show *Veronica Mars*. Since that time, he has appeared in a number of low budget movies, preferring to spend time concentrating on his charity work. Post-Police Academy Kim Cattrall appeared in *Mannequin* and *Big Trouble in Little China*, amongst other works, but it is her role as Samantha Jones in *Sex and the City* for which she will be forever known.

David Graf worked extensively in all manner of TV and movie roles, including *Lois & Clark, Malcolm in the Middle* and *The West Wing*. He died of a heart attack aged only 50 years old – both his father and grandfather had suffered the same fate at roughly the same age. Similarly, Bubba Smith worked steadily throughout the 1990s, making one-off appearances in various shows. He died in 2011 from heart disease and drug intoxication. After his one-and-only appearance in the series, Donovan Scott appeared in the short-lived Lucille Ball sitcom, *Life with Lucy*. Various roles followed, and since the year 2000 he has specialised in playing Santa Claus, appearing as the character (or a relation) in more than ten different shows and films.

As well as playing Commandant Lassard, George Gaynes appeared in the mid-80s sitcom *Punky Brewster*, which ran for over eighty episodes. He won positive notices for his work in *Vanya on 42nd Street* and also had a cameo in the Police Academy TV series. He retired from acting in 2003 at the age of eighty-six and passed away in February 2016. G.W Bailey, who appeared opposite Kim Cattrall in *Mannequin* and Steve Guttenberg in *Short Circuit* found success in TNT's *Bible* series, featuring in three different stories. He became a series regular on *The Closer*, in which he appeared in 108 episodes, and the show's spin-off, *Major Crimes*. Bailey is also noted for his extensive charity work with the Sunshine Kids Foundation.

Outside of the Police Academy series, Marion Ramsey did little film or TV work, though she did reprise her character for an episode of *Robot Chicken*. In contrast, Leslie Easterbrook worked consistently throughout the 1990s and beyond, in TV, film and voiceover roles. She took over the role of Mother Firefly in Rob Zombie's *The Devil's Rejects* when Karen Black dropped out. Easterbrook continues to work apace, already amassing over ten different roles in 2015. Finally, Michael Winslow, who was there from the first movie to the last TV show, continued to perform in all manner of roles, both as characters and himself. Since 2008, he has hosted the cable TV show, *Way Back Wednesday with Winslow* and tours his stand-up routine globally. In something of a mini-reunion, Winslow, along with Steve Guttenberg, Marion Ramsey and Leslie Easterbrook all appeared in the 2015 disaster movie, *Lavalantula*.

Over the years there have been many, many attempts at getting a new sequel or even a remake off the ground. In 2003, Maslansky announced plans to make an eighth movie after seeing the success of *Starsky and Hutch*. Most of the cast were said to be interested in returning, as was Hugh Wilson, but the plans were shelved in 2006. Two years later Winslow confirmed his interest to return and Steve Guttenberg told the BBC's Simon Mayo that he was working on a script with Warner Bros, with a plan to direct.

In 2010, the film was still in development with a new script being produced by David Diamond and David Weissman. That same year, Bobcat Goldthwait, now a director, issued a statement that Hollywood should reboot the series and confirmed that Guttenberg would return, and that the studio were hoping to secure Kim Cattrall and Sharon Stone too. In 2012, Michael Winslow revealed that Shaquille O'Neal had been approached to replace Hightower in the eighth movie and that Jeremy Garelick (who co-wrote *The Break*

Up) had been hired to write the script. At the time of writing, there have been no further entries produced but that all looks set to change in the near future. In April 2014, it was announced that acclaimed sketch show artists Key & Peele had been hired to co-produce a new movie with Paul Maslansky. Further news came in July 2015 when the duo confirmed that their sketch series would be coming to end after the current series and that Police Academy was their next project.

Although much of the goodwill earned by the first picture was squandered by its sequels, it remains one of the most successful comedy films of the 1980s. The original movie is by far the best of the series and musters some genuine laughs. Relatively tame by today's standards, it still has one or two risqué set pieces, and its ability to build on early jokes often pays off. While it may not have had the hard edge of *48 Hrs.* or the wit of *Ghostbusters*, Police Academy remains an enjoyable slice of 1980s comedy.

If Police Academy was your thing, try one of these…

Porky's

Set in the 1950s, Porky's is the tale of a group of high school students and their exploits with the opposite sex. In an effort to get one of their own to lose his virginity, they visit the local brothel of the title, but things go awry, leaving the group humiliated. While one swears revenge, the others continue in their pursuit of girls and sex.

While not the first sex comedy of the time, Porky's, more than any other film, is responsible for the genre exploding in the early 1980s. A failure with critics, it went on to become the fifth biggest release of 1982, making an astounding $105M from a budget of only $5M. Two direct sequels followed, along with many, many imitators. It was also a huge hit on video, and seeing it served as something of a rite of passage for many a schoolboy.

Trivia: Porky's was once the most successful Canadian movie ever produced, a title it held on to for 24 years, until it was usurped by *Bon Cop Bad Cop.*

National Lampoon's Vacation

The first (and best) in the series of Vacation movies, featuring the Griswolds. In an effort to bond with this family, Clark decides to drive them all across country to visit Wally World, a Disneyland-like theme park. Mishaps of all kinds befall the family, including crashing the car, getting tagged with graffiti, dealing with a dead aunt and the unfortunate fate of her dog.

Directed by Harold Ramis and based on a John Hughes short story he wrote during a blizzard, Vacation is a fantastic comedy with great leads in Chevy Chase and Beverly D'Angelo. The sequels didn't fare as well (though the Christmas one holds a soft spot for many) but this first movie still plays well and continues to stand up to repeated viewings.

Trivia: John Candy's part was added after poor test audience reactions to the original ending.

Stripes

Bill Murray and Harold Ramis star in this military comedy directed by Ivan Reitman. John Winger's life has hit rock bottom – he's lost his job, his girlfriend and his apartment. In a fit of desperation (or madness) he decides to join the army, dragging friend Russell Ziskey with him. Winger's devil-may-care attitude sees him clash with drill sergeant Hulka but also enables him to rally the troops when needed.

An hilarious comedy, with a great central performance by Murray. Warren Oates is also solid as Hulka, and the likes of Ramis, John Candy and John Larroquette provide excellent support. A huge critical and commercial success, the central team would reconvene a few years later to work on the mega-hit, Ghostbusters.

Trivia: It was originally written as *Cheech & Chong Join the Army*. When the duo wanted too much creative control, Reitman suggested they hire Harold Ramis to star and rewrite the script, knowing he would be able to convince Murray to join the cast.

Risky Business

There's a time for playing it safe and a time for...

Studio: Warner Bros. Release

Date: 5th August 1983

Director: Paul Brickman

Starring: Tom Cruise, Rebecca De Mornay

Budget: $6.2M – 2015 Equivalent: $14.9M

U.S Box Office: $63.5M – 2015 Equivalent: $152.7M

Joel Goodson is on the verge of graduating from high school, with thoughts of attending Princeton, like his father. Left alone for a few days while his parents are away, Joel inadvertently gets involved in a one-night stand with a call girl named Lana. But after his father's Porsche ends up in Lake Michigan, Joel needs the help of Lana, and her friends to raise the money to get it fixed before his folks return. Joel is about to find out more about life and business than he could ever learn in college.

Paul Brickman made Tom Cruise a star back in the early 1980s, yet his name is one that is all but forgotten nowadays. It is not unusual for a first time director to strike gold and go on to bigger things as result. In fact, in recent years, even a minor hit can secure a director a major picture deal, something to which the likes of Marc Webb and Colin Trevorrow can attest. Yet Brickman would do the opposite – while Cruise and Risky Business were blazing a trail back in the late summer of 1983, he chose to turn his back on the offers and money, and seemingly fade away.

Paul Brickman was born in 1949, the son of comic strip artist Morrie Brickman, and showed a flair for the arts from a young age. After graduating, he found work as a story analyst and camera assistant, but soon added scriptwriting to his resume. His first produced work was *The Bad News Bears in Breaking Training* (1977), the sequel to the well-received Walter Matthau/Tatum O'Neal baseball comedy. He donned an associate producer's hat for his next screenplay, the Jonathan Demme-directed *Handle with Care* (AKA *Citizen's Band*). Like many scriptwriters, it wasn't long before Brickman became disenchanted with the way his work was being handled by others and he realised that the only way to change that was to get out of the game or do the job himself. He wanted to make a film with humour and style all of its own – something that a high school version of himself would want to see.

With Ronald Reagan in power and the early excesses of the 1980s already rearing their heads, Brickman had some basis for his script. He hired a cabin in the middle of nowhere and, spurred on by seeing his friends switching from Philosophy to Business degrees, began to write *White Boys off the Lake*. By the end of the first week, he was sure the idea was a great one. By the second, he was still confident, but by the third he wasn't sure any of it was good and ended up finding a producer to help him decide.

He would later claim the script was his reaction to *The Graduate* and an effort to show the darker side of capitalism. The final lines of the screenplay were actually the first ones Brickman wrote, and he'd use them when it came to pitching the idea to various studios, now aided by producers Jon Avnet and Steve Tisch. Despite their best efforts, no-one was interested in what had now been titled Risky Business. As was the time, studios wanted another *Porky's*, another sex romp; they weren't interested in a serious script from what would be a first-time director, especially with no major star attached. However, when a friend passed the manuscript on to music producer David Geffen, they finally found an interested party who would be willing to give them both the money and the time to do the material justice. The Geffen Company, the film production arm, was still in its early days with only Robert Towne's *Personal Best* on its books, but Geffen was willing to give Brickman a shot at directing. He also encouraged him not to rush into casting and that he would know the right person for the lead when he saw him.

Brickman certainly took the statement to heart as casting on Risky Business stretched to almost a year. Producer Jon Avnet knew that the success of the film lay in the chemistry of the two leads, and during that period they auditioned a veritable who's who of Hollywood talent – both upcoming and established. Timothy Hutton was actually their first choice to play Joel Goodson but turned the offer down. Tom Hanks, Nicolas Cage and John Cusack all tested and at one point, Brian Backer was said to have been cast as the lead, as was Kevin Anderson. The female lead was equally as tough to cast. Kim Basinger and Sharon Stone both tried out for the part, the former apparently turning down the offer. Diane Lane was also interested, having been handed the script while working on *The Outsiders*, but her father forbade her from playing 'a twenty-something hooker'.

Rebecca De Mornay came into the casting process early on but was dismissed; partly it would seem due to a lack of experience – she had had one very minor role in Francis Ford Coppola's *One From The Heart*. Brickman and the producers continued to see others for the role and ended up coming back to De Mornay at around the same time they saw an upcoming actor called Tom Cruise. At this point, casting had been going on for many months, and most of the other parts had been filled – indeed according to Andrew Morton's account of the casting process in his book on Cruise, Kevin Anderson and Megan Mullally had been tentatively cast in the lead roles and had tested against other cast members (Mullally would end up with a blink-and-you'll-miss-it cameo) but Brickman still auditioned others as he wasn't sold on the leads.

Curtis Armstrong, who made his feature debut on the picture, had the part of best friend Miles nailed the second he walked in and consequently found himself playing against many of the prospective male leads. Armstrong had impressed the producers immediately and would later explain he based his character on someone he knew very well in high school. Similarly, Bronson Pinchot would make his film debut on Risky Business and also came with his character all mapped out. Brickman stated in a 2014 interview that having Armstrong and Pinchot be so perfect right off the bat helped him immensely, as everything else was chaotic.

Tom Cruise had gotten into acting during school. As a result of his family moving a great number of times, the young Cruise attended fourteen different schools in fifteen years. As a result of always being the new kid, he threw himself into sports to help boost his popularity, excelling at almost every one he tried out for. By fourth grade, he had gotten into drama and music, appearing in an improvised ensemble piece called *IT*. As a result of an injury picked up during a wrestling match, Cruise tried out for roles in *Godspell* and *Guys & Dolls* and soon swapped sports for acting full-time. His first on-screen credit was a bit-part in the romantic drama, *Endless Love*, which he followed up with a memorable turn as Cadet Captain

David Shawn in *Taps*, opposite Timothy Hutton. He then landed the part of Steve Randle in Francis Ford Coppola's *The Outsiders*. It was while working on that picture that he received the script for Risky Business (according to Diane Lane, it was Cruise who also gave her the script and suggested she try out for Lana).

Brickman wasn't sold on the actor based on his killer role in *Taps*, and when he dropped by the office still in his *Outsiders'* garb of greased back hair, fake tattoos and a greyed-out tooth, he was even more convinced Cruise wasn't right for the part. They did a short read through but as the actor told Cameron Crowe in a 1986 article for Interview magazine, he was terrible at doing a cold read of a script. Brickman dismissed the actor but Cruise asked if they could start again from the top, which allowed him to trying something different. Before long, they'd worked through half of the script. Cruise went back to filming on *The Outsiders* but returned to Los Angeles to audition again and met, the then already-cast, Rebecca De Mornay. Brickman wanted to see if the duo had chemistry but due to actor's commitment to The Outsiders, there was little time to do a screen test – Cruise flew in at 1am and needed to back in Tulsa by 10pm that night. This is how Paul Brickman found himself outside Tom Cruise's apartment block at 5am. The actor was running late and the director was about to give up when he finally emerged (He joked later that history could have been quite different had he not waited those extra five minutes).

They assembled at producer Steve Tisch's house. Cruise was still heavily built for his current role, but was now wearing a 'preppy' Adidas shirt and his hair was no longer slicked-back. His chemistry with De Mornay was apparent instantly. She could confidently boss him around, while he played both cool and naive to a tee. What impressed Brickman the most was when Cruise asked for the chance to replay scenes so that he could try out different things with his character. By the end of the screen test, no one was in any doubt that they had found their leads. The only remaining obstacle was Cruise's bulked up Outsider's frame. The producers told him he'd got a good shot at the part if he could slim down. Once work on the Coppola movie was completed, the actor lost 14 pounds thanks to jogging every day and went on a strict diet. Once he'd reached his goal, he stopped exercising and went back to eating normally to add on a layer of puppy fat.

As for the rest of the casting, Nicholas Pryor took on the part of Joel's father, with Janet Carroll portraying his mother. For the character of Guido the killer pimp, Brickman wanted someone with weasel-like qualities. He found them in Joe Pantoliano, an actor who to that point had mixed TV movie work with appearances in a number of televisions shows, including *M.A.S.H* and *Free Country*. However, as Brickman would shortly find out, not everyone was happy with Pantoliano's casting.

A summer 1982 shoot was planned in and around Highland Park, Illinois (the director's old stomping ground) with Warner Bros. putting up the $6.2M budget. The cast had a rare luxury afforded to them by its director, similar to that given to the cast of *Fright Night* by Tom Holland. A week before the shoot was set to commence, Cruise, Armstrong and co. all assembled in Illinois to read through and rehearse the script. More than that, Brickman wanted them to hang out and bond as if they'd grown up and attended school together. He hoped this would make the cast more relaxed around each other and more believable to the audience. However, while the budget stretched to rehearsals, it didn't cover clothing, hotel costs or a travel allowance, meaning the majority of the actors had to supply their own outfits and foot their own bills.

While Brickman may have been making his directorial debut on the picture, he had a crystal clear vision for how he wanted it to look and sound – right down to character movements for some shots (according to Curtis Armstrong). But this exacting nature would make the shoot a somewhat difficult one and push the already tight budget to its limits. The director wanted Risky Business to have a style quite different to other teen movies and was heavily influenced by Bernardo Bertolucci's *The Conformist*. Once shooting got under way, it became clear that Brickman and the cinematographer were going to have issues. Direction was ignored, shots were lit differently to how requested and anything out of the norm was dismissed as being too much work. The cinematographer was soon replaced by Reynaldo Villalobos, who gelled more with the director's vision. However, commitments to another picture saw him leave during production, to be replaced by Clint Eastwood's cinematographer, Bruce Surtees (the duo had worked together on seven films at that point).

A number of sequences caused the cast and crew a headache, magnified by Brickman's attention-to-detail. The first sex scene between Joel and Lana was a comedy-of-errors. It was meant to be dream-like – the doors would open and Lana would enter with wind blowing leaves into the room. In reality, the first attempt saw the leaves flop onto the floor in a pile. The second run through was the opposite, with leaves (and the cast's hair and clothes) flying everywhere. Much more adjustment was required before the shot could be completed. For Joel's iconic sunglasses, Cruise and Brickman ended up at a local optician during a break for lunch after the costume department could offer nothing suitable. The budget barely stretched to two pair. After the film's release, the Ray-Ban Wayfarers he wore become a bestseller for the company, helping revive its fortunes in the process.

The Porsche sequence, in which Joel desperately tries to stop his father's car from rolling into a lake, caused more problems. A perfect location had been found but it took Jon Avnet four months to convince the city to let them shoot there. When permission was finally granted, they were given just three nights in which to get the entire sequence. While the location was being prepared, shooting on other scenes was taking place elsewhere. When the producer arrived on set, he discovered to his horror that the fake dock had been built in the wrong place. It turned out that the production designer had taken it upon himself to set up the shot (which included the fake dock) in a different area because it allowed for the cityscape to be visible in the background.

The problem was this new location had no incline, so there was no way for them to shoot the Porsche slowly rolling away. Brickman was distraught when called to set, but having spent so long getting permission, Avnet refused to give in. He had three different crews, working for 24 hours to rebuild the dock in the proper location. The bad weather saw them unable to shoot for two of the three nights, meaning all the shots (including the dock collapse) had to be achieved on that final evening. In what would become a trademark of his career, Cruise did his own stunts, stumbling in front of the car to try and stop it, then jumping onto the bonnet as it came to a stop at the end of the dock. A diver had carefully worked to remove pins in the construction but as they only had one shot at it, they had no way of knowing if it would collapse on cue. More worrying was what would happen to the film's star when the dock and car fell into the water. For one of the few times during the shoot, luck was on its side – the car, Cruise and what was left of the dock, crashed into the water perfectly.

True to his word, David Geffen supported the project but after a visit to the set, he wasn't happy with Joe Pantoliano's performance. Over dinner with Paul Brickman that night, he strongly expressed his concerns and stated he wanted Pantoliano off the movie. The director refused to let him go; Geffen repeated his statement, and once again was met with refusal. They went back and forth for some time before Geffen eventually gave up. He received no further interference, though did go on to state that Geffen (or his people) supplied him with copious production notes, most of which he ignored. Unbeknownst to Brickman, in a few short months he'd be fighting tooth-and-nail with Geffen and Warner Bros. over the picture. In an interesting aside, Jon Avnet revealed in a 2013 interview that Pantoliano and Geffen had had words during the set visit, and it was for *that* reason and not for his performance, that the mogul wanted him gone. [When questioned, Avnet declined to comment on what had actually been said].

There would be one final difficult sequence that would cause issues for the cast and crew – the L-train love scene. The setup was in the script and during an extended dinner, Avnet and Brickman came up with the bizarre idea of using green screen to have the train come off the tracks and fly over the city as the couple make love. Rough footage was shot but it became evident almost straight away that it was completely laughable and simply didn't work. The pair joked on the DVD commentary that had it been used in the finished film, neither of them would have worked again. In the end, the production secured the use of an actual train for the shot and planned to film as it was being driven. Their window was extremely limited – they had the train (and the track loop) from 1am to 5am, and in that time they'd need to set up, get the shot and clear out before the public began to arrive. They hit a snag straight away when they realised that none of their equipment was weighted down. The train began to move and everything toppled over. Unable to reverse back to the station to reset, they had to wait for the train to complete a full loop before starting again.

When they actually began filming, Cruise and De Mornay had trouble getting into the moment. However, according to comments made in Andrew Morton's unauthorised biography, Brickman stated "It was hard to get them started, but it was harder to get them to stop". By now, their time was up and they still hadn't completed all the shots. Filming past their 5am deadline, early morning commuters were greeted by the sight of a single carriage slowly passing through their station with a naked Tom Cruise and Rebecca De Mornay simulating sex. The entire sequence took six weeks to stitch together during the editing process, partly because of the methods of the time, but also because of a strobe effect used to give the sequence its dream-like quality (Something Avnet suggested, having seen it used in a 1970s picture he'd worked on). Each time they had a finished piece, it had to be sent to the lab to be printed before they could see if it actually worked.

It is hard to believe that what would become Risky Business' most famous scene consisted of just one line in the script – 'Joel dances in underwear through the house'. The sequence was meant to signify the character's new-found freedom and independence, and while Brickman considered it a key moment for the character, he felt it was no more or less significant than any other part of the film. He had an idea of what it should consist of, and although he suggested that Joel dance around to the Bob Seger track *Old Time Rock and Roll*, he was equally happy to allow the actor to choose his own music. Cruise went through tape after tape but kept coming back to *Old Time Rock and Roll*. The duo got together one Sunday, when both actually had the day off from filming. They talked and walked through some ideas and decided to use the whole house rather than just one room.

Joel's entrance, in which he slides into view, took some experimentation to get right. Cruise tried it without socks, with socks and at one point even bounced into shot by way a mini-trampoline. Brickman liked the slide entrance but the actor kept sliding past his mark. In the end, Cruise waxed half the floor and left the other untouched, this allowed him a smooth entrance and a perfect stop. Various props were placed around the house and Brickman told his young actor to 'go wild'. Each time they rolled, Cruise tried different things, adding more and more as he went. All up the sequence took around half a day to shoot and ended up becoming one of the most iconic of the entire decade.

Risky Business shot for fifty days in total, and while the cast and crew moved on to other projects, the director began the long task of assembling his edit. Work had also begun on the soundtrack; in truth, that had commenced at the script stage, with Brickman choosing particular tracks that he thought would fit well with certain scenes. During the extensive casting stage, he'd heard the Phil Collins song, *In The Air Tonight* and knew it had to be in the picture. It would become Lana's unofficial theme; its sadness paralleling hers. For the instrumental tracks, electronic group Tangerine Dream were commissioned.

Work continued apace and a couple of additional scenes were shot in the January of 1983, the section with Lana talking while Joel plays with his train set being one of them. Cruise had to fit the extra work in between filming on his next movie, the sports drama *All The Right Moves*. Eventually, with the mix and soundtrack still to complete, the film had its first screening at the Writers Guild. The overall result was positive, but Warner Bros. and Geffen disliked the ending, feeling it was bittersweet and would leave cinema-goers on a downer. Brickman stood firm, and refused to alter it, stating that to do so would change the entire message of the piece. Neither side would back down and a long and protracted battle began.

The studio continued to push for a new ending and things turned ugly over the next six months. Warner Bros. threatened to fire Brickman while he was still working on the film's mix and hire someone else to shoot a new ending and complete the work. In amongst all this turmoil, the first Tangerine Dream tracks arrived – and they were far from what the production team had hoped for when they'd hired the band. Instead of using their own unique sound, the group had attempted to emulate a 1950/60s teen movie soundtrack. Brickman and Avnet were unsure how to proceed, and even discussed the possibility of scrapping the Tangerine Dream stuff and hiring a new group. Instead, whilst still in the midst of battle with the studio, the pair flew to Berlin and met with the musicians. Over the course of ten nights (the band preferred to work from 6pm into the early hours) they reworked the soundtrack, using new and existing material.

The fight with the studio continued, but a breakthrough was ultimately made. A new, more upbeat finale was shot, and Warner Bros. agreed to test the movie with both endings (whether this is how they convinced Brickman to shoot the new ending is unknown). A screening in San Diego saw the audience side with the studio, and that as good as sealed the deal for them. The director later stated that any other night, with any other audience, it could have easily gone the other way. As a result of the struggle, the studio refused to hold a premiere or even throw a cast and crew screening.

The marketing of the movie was difficult too, and the first poster, depicting a cartoon version of Tom Cruise in a bed full of girls surrounded by money, made Brickman question if the studio even knew what the movie was about. He suspected they thought (or hoped) that they had their own version of *Porky's*. He ended up taking the shot of the actor in his sunglasses that was used for the basis of the poster. The studio attempted to alter that too by giving Cruise a 'cheeky' wink. The director hated it and versions of his own shot were used to market the film. While he may not have been happy with the ending, he was incredibly proud of the picture and just prior to its release, went out to dinner with Cruise and De Mornay (who were now living together) and told them all their lives were about to change forever.

Risky Business was set to open in August 1983. A low budget movie with no major stars, made by a first-time director that contained themes of capitalism and prostitution. It's probably safe to assume that Warner Bros. would have been happy to break even on the picture. The fledgling stars did their best to sell the film on the talk show circuit but what really got people's interest, initially at least, were the reviews. Risky Business earned some of the best notices of any film released that year. All involved were singled out for praise, and many reviews noted the fantastic chemistry between its leads. Roger Ebert was equally impressed with Brickman's ear for dialogue stating that he 'has an ear so good that he knows what to leave out. This is one of those movies where a few words or a single line says everything that needs to be said'. The Tangerine Dream score came in for positive word too.

The film debuted on August 5th and had to contend with a number of major releases – many of which shared the same demographic. *National Lampoon's Vacation* was enjoying its second weekend in the number one spot and *Trading Places*, *Class*, *Staying Alive* and *Private School* were all still at more theatres than Risky Business would open in. And while *Krull* and *Return of the Jedi* weren't direct competition, they were still pulling in the crowds, the latter now in its eleventh week of release and showing little signs of slowing. On that opening weekend at 670 locations, Risky Business made an impressive $4.2M and dropped into third place. A week later, and with word-of-mouth spreading, it actually increased its takings, making $4.5M. In less than ten days the picture had recouped its budget. Buoyed by success, Warner Bros. added 198 screens for the third weekend and saw another rise in takings over the previous frame, though it was held off the top spot by new release, Easy Money.

After a month on general release, Risky Business had made almost $30M with barely a dip in week-to-week takings. Now at over 1100 locations, it saw a massive boost in its fifth weekend, making $6.3M (an increase of 31% on the previous frame). All told, it remained in second place for seven weeks and crossed the $50M threshold in week nine. The film stayed in the top ten for an incredible twelve weeks and didn't disappear until mid-November. When the dust had settled, Risky Business had made $63.5M in North America, against a budget of $6.2M and made Tom Cruise a star. It went on to become the tenth biggest movie of 1983. Like many releases of the time, it enjoyed an extended life on the home video market and influenced all manner of films and filmmakers.

While they'd been making the picture, Jon Avnet had been convinced the soundtrack was revolutionary, something that David Geffen disagreed with. He disliked many of the tracks they'd chosen and had even suggested they 'drop the dinosaur music' in reference to a Led Zeppelin track that had originally been chosen for one scene [it was replaced by the Talking Heads track, *Swamp*, which did actually contain the words "risky business"]. Initially, the soundtrack album wasn't released in North America, but when imports (and pirated copies) of it went on the rise, Geffen officially put out the album. Bob Seger's *Old Time Rock and Roll*, which had been a very minor hit upon its release in 1979, found a whole new generation of fans. Similarly, Tangerine Dream would state that 60-70% of their future success was as a result of working on Risky Business.

For Paul Brickman, with success came the attention, and in his own words, 'I had Hollywood coming at me full throttle'. He left Los Angeles almost immediately and did his best to keep everyone at arm's length. Even when studios sent him gifts and threw countless scripts and offers at him, he continued to resist, turning down the likes of *Forrest Gump* and *Rain Man* in the process. It would be seven years before he returned to directing, with *Men Don't Leave*, a remake of the French film *La Vie Continue*. It starred Jessica Lange,

Chris O'Donnell and Joan Cusack, and was produced by Jon Avnet. It barely registered at the box office, earning only $6M off a budget of $7M. He went on to contribute to the screenplay for the Clint Eastwood film *True Crime* in 1999. In 2001, he co-wrote the TV movie *Uprising*, again with Jon Avnet (who also directed). His only other credit in the last ten years has been on the short, *Allison*.

Jon Avnet went on to produce a great number of movies, TV shows and shorts, as well as finding time to write and direct in between. In the 1990s, he made *Fried Green Tomatoes, The War* and *Red Corner,* while producing the likes of *The Mighty Ducks* trilogy, *George of the Jungle* and *Up Close and Personal*. In recent years, he's worked primarily in television, directing a number of episodes for the show, *Justified*. Steve Tisch stuck with producing, working on *Big Business, Soul Man* and *Bad Influence* in the 1980s. He would later co-produce *Forrest Gump, The Long Kiss Goodnight* and *The Weather Man*. Most recently he produced the Jake Gyllenhaal drama, *Southpaw* and the Denzel Washington actioner, *The Equalizer*.

Curtis Armstrong moved on to further success with *Revenge of the Nerds* (and its two sequels) and opposite John Cusack in *Better Off Dead*. A recurring role in the TV show *Moonlighting*, as Herbert Viola, is the role for which he is probably best known to people of a certain age. He has continued to work primarily in television, amassing well over 75 credits in the likes of *The Closer,*

Supernatural and *New Girl*, as well as the animated works *Dan Vs,
The Emperor's New School* and *Robot & Monster*. Bronson Pinchot
had a memorable cameo in *Beverly Hills Cop* (which he reprised for
the third movie) before appearing in the long-running TV show,
Perfect Strangers. He has continued to mix TV and movie work and
recently appeared in the Liev Schreiber show, *Ray Donovan*.

In the years following Risky Business, Rebecca De Mornay took on
a number of different roles, but struggled to find the same level of
success. She played opposite Jon Voight in the well-received (but
criminally underseen) *Runaway Train*, before switching to the likes
of *Beauty and the Beast* and a misguided remake of *And God
Created Women*. The early 1990s saw a string of successes for the
actress, particularly her villainess role in *The Hand That Rocked the
Cradle. Backdraft, The Three Musketeers* and *Guilty As Sin* all
provided further chances for De Mornay to show her range. In recent
years, she's appeared in *Lords of Dogtown, Wedding Crashers* and
gave another menacing turn in *Mother's Day*. In 2012, she appeared
as Finch's mother in *American Reunion*.

As for Tom Cruise, he followed up his success with *All The Right
Moves*, before being absent from screens for almost two years thanks
to an extended shoot on Ridley Scott's, *Legend*. However, if Risky
Business had made the actor a star, his role in the 1986 action drama
Top Gun, shot him into mega-stardom, from which he has barely
looked back. While that film became the most successful of 1986,

Cruise was earning his dramatic chops opposite Paul Newman in Martin Scorsese's *The Color of Money*. Two years later, he appeared with Dustin Hoffman in *Rain Man* and won much acclaim as Ron Kovic in *Born on the Fourth of July*. Even lightweight fare such as *Cocktail* and *Days of Thunder* made money.

Ron Howard's *Far and Away*, in which he starred opposite then wife, Nicole Kidman, was something of a misfire, but Cruise followed this up with back-to-back hits *A Few Good Men, The Firm* and *Interview with the Vampire*. In 1995, he appeared in action thriller *Mission Impossible*, which began a franchise that is still going some twenty years later. He changed tactics yet again, winning awards and box office for his work on *Jerry Maguire* (which was heavily influenced by Risky Business and Joel Goodson according to director Cameron Crowe), *Eyes Wide Shut* and *Magnolia*, which some claim is still his best performance to date. He worked again with Cameron Crowe on *Vanilla Sky* before joining Steven Spielberg's ambitious science fiction picture, *Minority Report*. Even 'lesser' hits such as *Collateral* and *The Last Samurai* cleared over $100M apiece.

Cruise reunited with Spielberg on *War of the Worlds* in 2005, which at the time of writing remains the actor's most successful picture in North America. A year on saw the second *Mission Impossible* sequel, but by that point, issues in his private life were beginning to overshadow his career. *Lions for Lambs* in 2007 was seen as a low point and pretty much his only out-and-out flop (ensemble musical,

Rock of Ages aside). A split from long-term agent and production partner Paula Wagner didn't help matters either. Like a number of actors, Cruise subsequently found his success abroad overshadowing that in North America. *Knight & Day*, in which he starred opposite Cameron Diaz stretched to $76M domestically, yet overseas earned a staggering $185M. *Jack Reacher*, *Oblivion* and the fantastic *Edge of Tomorrow* all followed that same path, with the latter clearing $269M. With the massive success of the fifth *Mission Impossible* movie, *Rogue Nation* in 2015, Tom Cruise arguably remains the biggest film star in the world.

To this day, Paul Brickman maintains his ending to the film remains the stronger one. It would be 30 years before an audience got to see his version when it was screened intact to mark the film's anniversary. While the fashions have aged somewhat, the themes within the picture still resonate and seem as relevant as they ever did. Similarly, its soundtrack may be very much of the time, but that doesn't detract from how impressive it still sounds. The iconic dance sequence is still emulated (and spoofed) to this day. By trying to create more than just another teen movie, Risky Business continues to find fans and remains one of the best movies of the decade.

Similar to Risky Business…

Weird Science

After defining a generation with *The Breakfast Club*, John Hughes
wrote and directed this teen-fantasy comedy which sees Anthony
Michael Hall and Ilan Mitchell-Smith creating the perfect woman
via their computer. When the fantasy becomes a reality in the guise
of Kelly LeBrock, the duo finds themselves in over their head –
especially when a huge house party they've thrown is overtaken by a
motorcycle gang.

Weird Science plays like the ultimate geek fantasy, the high school
nerds getting the girls and the popularity – all thanks to their
computer skills. There's much to enjoy here, including an obnoxious
Bill Paxton and a great sequence with Hall's parents, and Hughes'
writing elevates proceedings above the normal teen-sex comedy. In
fact, despite the 'It's Purely Sexual' tagline, the film contains little
that would score it a PG-13 rating these days. Passed over by *The
Breakfast Club* and *Ferris Bueller's Day Off*, Weird Science still
offers plenty of lightweight laughs.

Trivia: After expressing a desire to work with other filmmakers,
Anthony Michael Hall found himself completely shut out of John

Hughes' life, missing out on parts in *Ferris Bueller's Day Off* and *Pretty in Pink* in the process.

Stand by Me

Even all these years later, it's incredible to think that Stand by Me still ranks as one of the best Stephen King adaptations ever committed to film. Directed by Rob Reiner (who would go on to direct the equally brilliant, *Misery*) Stand by Me stars Wil Wheaton, Corey Feldman, River Phoenix and Jerry O'Connell as four friends who hope to become local heroes by locating a dead body.

The bittersweet tale has more in common with a John Hughes picture than the horror you'd normally associate with King, yet has a much darker edge running through it. The four leads display a maturity beyond their years, as they're portrayed as being scared, brave and ultimately, defiant. Overshadowed by other teen-centric pictures, Stand by Me remains a powerful coming-of-age saga.

Trivia: *Different Seasons*, the book of short stories from which Stand by Me was taken, also contains *Rita Hayworth and the Shawshank Redemption* and *Apt Pupil*. The fourth story, *The Breathing Method*, is the only one not to make it to the screen.

Ferris Bueller's Day Off

One of the best examples of 1980s escapism, Ferris Bueller is the simple tale of a popular guy who decides to skip school and spend the day with his girlfriend, Sloane, and best friend Cameron. Matthew Broderick is superb as the titular hero, but credit must also go to Alan Ruck as his downtrodden friend, who might just be having the best day of his life. A red Ferrari and the city of Chicago could be billed as co-stars, so central are they to the film.

The picture also contains memorable turns from Jeffrey Jones, as the high school principal on a mission to catch Ferris out, and Jennifer Grey as Jeanie, his overshadowed sister. Proceedings are backed by an eclectic soundtrack, hand-picked by Hughes himself and featuring the likes of The Beatles, Yello and Dream Academy. A $70M hit back in 1986, Ferris Bueller's Day Off is still endlessly watchable to this day.

Trivia: *Clue* director Jonathan Lynn directed the pilot episode of the Ferris Bueller TV series, which ran for 13 episodes in the early 1990s.

Clue

It's not just a game anymore.

Studio: Paramount

Release Date: 13th December 1985

Director: Jonathan Lynn

Starring: Tim Curry, Madeline Kahn

Budget: $8M – 2015 Equivalent: $17.8M

U.S Box Office: $14.6M – 2015 Equivalent: $32.5M

Six strangers each receive a mysterious letter inviting them to attend a meeting at a house in the country. Mrs White, Miss Scarlet, Mrs Peacock, Mr Green, Professor Plum and Colonel Mustard don't know each other, or so it seems, but each shares the same dark secret. Six Strangers, Six Rooms, Six Weapons....Should murder be this funny?

Inspiration for a movie can come from all manner of places and over the years that list has expanded far beyond what many thought possible. Books and plays soon gave way to comics, short stories and poems as the bases for film, while real-life events and mythology added further to the medium. The common theme was that there was a plot or narrative of some kind that could be adapted or expanded upon, no matter how flimsy the source. But when it was announced that Paramount Pictures were intending to make a movie based on the board game Cluedo, many thought Hollywood had really begun to scrape the barrel. Indeed, even the film's eventual director described it as "...the dumbest thing I ever heard." when it was pitched to him in the early 1980s.

Cluedo was invented by Anthony E. Pratt during the Second World War. Originally titled *Murder!*, Pratt and his wife Elva, who helped with the design, envisaged it as a new board game for families to play in bomb shelters during air raids. He applied for the patent in 1944 and presented the design to Norman Watson of Waddingtons. Watson snapped it up immediately, renaming the game Cluedo (a play on the word Clue and Ludo) but post-war shortages of material meant it didn't actually launch until 1949. It received a simultaneous US release, where it was licensed by Parker Brothers and renamed Clue. The game went through various changes during its design, with the character, room and weapon count all being altered and reduced. However, once released, the game remained virtually unchanged for almost 60 years.

Cluedo proved incredibly popular and for many children, marked their first foray into more mature game playing. One such fan was producer Debra Hill who, in a 1985 interview with the New York Times, talked about how she loved that it was a game of deduction rather than memorisation. Hill got her start in the business as a production assistant, but it was her work with John Carpenter for which she would become known. The duo first collaborated on *Assault on Precinct 13*, Carpenter as director, and Hill as script supervisor and assistant editor. While the picture wasn't a hit and didn't gain critical respect for a number of years, it set up a very fruitful partnership (both personal and professional). Their next collaboration was on the hugely successful *Halloween*, which Hill co-wrote and produced. It was around the time of working on *The Fog* that she was able to secure the rights to bring Clue to the silver screen. A deal was set up at Universal pictures under the supportive eye of the president of film production, Ned Tanen.

John Carpenter wouldn't be available to direct (if he was ever considered) due to finishing up work on *The Fog* and prepping his next picture, *Escape from New York*. Instead, Hill turned to John Landis, who had come to prominence with *Animal House* and *The Blues Brothers* and was currently enjoying success with *An American Werewolf in London*. Landis loved the idea but was stuck on how to bring the game to the screen, other than to inform Hill that the movie should not reference the game – it had to work for those who had never played it. He created a rough outline for the central plot but quickly realised he'd need to hire a writer to better shape the ideas and find a solution to the ending, or rather, the endings. In what was hoped to be a brilliant piece of promotion and provide a boost to the box office, it was decided that Clue should be distributed with four different endings, any one of which could logically tie up with what had come in the first two thirds of the movie. The general public wouldn't know which ending they'd see and it was hoped there would be a large percentage of return business as people tried to catch all four endings.

In October 1982, Landis turned to famed playwright Tom Stoppard in a hope of getting him to write Clue. Negotiations took place over the next couple of months and Stoppard flew out to meet with Landis in January of the next year. The writer agreed to take on the project but by March was struggling to bring the ideas together, telling Landis as much. The director discussed moving the location of the story to England, or another locale, if it would make it easier, and even went as far as suggesting the crimes in the story be unsolvable. The basic outline was expanded and characters began to have some backstory. The unique device of having four different endings (with four different killers) was also in place, and would prove to have a far-reaching impact upon the film.

A couple of weeks later, Stoppard wrote again to Landis and admitted defeat. He had completed roughly half of the script but was unhappy with the way it was developing. He'd found the central puzzles too difficult to reconcile and for the first time in his writing life, had a project he couldn't complete. By April, the two had gone their separate ways, and Clue was in need of another writer. There's conjecture here, perhaps clouded by time. According to transcripts of their meetings, Landis and Stoppard collaborated for only a few months (spending approximately two months on the writing itself). However, in a 2013 interview with Buzzfeed, Landis claimed Stoppard worked on the script for almost exactly a year before admitting defeat and returning his entire fee. Despite the differences in the length of time involved, it is confirmed by others that Stoppard did indeed return his payment.

Landis consulted with Stephen Sondheim and Anthony Perkins, who had written the Hollywood murder mystery *The Last of Sheila* together. The duo were very enthusiastic and had some great ideas, but asked for far too much money to be a feasible option. Further writers were entertained including PD James and Alan Ayckbourn, but none could crack the story, especially the puzzle of the four endings. One other notable contributor was playwright Warren Manzi, whose work actually pre-dates that of Tom Stoppard. Manzi turned in a 152-page script but it had little in common with any other version (or with Landis' ideas). A small review on the Art of Murder website (which dates the script as March 1982) describes details involving a writer, his genius daughter and an editor, who are tracking a killer who seems to be using the game as the basis for his crimes. The script contains a single ending and doesn't appear to have had any further development past the initial draft.

By now some time had passed; Hill had produced *Escape From New York* and two further *Halloween* sequels, along with the Stephen King adaptation *The Dead Zone*. Landis, too, had been busy, directing the Eddie Murphy/Dan Aykroyd smash hit *Trading Places*. But tragedy had struck on the 1983 picture, *Twilight Zone: The Movie*, when three actors were killed during the filming of Landis' segment. He went on to direct the legendary video for Michael Jackson's *Thriller* but the shadow of what had happened on the *Twilight Zone*, along with the impending court case, was constantly on his mind. In the meantime, Ned Tanen had left Universal Pictures and with him gone so too was the support for Clue. Fortunately, when the executive re-emerged at Paramount, the project was able to find a new home, and one of the picture's executive producers was about to find the man who would finally crack the mysteries of the script.

Jonathan Lynn was born in Bath in 1943 and after leaving school went to study law at Pembroke College in Cambridge. He soon caught the acting bug and appeared in the Footlights revue, Cambridge Circus (which included a run on Broadway). He switched to acting full-time and made his West End debut in *Green Julia*, for which he won a Most Promising Actor award. This was followed up by an appearance in the original West End production of *Fiddler on the Roof.* But acting alone couldn't pay the bills, so Lynn supplemented his income by writing for various sitcom and sketch shows including one of the forerunners to Monty Python and The Goodies, *Twice a Fortnight* (which featured Michael Palin, Graham Garden, Terry Jones and Bill Oddie).

More writing work followed on the likes of *Doctor at Large* and *Doctor at Sea*, along with a memorable appearance on sitcom *The Liver Birds*. By the early 1970s, Lynn and writing colleague George Layton took over scripting duties on the successful LWT series *On The Buses*, while the usual team were preparing the movie adaptations. While far from what Lynn was used to working on, he joked in a Den of Geek interview that it was the only time an episode of *On The Buses* scored a rave review from The Times.

Lynn was also directing a lot of theatre, but it was his work on political satire *Yes Minister* (which he co-created and co-wrote with Antony Jay) for which he would become best known. The show debuted on the BBC in 1980 and was an instant hit with audiences as well as being a critical success, winning BAFTA Best Comedy awards three years running. It was while directing *Loot* at London's National Theatre that Lynn took a call from his agent, who informed him that producer Peter Guber wanted to discuss a movie-writing project with him. Lynn was surprised, having never heard of Guber (or how Guber could possibly know of him) but agreed to take a meeting.

By this point in his career, Peter Guber was already a successful film producer. He'd begun his career at Columbia Pictures, and when he left he was granted a three-picture deal with the company. His first full producing credit was on the 1977 hit, *The Deep*, which he followed up a year later with the critically acclaimed *Midnight Express*. The picture earned seven Academy Award nominations and helped Guber win the Producer of the Year award from the National Association of Theatre Owners. He merged his Filmworks Company with Casablanca Records and had great success with the likes of Donna Summer, The Village People and Kiss. Forays into TV show producing followed and, in 1979, he formed Polygram Pictures, which went on to distribute the first Simpson/Bruckheimer smash, *Flashdance*. By 1983, he'd sold the company and formed a new producing partnership with Jon Peters. The duo were set up as executive producers on Clue, and in Jonathan Lynn, Guber was convinced he'd found his writer.

Lynn explained in a 2013 interview that Guber told him before he'd even sat down for their first meeting, that he had the perfect project for him. He went on to explain the rough outline of Clue, and in what capacity he needed Lynn – he would hire him to write the script from which John Landis would direct the movie. Despite Lynn stating the board game had no story, Guber insisted he fly out to Hollywood and meet with Landis. Years later, Lynn mentioned the only reason he'd initially agreed to meet John Landis was because he'd never flown first class before.

Having pitched the story so many times over the years, Landis was now an expert. He bowled Lynn over with his enthusiasm. He ran through the first half of the plot, detailing that the six characters were victims of a blackmail scheme and that they'd all been asked to attend a meeting. Each person is given a weapon, the lights go out and when they come up again their host, Mr Boddy, lies dead on the floor. By this point, Landis was bouncing around the room, shouting and screaming. He explained further murders take place and that suddenly the butler announces 'I know who did it!' Lynn, now on the edge-of-his-seat, asked who did do it, to which Landis replied 'That's what I need a writer for!'

However, once back at his hotel, the enthusiasm was gone and Lynn was at a loss for what to do. At his agent's behest, he came up with a few ideas and met up with Landis the next morning, who loved what he'd come up with and set about getting Lynn officially signed on-board to write the script. Again, the mandate came down – Clue must have four different endings, each that can work independently of the other and make sense with the first two thirds of the picture.

Lynn returned to the UK and got to work. Early in the script's development both writer and director realised that the key character wasn't any of the main six but rather Wadsworth the butler.

Wadsworth served as the perfect storyteller and amateur sleuth, allowing the audience to understand the evening's events – and perhaps even being part of the master plan. The character of a butler had appeared in Stoppard's script (where he was known as Cleese) but not to the extent or importance that he'd have in this new version. Lynn opted to set the film in the 1950s allowing him to play up the communism/McCarthyism angle. Part of the inspiration came from people Lynn knew who'd lived through this time and had found themselves blacklisted in Hollywood and forced to work overseas. It also added to the mystery and paranoia of the story; anyone could be a suspect – or victim.

The first draft ran for around 200 pages and was completed in the May of 1984. It took a week to write the first act but nearly three months to figure out the second. Lynn told the New York Times that the final 'who did what' act was hastily written on an eleven-hour flight to Los Angeles. The main differences from the finished script at that point were the story's location (Florida in the first draft) and the darker nature of the plot, which amped up the Communism aspect. All four endings were also present at this point, with a nastier ending for at least one of the killers. Furthermore, it was Lynn who came up with the idea that the colour character names (from the board game) would actually be pseudonyms.

There was more work required and Lynn took another pass (presumably based on notes from Landis), completing the second draft in June. It still ran very long and even at this early stage, there was much material that never made the finished picture (or even the shooting script). He'd make one further pass, further refining the endings and Wadsworth's explanation. In all, it took roughly six months to create and finalise the screenplay – and that didn't include revisions that would take place once the production moved forward. It is also worth pointing out that over the years, many have cited the influence of Neil Simon's *Murder by Death* on Clue, however Lynn (to this day) has never seen the picture and puts the influence on both pieces of work down to the writings of Agatha Christie and Dorothy L Sayers.

Landis, Debra Hill and executive producers Peter Guber and Jon Peters loved Lynn's work on the script and prepared to greenlight the picture into pre-production. There was just one snag – it had taken so long to reach this stage that John Landis was no longer free to direct the picture. He'd already agreed to take the reins on the Chevy Chase/Dan Aykroyd comedy, *Spies Like Us*. There was speculation that the director passed on Clue because he needed a 'big money picture' to help towards the impending *Twilight Zone* court case, for which he faced an involuntary manslaughter charge. In reality, Clue had been in development for many years and it was more a case of scheduling conflicts than anything else (the court case was eventually settled in 1987). Indeed, the director even stated that he'd have been happy to make the picture, but it would be at least another year before he could go into production.

This could easily have been the end of Clue. Despite the time spent on the many versions of the story and script over the years, it was still a low-key project. However, by this point, the director and writer had become good friends and after seeing a Georges Feydeau theatre farce that Lynn had directed in London, Landis suggested to Paramount production chief Dawn Steel that Lynn be offered the chance to make the picture. He argued that the writer had such enthusiasm for the story and knew the plot strands better than anyone else. Moreover, as this would be his first feature directing gig, the studio would be able to get him for scale wages – much less than Landis would cost them. While Lynn may not have directed film before (save for a 25 minute short in the early 1980s), he did have extensive experience working in theatre, having worked on more than fifty productions. As he would soon find, directing film and theatre were two entirely different beasts.

The screenplay was refined further (though not shortened) into what would become the shooting script. The online Cluedo resource, The Art of Murder, mentions that revisions came in February, March, April and July (the month the picture was shooting). Paramount put up a budget of $8M, one million dollars of which would go on Clue's huge multi-roomed set. Filming was set to commence in the summer for a December 1985 release. With Lynn and the script now signed off, Landis went off to Europe to shoot *Spies Like Us*, and work on casting the seven principal roles got underway. While he didn't have complete control over who would play who, Lynn stated that he was lucky that the majority of the people the studio suggested fit perfectly into their roles.

Again, the key to it all was Wadsworth. The character had so many different layers and essentially takes over the final third of the picture, with pages of explanatory dialogue and actions. Around the time of writing Clue, Lynn had been working on a version of Joe Orton's *Loot* with sitcom star Leonard Rossiter. He thought the actor would be perfect as Wadsworth but during a performance of the show in October 1984, Rossiter collapsed and died. John Cleese was said to be up for the part (being perhaps an inspiration for Stoppard's butler, Cleese) but there's little evidence he auditioned. Lynn then looked to Rowan Atkinson, who had enjoyed success in *Not he Nine O'Clock News* and more recently as Edmund Blackadder. He sent Paramount tapes of Atkinson's shows and stand-up routines (which were more physical comedy than traditional stand-up) in hope they would allow him to be cast. He may have been someone in the United Kingdom but the studio had never heard of him and pushed for a 'named' star instead.

Finally, Tim Curry was cast in the role. For the studio, he was a big enough name and had the theatricality the part needed – and it also helped that he and Lynn had been friends in school and had known each other since they were fourteen years of age. Curry had begun his career in a production of *Hair*, where he had a fateful meeting with Richard O'Brien. Some years later the pair met again when O'Brien was looking in a local gym for a muscleman to feature in a musical he was writing. He urged Curry to contact the show's director Jim Sharman and gave him the script for *The Rocky Horror Show*. He ended up cast as Dr Frank N. Furter, a role with which he would become synonymous. *The Rocky Horror Show* was a huge success, and became one of the longest run shows in history. Curry reprised the role for the 1975 movie, *The Rocky Horror Picture Show*. Much more theatre and movie worked followed, and by the time of his casting in Clue, he'd just finished an extensive shoot on the Ridley Scott fantasy, *Legend*.

Six more actors were required for the main cast, three men and three women; they'd consist of established comedy players, though perhaps not quite household names. For some of them, Clue wouldn't be their first time working together either. For the role of Colonel Mustard, Lynn went with Martin Mull. The actor came to prominence in the soap opera parody, *Mary Hartman, Mary Hartman*, and its spin-off, *Fernwood 2 Night* in 1976 and 1977 respectively. He'd already had minor success as a singer/songwriter but acting soon became his mainstay. He loved the script for Clue and had been a fan of the original game. He was also impressed by the cast that was being assembled – one of which he'd already worked with on his movie debut, *FM*, that being Eileen Brennan.

In contrast to Martin Mull, Eileen Brennan was an established actress of some standing by the time she worked on Clue. While she didn't make her film debut until 1967, she'd already appeared in numerous stage plays and musicals, including *Arsenic and Old Lace, The Miracle Worker* and the first Broadway production of *Hello Dolly!* She went on to mix theatre, TV and movie work through the late 1960s and early 70s, receiving a BAFTA award for her work on Peter Bogdanovich's *The Last Picture Show*. Of further note was her part in *Murder By Death*, an Agatha Christie spoof written by Neil Simon. The role for which she would become famous came in 1980, that being Captain Lewis in the Goldie Hawn comedy, *Private Benjamin.*

The part won her many positive notices and was nominated for an Academy Award. She reprised the role for the short lived (37 episodes) TV show of the same name, winning a Golden Globe and a Primetime Emmy. Her career was put on hiatus however in 1982 after she suffered a near fatal car crash, which crushed her legs, damaged her jaw and nose and even pulled her eye from its socket. It would be three years before Brennan acted again and during the recovery period she had become addicted to painkillers. Prior to taking on the part of Mrs Peacock, she had completed a stint in rehab for the addiction. Clue would mark a return to film for the actress, her first role since 1982's *Pandemonium.*

Curiously, Brennan and Mull had also appeared in episodes of the hit sitcom, *Taxi*, which is where the third member of the Clue cast came from. Christopher Lloyd had made his debut in the hit movie *One Flew Over the Cuckoo's Nest*, playing Max Taber. He appeared opposite Jack Nicholson and Danny DeVito again in the 1978 picture *Goin' South*. Initially his part in the sitcom *Taxi* was a guest role, which he reprised in the show's second season. Before the run had ended, he was upgraded to being a regular cast member and appeared in the next three seasons (84 episodes in all – up to the show's end). At the same time, he was appearing in more movies, including the 1983 Michael Keaton comedy, *Mr Mom* (which also featured Martin Mull). He followed this up with appearances in *Star Trek III: The Search for Spock* and *Buckaroo Banzai*, as well as more one-off appearance in various TV shows, including the pilot episode of *Street Hawk*. It was while playing Professor Plum in Clue that Lloyd became an international star thanks to the release of the smash hit movie *Back to the Future*.

As Mr. Green, Lynn cast Michael McKean. Again, the actor was a well-established comedy player, though at that point known more for his TV work. After graduating from college he formed part of a comedy troupe with Harry Shearer and David Lander. In 1976, Lander and McKean were cast in the sitcom *Laverne & Shirley*, where they played versions of characters they'd created (and perfected) in college. So successful were the characters that they even had their own spin-off album, on which they were accompanied by one Nigel Tufnel (aka actor Christopher Guest). When his work on *Laverne & Shirley* came to an end, McKean once again teamed up with Shearer and Christopher Guest to work on the epic mockumentary, *This is Spinal Tap*. While not a huge success on its initial release in the March of 1984, it would go to become the ultimate cult movie. By the point of him joining the cast of Clue, McKean was in cinemas as Andy Richardson in *D.A.R.Y.L.*

For the role of Mrs White, legendary actor and comedian Madeline Kahn was chosen. She got into acting after following the path of her mother, and actually subsidised her earning as a singing waitress in a Bavarian restaurant (where she discovered she had a talent for opera). After graduating she appeared in *Kiss Me, Kate*, but her part in theatrical flop *How Now, Dow Jones* was actually written out before the show got to Broadway. She continued to land work and was even able to call upon her former opera talents when she performed in *Candide*. In 1972, she made her movie debut opposite Barbra Streisand and Ryan O'Neal in *What's Up, Doc?* for which she earned a Golden Globe New Star nomination. The picture marked her first collaboration with director Peter Bogdanovich. A year on, she scored her first Academy Award nomination for *Paper Moon* (again for Bogdanovich), along with winning a Tony for *In the Boom Boom Room*.

1974 saw Kahn appear in not one but two Mel Brooks movies, *Young Frankenstein* and *Blazing Saddles*, in which she gave a memorable turn as Lily von Schtupp. Curiously, she only got the part in *Saddles* after being fired from the Lucille Ball picture, *Mame*. According to the Wikipedia entry, Ball and Kahn had creative differences and she was let go. Ball claimed the actress wanted off the picture to work on the Mel Brooks movie. Years later, Kahn confirmed she was actually fired. She would once again be nominated for an Academy Award (for *Blazing Saddles*) and a Golden Globe (*Young Frankenstein*). Further collaborations with Brooks and Bogdanovich followed, and interestingly, so did a role in *The Cheap Detective*, the follow-up to *Murder by Death*, that also featured Eileen Brennan. This wasn't the first time the duo had worked together, that would be the Bogdanovich flop, *At Long Last Love*. The actress continued to mix theatre and film work, appearing in six movies in two years. She also re-teamed with Marty Feldman (her co-star in *Young Frankenstein* and *The Adventure of Sherlock Holmes' Smarter Brother*) on the ill-fated *Yellowbeard* (Feldman died during its production).

When Jonathan Lynn heard that Madeline Kahn was interested in the role of Mrs White, he went back to the script and wrote further scenes and dialogue for the character. Speaking around the time, Kahn stated she was nervous about doing a farce with a first-time director but when she discovered Lynn had directed numerous farces on stage (which she considered even tougher than doing it for film), the actress signed on-board. That left just one more central role to fill, that of Miss Scarlet. For the part, Lynn was able to secure one the biggest stars in the world at that moment, Carrie Fisher. The actress was riding on high on the success of the *Star Wars* trilogy, in which she had portrayed Princess Leia. She loved the script for Clue and met with Lynn to discuss it. At the time, the director dismissed Fisher's tripping over chairs as clumsiness, and she explained her 'sniffing' as being nothing more than a bad bout of hay fever.

Fisher signed on-board as the final lead. The remainder of the roles to be filled on Clue were minor ones, except for that of Mr Boddy and Yvette the maid, who accompanies the leads on their search of the mansion. According to Colleen Camp (who won the part), it was hotly contested and the likes of Demi Moore and Madonna had tried out for it. Camp went the extra mile for her audition, renting an actual maid's outfit. Lynn thought she was hilarious and ended using Camp's bosom to the film's advantage. Of all the roles, Mr Boddy was the one the director had the least say in casting. The man who eventually got the part was Lee Ving, the lead singer in punk band Fear, who had appeared in the Penelope Spheeris documentary, *The Decline of Western Civilization.*

After an aborted *Saturday Night Live* performance (their set was cut short and replaced with a pre-recorded performance) the band gained something of a reputation – more so when Ving claimed they'd caused $500,000 worth damage on the *SNL* stage, which because he was 'professional, he'd counted it up himself' [The actual figure was closer to $10,000 but many news outlets at the time ran with Ving's number]. The singer/actor wasn't the kind of person Lynn could see in the role but having rejected other cast choices that Paramount sent his way, he felt committed to say yes to at least one of them.

Kellye Nakahara appeared as the cook Mrs Ho, Bill Henderson played the Cop and in an uncredited role, Howard Hesseman was The Chief. Go-Go's singer Jane Wiedlin also had a very memorable cameo as the Singing Telegram.

With so much talent on set and the need for them to work in close quarters for many of the scenes, there was a chance that egos would clash, but this was wisely avoided by ensuring each of the principal cast received the same fee ($100,000), billing and trailer. While the casting was taking place, work was well under way on construction of the huge mansion stage (designed by Les Gobruegge, William B. Major and Gene Nollman and was based on the work of production designer, John Lloyd). With the exception of the ballroom, all of the rooms were constructed on a Paramount soundstage – the same one that had housed *Rear Window*'s apartment courtyard. The ballroom scenes were shot on location in the house that also served for the film's opening external shots.

A week out from shooting commencing, Carrie Fisher called Jonathan Lynn to say she was in rehab. The director wasn't sure what she meant, but was suspicious when she said she still wanted to do the film and that they'd let her out in the day to work, providing she returned back to the clinic each night. He spoke to Debra Hill and Dawn Steel about the situation and neither could see the issue. Unbeknownst to Lynn, both were cocaine users – as was half of Hollywood he'd later discover. When the insurance company covering the project got wind of the situation, they refused to allow Fisher's participation, leaving Lynn scrambling to find a new Miss Scarlet with only days to go.

He turned to Lesley Ann Warren. Like much of the cast, she'd begun her career in the 1960s, initially training as a ballet dancer before being accepted into the Actors Studio (at 17 years old, she was said to be the youngest they'd ever accepted). She narrowly missed out on a part in the movie version of *The Sound of Music*, making her credited screen debut in Rodgers & Hammerstein's *Cinderella* instead. Her first feature role was as Cordelia 'Cordy' Biddle in *The Happiest Millionaire* (1967). She landed the female lead in *Mission: Impossible*, but lasted only a single season and was released from her contract due to her lack of experience – ironic considering she scored a Golden Globe nomination for her work on the show.

In 1976, she won the award for her work in Harold Robbins' *79 Park Avenue*, and was nominated again for her part in *Victor/Victoria* in 1982, along with earning an Academy Award nod. She also tried out for the part of Lois Lane in *Superman The Movie*, but lost out to Margot Kidder (Warren had actually played Lois Lane in *It's a Bird...It's a Plane...It's Superman*, a TV adaptation of the Broadway musical). Warren already had a link of sorts to Clue – executive producer Jon Peters was her ex-husband, though the pair had been divorced over ten years by the time she got the part. She knew little of the board game and was on holiday when she got the call to play Miss Scarlet.

Before shooting commenced, Jonathan Lynn assembled the cast on the Paramount lot and screened Howard Hawk's *His Girl Friday*. He wanted the cast to study the delivery of the dialogue, the clipped words and speed in particular. This meeting of the cast helped them form a bond that Lynn both welcomed and regretted once filming got under way. That said, despite Madeline Kahn and Eileen Brennan having been good friends prior to Clue, the former struggled with how to deal with latter's stint in rehab and sadly kept interaction with her to a minimum. [According to Brennan, in an interview for Kahn's biography, the two barely spoke in the years after].

The shoot was scheduled for fifty days with the vast majority of time being spent on the huge mansion set that was now finished and finely furnished (by Thomas L. Roysden) with vintage pieces loaned from private collectors including the Teddy Roosevelt estate. Filming actually commenced in the late May/early June of 1985 for a December release. Lynn quickly realised that directing theatre and film were two vastly different things. The placement of props, characters and general framing were reduced drastically on film by what the camera actually saw as opposed to what a theatre audience saw. This gave him more than few headaches but caused few, if any delays.

The bigger problem was with the cast, albeit in a good way. Unlike most movies which have two or three leads and a number of supporting roles, Clue had seven major players, who all shared a good portion of screen time together. They were often in hysterics during takes, and shots would have to be reset again and again. Most of the cast members that have been interviewed in the years since the film's release have said how bad they felt for Lynn having to deal with their antics.

According to Martin Mull, Michael McKean began pre-empting each take with the phrase 'Something terrible has happened here' in an effort to get them all back into character – though this often made things worse. Tim Curry didn't always take kindly to the interruptions, as he made the effort to memorise huge swathes of dialogue and action cues. The advantage of filming on one large set meant they could shoot mostly in sequence, making continuity much easier to maintain – something they had to do to make sure all four endings matched up with the first part of the picture.

Despite the laughs, Lynn gave the actors no room for improvisation. The script was shot almost word for word to keep some semblance of order. It also meant they could shoot quickly – six or more actors who appeared in many of same scenes, all trying their own ideas, would have added another fifty days to the shoot. Of all the cast, Madeline Kahn found this the toughest. Having worked with Mel Brooks (and Gene Wilder) on a number of occasions, she was used to being encouraged to add her own spin to dialogue and actions. Eventually, towards the end of the shoot and in a pivotal scene for her character, Kahn asked if she could try something. For once, Lynn gave her permission. The line in the script called for Mrs White to simply say 'I hated her so much that I wanted to kill her'. Instead of leaving it there, Kahn went into overdrive and the infamous 'Flames on the side of my face' scene was born. The actress altered things on subsequent takes and Lynn found it so funny he agreed to use it instead of what was scripted.

The props on the set weren't just for show either. When the cast discovered the billiard table in one of the rooms, they set about having it professionally balanced so they could play between calls to the set. It soon began to draw both cast and crew during the downtime. However, due to costumer designer Michael Kaplan's insistence that everyone be dressed in period garb, Lesley Ann Warren found herself unable sit or bend thanks to her bone corset. Instead of playing pool between shots, she was on a slant board complete with arm rests.

One scene in which there was no room for jokes was the chandelier crash that nearly ends up killing Colonel Mustard. The stunt coordinator prepared the shot but mindful of John Landis' *Twilight Zone* accident, Lynn made sure Martin Mull was a good distance away before it crashed down. Upon reviewing the shot, he realised the actor was probably a bit too far from the event but decided not to push his luck and printed the shot as was. In a 2013 interview, Mull claimed that the prop master (who would drop the chandelier) did a great job of terrifying him just prior to the scene taking place by appearing to be drunk and slurring his words.

The shoot came to an end late summer and Lynn was soon assembling his edit. He kept things incredibly lean and a lot of footage (and potential laughs) was left on the cutting room floor. This post-production and editing period was very hard on the fledgling director due to commitments in the UK for *Yes, Prime Minister*. In a June 2015 interview for the Movies and Stuff podcast, he talked about having to split his week between Los Angeles and England – four days in one, three in the other – for ten weeks. It was during this period that it was decided the fourth ending didn't work and the decision was made to remove it completely. Of all the endings, the fourth was the darkest and that may well have been part of the reasoning for its removal. Still, Paramount had their three endings and the unique plan for Clue was about to come into play.

Jonathan Lynn was never a fan of the idea to release three different versions of the movie into theatres. He'd worked incredibly hard on ensuring all three endings worked logically with what came before, and it seemed a shame that audiences might not venture out to see the other two endings. Further, he felt that it robbed the picture of some of its genius – with only one ending attached Clue was just like any other picture – its brilliance shone when all three were shown together. The studio pushed ahead with their plan, working on the idea that audiences would be intrigued by whichever ending they saw and would seek out the other two. Unfortunately, as they would soon discover, Lynn's fears were well founded.

Critics were not kind to Clue and more than a few took offence at Paramount's insistence on releasing three different versions of the film. This wasn't helped by the studio failing to inform critics which letter referred to which ending (they were named A, B and C in newspaper adverts). People were left confused, unsure if they needed to see all three endings or how to avoid seeing the same ending twice (or thrice). Some cinemas referenced the lettered ending with their showtime listings in an effort to help out their patrons. The idea of getting repeat business backfired spectacularly – instead of going three times, audiences simply didn't bother going at all.

The picture opened on December 13th up against the *Romancing the Stone* sequel, *Jewel of the Nile*. *Rocky IV* was still doing great business and John Landis' *Spies Like Us* had already made over $16M in the fourteen days since opening. Clue was in 1,006 theatres initially though it is unclear if they had three prints (one with each ending, which they rotated) or were only issued one with a specific finale. Whichever it was made little difference. Clue placed sixth on that first weekend, with a disappointing $2M. A week later and with three new releases (and a re-release of *101 Dalmatians)* added to the mix, the movie found itself already out of the top ten. While its weekend-to-weekend drop was only 30%, because its initial start was so poor it made little difference.

Things improved a little by weekend three and the film made it back into the top ten, but this was due more to the post-Christmas holiday period (when almost every film receives a boost) than any word-of-mouth. Clue lasted only five weeks on general release and made $14.6M. It may have covered its production budget but prints and advertising costs would have still put it in a loss. There were also the costs involved in developing it originally, for both Universal and Paramount. However one dressed up the numbers, it was still a flop.

For Jonathan Lynn, it was even more crushing. While finishing up work on the picture he'd signed a deal to direct the Steve Martin comedy, *Roxanne*. However, within ten days of Clue opening, he was replaced by Fred Schepisi. He returned to England, and it would be five years before he would direct another picture. *Nuns on the Run*, which Lynn also wrote, was a hit in the UK and a minor success in North America. He returned to the US in 1990 to direct the pilot for the short-lived *Ferris Bueller* TV show. He then became a director-for-hire on *My Cousin Vinny*, which was both a critical and financial success, earning star Marisa Tomei a best actress Academy Award.

It was around this time that Lynn discovered Clue had taken on a life of its own. No longer was it shunned or slated, rather it was being celebrated. Upon release on VHS, the film had all three endings restored, playing one after another, with title cards in between each one suggesting that this was how it could have ended. Thanks to a lack of nudity and bad language, Clue had become a staple on basic cable channels, where it could be screened at any time of the day as a family film. The advent of the internet furthered its life as fan pages and theories were put forth onto websites, including the rumour that there was once a version with six endings – with a different guest being the killer in each one.

There are regular screenings of the film, some of which Jonathan Lynn has attended, complete with a Q&A session at the end. A shadow cast performance, in which real actors perform in front of a screen playing the movie, is also a regular (and popular) occurrence in Los Angeles. The TV show *Psych* even organised a Clue reunion of sorts for its 100th Episode. Martin Mull, Lesley Ann Warren and Christopher Lloyd featured in a wacky murder mystery plot set within a huge mansion. Sadly, it seems Paramount are still stinging from the film's failure – it received only a bare-bones DVD and Blu-Ray release in recent years. Despite Jonathan Lynn offering to do a commentary for a possible 30th anniversary edition, Paramount refused to entertain the idea.

After working on Clue the cast and crew went their separate ways. Christopher Lloyd enjoyed success with the *Back to the Future* sequels, along with a nightmare-inducing role in *Who Framed Roger Rabbit*. In 1991, he played Fester Addams in Barry Sonnenfeld's big screen adaptation of *The Addams Family*. He reprised the role two years later for the sequel. Over the next two decades, Lloyd worked seemingly without a break in all manner of TV shows, TV movies and films. In recent times, he's had a recurring role on the show *Granite Flats*, provided his voice to a character in *The Simpsons* and appeared in *Sin City: A Dame to Kill For* and Seth MacFarlane's *A Million Ways to Die in the West*.

Similarly, Martin Mull has worked consistently since the release of Clue, favouring TV work over film. Various one-off appearances in the likes of *The Golden Girls, Lois & Clark* and *The Larry Sanders Show* came alongside recurring roles in *Rosanne, The Ellen Show* and memorable turn as Mr Kraft in *Sabrina the Teenage Witch*. Of late, Mull has been seen in *Arrested Development, Two and a Half Men* and *Dads*. He is also something of an accomplished artist, his work appearing in solo and group exhibitions. He has provided art for books and album covers, including the Steve Martin/Edie Brickell collaboration, *Love Has Come For You*.

Like Tim Curry, Michael McKean has not one but two cult movies to his name. His work on Clue has been overshadowed by the continuing popularity of *This is Spinal Tap*. In the years since its release, he's appeared as David St. Hubbins on numerous TV shows and Spinal Tap performances. Like Christopher Lloyd and Martin Mull, McKean has worked on a variety of TV shows and movies. He's also lent his voice to a vast array of cartoon characters, both as one-offs and recurring characters. He also became (at the time) the oldest regular member of the *Saturday Night Live* cast and, according to Wikipedia, the only person to ever appear as a musical guest, host and cast member (in that order) in the show's entire history. In 2015, he appeared as Chuck McGill on the AMC show, *Better Call Saul* and for 2016, he'll reprise the character Morris Fletcher in *The X-Files* revival.

After finishing work on Clue, Lesley Ann Warren appeared opposite Whoopi Goldberg in *Burglar* and with James Woods in the James Ellroy adaptation *Blood on the Moon*, released as the movie, *Cop*. Notable roles in the 1990s included (amongst many others) *Life Stinks, Color of Night* and *The Limey*. She switched back to TV for a four-episode stint on *Will & Grace* and played Teri Hatcher's mother on *Desperate Housewives*. She followed this up with a regular part on *In Plain Sight*. In 2013, she played Steve Jobs' mother in the Ashton Kutcher picture, *Jobs*.

Eileen Brennan made up for lost time in the second half the 80s and well into the 1990s, racking up a variety of credits, both film and TV related. She reprised her *Last Picture Show* role for the 1990 sequel, *Texasville*, before going on to appear in the new *Dennis the Menace* show, *Murder She Wrote* and *E.R.* She worked on *Will & Grace* for six episodes and on *7th Heaven* for another nine. Her final credit is as Gram Malone in 2011's *Naked Run*. Eileen Brennan died from cancer in July 2013.

The brilliant Madeline Kahn struggled to find work that fully utilised her talents in the years after Clue. She worked opposite George C. Scott on the short-lived sitcom, *Mr President* then appeared in ensemble comedies *Betsy's Wedding* (1990) and *Mixed Nuts* (1995) with Steve Martin, Juliette Lewis and Rob Reiner. She worked on the Mary Tyler Moore drama, *New York News*, which lasted for a single season. Kahn also provided the voice of Gypsy Moth in Pixar's *A Bug's Life*. She went on to win a regular role on *The Cosby Show* before succumbing to cancer in 1999, aged just 57.

Tim Curry followed up Clue with a bizarre cameo in *The Worst Witch* along with a role opposite Bill Paxton in *Pass the Ammo*. In 1990, he appeared with Sean Connery in *The Hunt for Red October* and gave a memorable (and utterly terrifying) turn in the Stephen King TV movie, *IT*, as Pennywise the clown. Further movie work followed, including *Home Alone 2, Congo* and *The Three Musketeers*, opposite Kiefer Sutherland and Charlie Sheen.

However, it was for his voiceover work that Tim Curry would be known throughout the decade and well into the next. His voice appeared in countless cartoons running into thousands of episodes, including (amongst many, many others) *Gargoyles*, *The Wild Thornberrys, Hey Arnold, Scooby Doo* and *Rugrats*.

His work wasn't limited just to cartoons, he continued to act in movies, TV shows and lent his voice to numerous video games, notably the *Gabriel Knight* series. Theatre, where he got his start, wasn't neglected either, with parts in *A Christmas Carol* and *My Favourite Year*, for which he earned his second Tony nomination. 2004 saw Curry take the lead in *Spamalot*, which opened in Chicago before moving to Broadway (it sold an incredible one million dollars' worth of tickets in 24 hours). He would win a third Tony nomination for his work. The show transferred to the West End and the actor went with it, earning a Laurence Olivier nomination as well as a Theatregoers' Choice Award. Sadly, the actor suffered a major stroke in 2012 and was all but absent from public life over the next three years. However, he continued to provide his voice for the likes of *Randy Cunningham: 9th Grade Ninja* and *The Clone Wars*. Curry made a rare public appearance in 2015 to collect a Tony Lifetime Achievement Award. More recently he joined a cast reunion of *The Rocky Horror Picture Show* arranged by Entertainment Weekly and will play the narrator of the show in a new live TV event.

As for the talent behind the camera – Jonathan Lynn directed the aforementioned *Nuns on the Run* and *My Cousin Vinny*. He then dealt with American politics in the Eddie Murphy comedy, *The Distinguished Gentleman* and helmed the Steve Martin *Sgt. Bilko* remake. In 2000, he saw success with *The Whole Nine Yards*. In 2013, he returned to the small screen, writing and directing a new version of *Yes, Prime Minister*. He remains incredibly proud of his work on Clue and states that of all the projects he's been involved with, it remains the one for which he still receives the most fan mail.

John Landis followed *Spies Like Us* with *The Three Amigos* and later worked again with Eddie Murphy on *Coming to America* and the misfire, *Beverly Hills Cop 3*. An attempt to revive his earlier success with *The Blues Brothers 2000* fell flat with audiences in the latter part of the 1990s, as did comedy *The Stupids*. His most recent theatrical release was dark comedy, *Burke & Hare*, which featured Simon Pegg and Andy Serkis.

Clue was and remains a slice of pure brilliance. The genius of setting the picture in the 1950s gives it an ageless quality, making it seem as fresh today as it did thirty years ago. The chaotic yet logical way in which all the pieces fit together means each ending can be enjoyed independently, but the picture really soars when they're put altogether. Tim Curry gives a breathless, career-best performance and he is ably supported by the rest of the strong cast, with Martin Mull and Madeline Kahn being standouts. Clue is one of the brightest of all the hidden gems the 1980s had to offer and remains a must-see for all.

If you liked Clue, you may enjoy one of these…

The 'Burbs

Joe Dante's dark suburban comedy sees a bored Tom Hanks suspecting his new neighbours might have a murderous secret to hide. While wife Carrie Fisher rolls her eyes, Hanks and Rick Ducommun, aided (and hindered by) Bruce Dern and Corey Feldman begin to investigate the mysterious Klopek family.

After *Gremlins*, director Dante had little problem twisting everyday life into something a little more subversive. Hanks too, had little issue playing the everyman whose paranoia quickly surpasses logic. The film was only a minor hit upon release but gained a deserved audience over the years.

Trivia: The original scripted ending was much more downbeat, but when Tom Hanks joined the project it was re-written. Rumours persist that this darker ending was shot but has never seen the light of day.

Who Framed Roger Rabbit?

Robert Zemeckis' ground-breaking combination of live action and animation, starring Bob Hoskins, proved that the two mediums could work together seamlessly. The backdrop to all this is the murder of Marvin Acme – and the prime suspect Roger Rabbit. Having lost his brother to a 'toon', Hoskins' Eddie Valiant has more than an axe to grind but (very) reluctantly agrees to help Roger clear his name.

It isn't all laughs, thanks to Christopher Lloyd's truly frightening Judge Doom, a character who's given kids (and adults) their fair share of nightmares in the years since the film's release. While other pictures utilised the same methods, few have come close to its brilliance, in part because Roger Rabbit used the animation as another character, rather than making it a gimmick.

Trivia: With a budget of $30M, the film was most expensive animated feature in cinematic history, at that point.

Without a Clue

An alternative take on Sherlock Holmes and Dr Watson, Without a Clue stars Michael Caine and Ben Kingsley as the legendary detective and his partner respectively. The twist being that Holmes doesn't exist, and it is Watson who solves the crimes and writes the stories. Forced to bow to public demands, Watson has to hire an out-of-work actor to 'play' Holmes.

Things only get more complicated when the government seeks Holmes' help to solve a major crime – and will accept no one but the 'famous' detective, much to Watson's annoyance. The plot is almost secondary to the interplay between the leads, and they're ably backed by the likes of Peter Cook, Jeffrey Jones and Lysette Anthony.

Trivia: Michael Caine and Lysette Anthony appeared together in the Victorian murder mystery, *Jack the Ripper*, which was also screened in 1988.

-----

80 From the 80s – Sources

80 From the 80s couldn't have been written without help from a vast number of websites, magazines, YouTube videos and DVDs, along with their commentaries and special features.

The Internet Movie Database and Wikipedia were an endless source of help. Not only the individual pages related to the specific movie I was covering but in discovering more about each actor, actress, director, producer, writer and musician. Wikipedia in particular was an invaluable resource for information on special effects teams, filming techniques and technical jargon.

One further source that I must single out is the exhaustive website, Box Office Mojo. With box office information dating right back to the start of the 1980s, the site was invaluable in providing screen counts, release dates, competition and of course, box office figures.

The following provided further insight and information on individual films –

Krull

Bad Ass Digest
The Hollywood News

The New York Times

Fast-Rewind

Filmtracks

Cast & Crew DVD Commentary Track

Flash Gordon

The Encyclopaedia of Science Fiction

Sci-Fi Chronicles

Maxim (December 2012 issue)

Io9

Starlog (Issue 41)

Dino: The Life and Film of Dino De Laurentiis

WarGames

Wired (July 2008 issue)

John Badham – The Hollywood Interview

Venturebeat

Allmovie

Imsai.net

My Life as a Mankiewicz: An Insider's Journey through Hollywood.

Yahoo Movies

The Salon

Romancing the Stone

Time Magazine

Diane Thomas' Biography

Entertainment Weekly (August 1991)

American Film (July/Aug 1988)

Send Yourself Roses: The Memoirs of Kathleen Turner

The LA Times

Fast-Rewind

The Wrap

Cinefax

Blockbuster: How Hollywood Learned to Stop Worrying and Love the Summer By Tom Shone

Mannequin

Roger Ebert's Chicago Sun Times' Review

The New York Times – Joseph Ferrell's obituary

The Morning Call – February 1987

Moviefone

Snakkle.com

Fast-Rewind

Phillymag (December 2013)

The Last Starfighter

Crossing the Frontier: The Making of the Last Starfighter Featurette

Io9: Everything you never knew about the making of The Last
Starfighter (July 2014)

/film

Fast-Rewind

Ohio State University CG History Page

Starlog

The A.V Club: Enter a backstage history of The Last Starfighter
(July 2014)

Popcultureaddict

Gremlins

Flight in America: From the Wrights to the Astronauts

Behind the Scenes DVD Featurette and Commentary

Empire Magazine: Gremlins Reunion June 2014

Associated Press: PG-13 Remade the Hollywood Ratings System

Mentalfloss

Film Divider

Heathers

Entertainment Weekly: Heathers – An oral history

Qnetwork: Heathers DVD Review

Heathers DVD Documentary: Swatch Dogs and Diet Coke Heads

Movieline

Variety

Topless Robot: 10 Secrets about the History of Heathers

Moviepilot

Mentalfloss

Fletch

Fletchlives.net

Entertainment Weekly: The Curse of Fletch

Movie Magazine (Summer 1985)

New York Post: Fletch Fanatics

The Globe and Mail

The A.V Club Interview: Tim Matheson

The Times (26th September 1985)

Time Magazine: 10 Questions: Chevy Chase

Los Angeles Times

Variety

Redbull Musical Academy: Harold Faltermeyer

Silent Bob Speaks

The Lost Boys

Venice Magazine: Joel Schumacher: Safe in the Dark

MTV.com: Corey Feldman Interview

80s Music Channel

Total Film: The Story behind The Lost Boys

Vulture

Indiewire

New York Magazine

Biography.com

Lostboys.wikia

Screencrush

The Hollywood Interview

Den of Geek

IGN.Com

Gamesradar

Herocomplex

The AV Club Interview: Joel Schumacher

Movline

GeekTyrant

The Secret of My Success

New York Times (15th April 1987)

Inside The Actor's Studio: Michael J. Fox

People Magazine (April 3rd 1989)

Fast-Rewind

The Autobiography of David Watkin

Lucky Man: A Memoir: Michael J. Fox

Young Sherlock Holmes

New York Times: Imagine Sherlock Holmes as a Boy (Dec 1985)

Filmsite.org: Visual and Special Effects Film Milestones

Listal.com

Design.osu.edu: CGI in the Movies

Kent Film Office

film.menu

Cinefex (Issue 26)

Starlog

People Magazine

Film-news.co.uk

Dragnet

Los Angeles Times: Just the Facts, Mank: (22nd March 1987)

My Life as a Mankiewicz: Tom Mankiewicz

The Ultimate Writer's Guide to Hollywood

People Magazine: July 1987

48 Hrs.

Film International: Walter Hill: Last Man Standing (June 2004)

Movie City News

YouTube: Delirious – The Eddie Murphy Interview

YouTube: Mary Hart interview Eddie Murphy for Entertainment Tonight

Steven E. de Souza on Twitter

No Exit: The Nick Nolte Documentary.

The Directors Guild – The Walter Hill interview

Fright Night

Shock N Roll Issue 2: Mr Holland's Opus

Choice Cuts: Tom Hollland's Fright Night Tour

Dread Central: Fright Night Retrospective: All Parts

Pirate Commentaries

Icons of Fright

Fright Night Press Kit

Nino7500's YouTube Channel: Fright Night Stars Discuss the Movie

Fright Night Reunion Q&A

The Projection Booth: Fright Night

Monsterpalooza: Fright Night Panel

Fangoria (August 1985)

Days of the Dead: Fright Night Reunion Panel

Stephen Geoffreys Discusses Fright Night

New York Times

Los Angeles Times

Fright Night Wikia

The Sure Thing

Road to the Sure Thing DVD Featurette

The Sure Thing DVD Trivia track

Cobra

The Role That Changed My Life: Season 1 Episode 4

Movie Geeks United: Summer of 1986: Cobra

People Magazine: 26th May 1986

USA Today

Sun Sentinel

Movie Legends Revealed

GeekTyrant.com

New York Times

Ain't It Cool News

Movie Geeks United Podcast

Fast-Rewind

Police Academy

Jog Road Productions: Interview with Paul Maslansky (YouTube)

Making of Police Academy – DVD Featurette

Police Academy 20th Anniversary – DVD Cast Commentary

Fast-Rewind

Uproxx

New York Times

Risky Business

The Bottom Line

Movieline

People.com

Yahoo

Chicago Tribune

UCTV: Script to Screen: Risky Business (YouTube)

The Uncool

Rolling Stone Magazine

The Salon

Mental Floss

EddieonFilm

Tom Cruise: An Unauthorized Biography – Andrew Morton

Risky Business: Blu-Ray Featurette

Risky Business: Blu-Ray – Commentary

The Merv Griffin Show: Tom Cruise Interview

Clue

Buzzfeed: Something Terrible Has Happened Here – The Making of Clue

Interview with Jonathan Lynn: Boxcar Theatre YouTube Channel

Combat Radio: The Jonathan Lynn Interview

Cinematheque: Facebook page interview: Jonathan Lynn

The Art of Murder website

Den of Geek: Jonathan Lynn Interview

Den of Geek: Tim Curry Retrospective

New York Times: Off the Board, Onto the Screen for Clue

Movieline

Jonathan Lynn – On twitter and via email correspondence

Further sites that assisted in providing information across all the movies covered in this book –

The Numbers

Rotten Tomatoes

Den of Geek

Fast-Rewind

Worldwide Box Office.com

The Starlog Archive

Dollartimes.com

Acknowledgements

80 From the 80s couldn't exist without the support of the following people. For all the upvotes, shares, retweets, kind words and support. My eternal thanks to the following...

Nic, lordcookie, Thushan Kumaraswamy, Glasgowchivas, JoeK, Jammy, Jonamok, Kerraig, Rumblecat, luth714, Sandman, Monkeyboy, Chosty, FishyFish, Sabreman, Nathan Wind, Strategos, Plissken, Gmass, AK Bell, Neo Elite, CarloOos, jeebus, Gabe, Treble, Carlos Valderrama, SeanR, Spagmaster Swift, Don Wiskerando, smac, RFT, Spleen, Azrael, mr_woo, Moora, Punished Smitty, Cheeko, Wiper, Tenrou, TehStu, gismo1990, Fireproofradiator, Fuddle, John C, mdn2, Kevvy Metal, Retroguy, Dimahoo, Pob, MDY, Davros Sock Drawer, geldra, jon_cybernet, Orion, Skeez, Mortis, Mentazm, Mr Gerbik, sidewaysbob, Strider, RaoulSilva, Andy_why, Fry Crayola, Chewylegs, Rowan Morrison, Silent Runner, Stefcha, Seamonster, Colonel Panic, Laine, Mr Do 71, Pete, Jim, The Hierophant, Jim, Creamstick, Delargey, Staplehead, JohnnyNolan, Tempy, Poet, The Bag, Villenium, Space Monkey, Scouser_in_exile, Yoshimax, Nifta, Textface, Gommy, Deniable Asset, Hungry Joe, Cras, Thwomp, Krenzler, Jack Walsh's Coffee Shop, Roboattack, The Disco, Lucas, Merman, Gregory Wolfe, Down By Law, Brunceling, Jon, Lofarius, top-cat, Mr Monday, Ivanho, Wev, Robo_1, Danster, Vimster, Mighty Mo,

Jackie B, JPickford, Ste Pickford, Scott Mendelson, Steven E de Souza, Jonathan Lynn, Jon B, Angela G, Emmabob, Amanda S, James Cornelius Bird, Brandon Peters, Steve Robinson, Chris Hall, Angela Garry, Ste Pickford, Geraldine Brown.

About the Author

Lane Myer is the author of 80 From the 80s and Box Office: The Collected U.S Box Office Reports. He lives in Melbourne with his wife and two children, neither of which seems to be interested in watching Ghostbusters.

The End...?

17950189R00252

Printed in Great Britain
by Amazon